# MONEY
### *thoughts*

# BRUCE BOND

# MONEY
## *thoughts*

## The ABC of
## Money Management

# Lothian Publishing Company
MELBOURNE · SYDNEY · AUCKLAND

All details and figures quoted in this book were pertaining at the time of going to press or the best available at that time. Any facts, figures, conditions and regulations quoted herein are presented as information in good faith but neither the author nor the publisher will bear responsibility or liability for any action taken by any person, persons or organisation on the purported basis of information supplied here.

First published 1986
Reprinted 1987 (twice), 1988
This second and revised edition first printed 1990

National Library of Australia
Cataloguing-in-Publication data

Bond, Bruce, 1928– .
   Money thoughts: the ABC of money management.

   Rev. ed.
   ISBN 0 85091 413 2.
   ISBN 0 85091 392 6 (pbk.).

   1. Finance, Personal – Australia. 2. Financial institutions
   – Australia. 3. Financial institutions – Australia –
   Investments. 4. Investments – Australia. I. Title.
332.02400994

Typeset by Bookset Pty Ltd
Printed in Australia by The Book Printer

# Contents

# Acknowledgements

The author acknowledges with appreciation and thanks the overwhelming co-operation and assistance of the following:

The Australian Bank Ltd
Australian Guarantee Corporation Ltd
Barclays Bank
BHP
Challenge Bank
Commonwealth Bank
Commonwealth Department of the Treasury
CSR Ltd
Eric J. Morgan & Co.
Friends' Provident
Macquarie Bank Ltd
State Bank of NSW Investment Advisory Service
Treasury Corporation, NSW
Telecom Australia
NSW Corp. Affairs Commission
Norths — Stockbrokers
Potter Partners — Stockbrokers
Sydney Stock Exchange Ltd — Investment Advisory Service
TPF&C — Actuaries and Management Consultants
Trade Practices Commission
Westpac Bank
St George Building Society

# Foreword

Over the past ten or so years Australia has experienced an investment revolution. New products are being introduced almost daily, accompanied by the appropriate and, in some cases, inappropriate publicity. Today's investor has a bewildering range of options from which to choose.

With the Commonwealth Government making it clear that it wants retired Australians to be as independent as possible from social services, and offering some tax incentives and tax-free benefits, now is a very good time for ordinary Australians to become totally involved in investment and the world of finance.

Competition for the investor's dollar has become so fierce that a new breed of so-called 'advisors' (salespersons) has appeared, with investors — particularly retirees — in their sights. And so the most crucial questions remain. Which investment, or range of investments, should you choose? And, more importantly, to whom do you turn for caring and unbiased advice? It is time for a cautious and common-sense attitude to be adopted by everyone. Intelligent enquiry and recourse to second, or even third and fourth, opinions before any major investment decisions are made are essential. So in reality it is *back to basics*, and that is what this book is all about — common-sense money management combined with an understanding of the investment avenues and opportunities that exist.

This is not a dry textbook of facts but a combination of information about the range of investments available and how the money markets operate, advice and opinion on personal finance, and important case histories.

# Banks, Building Societies and Credit Unions

**A Link with the Bank**

A link with a bank and a regular pattern of saving are essential if you need to borrow money by way of housing loan, overdraft, personal loan or credit card.

To have a good credit rating is one of your greatest assets. It *counts* when you ask for a loan and could influence the rate of interest you will be charged. The sooner your link with a bank is established the better, especially if you are saving to buy your first home or starting off in a business.

Always remember a caring bank manager is worth his/her weight in gold, so make sure you keep in touch. In some instances it might be in your best interests to move with the manager if he or she is transferred to another branch, rather than suffer the frustration of 'training' another manager. And do not forget to do the right thing by the bank. If you want to exceed your overdraft limit ask your bank manager first. Apart from saving you money it could also save you a lot of embarrassment.

If you are saving to buy a home you must of course meet the bank's requirements to qualify for a loan.

This might mean investing with the bank for a specified period, but you don't have to leave it in an old-fashioned savings account earning miserable interest.

You can still qualify for the loan if you open one or more of the many deposit and investment accounts which are now available. The important thing to remember is to make your money work for you.

**A Second Bank Account**

Even if you have a good credit rating it's not always possible to borrow money from your bank when you want to.

If your bank manager refuses your loan application don't rush in and close your account as most people would probably do. Shop around and see if another bank will provide the loan.

The easiest solution is to look in the newspaper for a bank which is advertising the opening of a new branch office. As the new branch will be trying to attract as many customers as possible it could be to your financial advantage to open a second bank account with them. But still keep on good terms with your original bank in case of future needs.

**Savings Banks — don't waste investment funds**

One would not normally look upon a Savings Bank Account as an investment and yet millions of people do. They have had the account from birth, it is convenient and the money is safe. It is also part of that vital link with the bank, but as an *investment* an old-fashioned Savings Bank Account is a sheer waste of money for, with inflation and taxation, the miserable interest rates just cannot compete.

There are other forms of high yielding, safe investment alternatives inside and outside the banking system and each should be considered. So, if you have any *surplus* money in an old-fashioned savings account paying nominal interest, look around for better alternatives.

**Interest Bearing Deposits**

Like Savings Investment Accounts, Interest Bearing Deposits can serve a useful purpose, and the interest rates are in some cases far more competitive and realistic. But with longer term deposits a cautious approach should be adopted, for if interest rates do go up your interest stays the same until your deposit matures. In an emergency it is possible to arrange with the financial institution to withdraw before the due date, but if you do your interest will probably be reduced.

However, it should be noted that the banks will not allow this 'early withdrawal' privilege just to enable you to invest in a higher income producing investment; and rightly so, for many people don't realise that the lodgement of an interest bearing deposit creates a formal contract. This again emphasises the need to plan your investment programme wisely.

The number and variety of accounts and investments offered by banks is literally overwhelming, but excellent guides would be those of the Commonwealth Bank and Westpac, which are as follows.

## COMMONWEALTH BANK

### Investment Accounts

(Effective interest rates apply when interest is added to principal and not withdrawn).

STANDARD TERM DEPOSITS                    Up to 17.50% p.a.
Interest calculated daily and credited every six months and/or at maturity

$500 to less than $50,000

| | |
|---|---|
| 1 to less than 3 months | 12.00% p.a. |
| 3 to less than 4 months | 16.00% p.a. |
| 4 to less than 6 months | 16.75% p.a. |
| 6 to less than 7 months | 17.25% p.a. |
| 7 to less than 13 months | 15.50% p.a. |
| 13 to less than 24 months | 14.50% p.a. |
| 24 to 60 months inclusive | 13.50% p.a. |

$50,000 to less than $100,000

| | |
|---|---|
| 1 to less than 2 months | 14.00% p.a. |
| 2 to less than 3 months | 15.00% p.a. |
| 3 to less than 4 months | 16.75% p.a. |
| 4 to less than 6 months | 17.00% p.a. |
| 6 to less than 7 months | 17.50% p.a. |
| 7 to less than 13 months | 15.75% p.a. |
| 13 to less than 24 months | 14.50% p.a. |
| 24 to 60 months inclusive | 14.00% p.a. |

$100,000 and over

| | |
|---|---|
| 7 days to 60 months inclusive | Rates on request |

COMPOUND INTEREST TERM DEPOSITS
Up to 16.37% p.a. effective
Interest calculated daily and compounded every six months and paid at maturity.

Effective yield for a term of 12 months

| | |
|---|---|
| $500 to less than $50,000 | 16.10% p.a. |
| $50,000 to less than $100,000 | 16.37% p.a. |

The flat rates applying to Compound Interest Term Deposits are the same as those applying to Standard Term Deposits.

REGULAR INCOME TERM DEPOSITS   Up to 15.75% p.a.
Interest calculated daily and payable every 28 days
Minimum Deposit $2000
Minimum Term 12 Months
Personal Customers Only

$2000 to less than $50,000

| | |
|---|---|
| 12 months | 15.50% p.a. |
| 13 months to 23 months inclusive | 14.25% p.a. |
| 24 months to 60 months inclusive | 13.25% p.a. |

$50,000 to less than $100,000

| | |
|---|---|
| 12 months | 15.75% p.a. |
| 13 months to 23 months inclusive | 14.25% p.a. |
| 24 months to 60 months inclusive | 13.75% p.a. |

## CASH MANAGEMENT CALL ACCOUNTS — AT CALL
Minimum Balance $5000
Minimum Transaction $1000
Interest is calculated on the full balance each day according to movements in the Short-term Money Market and is credited quarterly on the first working day of March, June, September, and December

## SECURITY PLUS INVESTMENT ACCOUNTS — AT CALL
Up to 16.42% p.a. effective
Minimum Balance $5000
Minimum Transaction $500
On Full Balance

| | | Effective yield |
|---|---|---|
| $50,000 and over | 15.50% p.a. | 16.42% p.a. |
| $20,000 to $49,999 | 14.50% p.a. | 15.30% p.a. |
| $5000 to $19,999 | 12.50% p.a. | 13.09% p.a. |

Interest is calculated on the daily balance and is payable quarterly on the first working day of March, June, September and December. Interest is not paid on deposits held for less than one month or where the account balance is below $5000.

## SAVINGS INVESTMENT ACCOUNTS — AT CALL
Up to 14.49% p.a. effective

Minimum Balance $500
Minimum Withdrawal $100
On Full Balance

| | | Effective yield |
|---|---|---|
| $50,000 and over | 14.00% p.a. | 14.49% p.a. |
| $20,000 to $49,999 | 13.00% p.a. | 13.42% p.a. |
| $10,000 to $19,999 | 12.00% p.a. | 12.36% p.a. |
| $2000 to $9999 | 10.00% p.a. | 10.25% p.a. |
| $500 to $1999 | 8.50% p.a. | 8.68% p.a. |

Interest is calculated on the daily balance and is payable half-yearly on the first working day of June and December. Interest is not paid on deposits held for less than one month or where the account balance is below $500.

### Transaction/Savings Accounts

## KEYCARD SAVINGS ACCOUNTS — AT CALL
Up to 13.50% p.a.

| On Full Balance | |
|---|---|
| $50,000 and over | 13.50% p.a. |
| $20,000 to $49,999 | 12.00% p.a. |
| $10,000 to $19,999 | 11.00% p.a. |
| $2000 to $9999 | 9.00% p.a. |
| Less than $2000 | 8.50% p.a. |

Interest is calculated on the minimum balance each calendar month and is payable on the first working day in June.

## PASSBOOK ACCOUNTS — AT CALL

| | Up to 6.00% p.a. |
|---|---|
| On that part of the balance over $4000 | 6.00% p.a. |
| Up to and including $4000 | 3.75% p.a. |

Interest is calculated on the minimum balance each calendar month and is payable yearly in June.

## APPROVED DEPOSIT FUND

This facility is available for the lodgment of Eligible Termination Payments only.

At 31 December 1989 the assets of the Fund were earning 13.32% p.a. after tax and fees. A continuation of current interest rates should see depositors receiving a rate of return greater than the current rate over the income period to 30 June 1989.

| | |
|---|---|
| Earnings credited for the six months ended 31/12/89 | 10.56% p.a. |
| Net yield for twelve months ended 31/12/89 | 11.47% p.a. |

## COMMONWEALTH DEVELOPMENT BANK HIGH YIELD DEPOSITS

| | Up to 15.75% p.a. |
|---|---|

Minimum Deposit $10,000
Maximum Deposit $250,000

| | |
|---|---|
| 2 Years | 15.75% p.a. |
| 3 Years | 15.00% p.a. |
| 4 Years | 14.00% p.a. |
| 5 Years | 14.00% p.a. |

Interest is calculated on a daily basis and is payable every three months from the date of lodgment.

## COMMONWEALTH MORTGAGE FUND

| | |
|---|---|
| The annualised rate for the 12 months ended November 1989 | 14.16% p.a. |
| Earning rate for the quarter ended November 1989 | 15.505% p.a. |

Application for units may only be made on the application form attached to the current prospectus ADB 1151.

Neither Commonwealth Bank of Australia nor the Commonwealth of Australia nor the Commonwealth Management Services Limited guarantees the performance of the Fund, nor the return of Capital.

## Westpac Interest-bearing Deposits (IBDs)

| Term | Interest rate |
|---|---|
| | **$500 to less than $50,000** |
| Interest paid at maturity (normal): | |
| 7 days to less than 1 month | 10.00% p.a. |
| 1 month to less than 3 months | 11.50% p.a. |
| 3 months to less than 4 months | 14.50% p.a. |
| 4 months to less than 6 months | 16.50% p.a. |
| 6 months to less than 13 months | 15.25% p.a. |
| 13 months to less than 25 months | 14.50% p.a. |
| over 25 months | 13.50% p.a. |
| Interest paid monthly: | |
| 3 months to less than 4 months | 14.00% p.a. |
| 4 months to less than 6 months | 16.00% p.a. |
| 6 months to less than 13 months | 14.75% p.a. |
| 13 months to less than 25 months | 14.00% p.a. |
| over 25 months | 13.00% p.a. |
| | **$50,000 to $250,00** |
| Interest paid at maturity (normal): | |
| 7 days to less than 1 month | 11.50% p.a. |
| 1 month to less than 2 months | 13.50% p.a. |
| 2 months to less than 3 months | 15.00% p.a. |
| 3 months to less than 4 months | 16.50% p.a. |
| 4 months to less than 6 months | 17.00% p.a. |
| 6 months to less than 13 months | 15.50% p.a. |
| 13 months to less than 25 months | 14.50% p.a. |
| over 25 months | 13.50% p.a. |
| Interest paid monthly: | |
| 3 months to less than 4 months | 16.00% p.a. |
| 4 months to less than 6 months | 16.50% p.a. |
| 6 months to less than 13 months | 15.00% p.a. |
| 13 months to less than 25 months | 14.00% p.a. |
| over 25 months | 13.00% p.a. |

Rates effective 22 May 1989 and subject to change without notice.

**Overdraft, Borrowing Money**

Apart from loans from family or friends (and always do it on a business basis), one way of borrowing money is with a bank overdraft. With an overdraft the interest rate is calculated daily on what you owe. This means that if you borrow $5000 and repay $4000 you will pay interest only on the $1000 still owing.

If your bank cannot or will not give you an overdraft, they may offer you a personal loan. The money can be borrowed for a variety of needs, including a holiday. But once again, interest rates on personal loans vary, so it will pay to shop around. Do not forget Visa, Mastercard, Bankcard etc. for, even if there is no 'free credit' period, in some cases, interest rates are lower than personal loan interest rates.

**Credit Card Borrowing: Shop around**

Continuing interest rate increases on credit/debit cards reinforce the need to shop for the best deals.

These could be available through the old banks, building societies, credit unions or some of the new banks. Interest rates on Bankcard, Mastercard and Visa have risen significantly in recent times, some to as high as 24 per cent.

Subject to what credit limit you are allowed, Westpac's Mastercard interest rate of 19.2 per cent, even without a free credit period, is not unattractive. Nor is National Mutual Royal Bank Visa, which has an interest rate of 19 per cent.

On Bankcard, and with some Visa cards, provided you pay in full within a specified period, there are no interest charges. But make sure your credits go through by the due date, otherwise you will be up for interest.

**New Banks**

Over the past few years we have seen the creation of a number of new Australian banks including the Australian Bank, the Macquarie Bank and the Challenge Bank, which was formerly the Hotham Building Society. However, since deregulation was announced we've seen a number of so-called foreign banks opening their doors and they have certainly shown their aggressive competitiveness in attracting new customers.

By way of illustration some of the new banks have been offering extremely attractive interest rates on a range of term deposits and Cash Management Trusts, and rates of 15.5–16.5 per cent per annum cannot be ignored, either by investors or their competitors. Some of the 'new' banks making their mark include:

Barclays Bank
CitiBank
Lloyds Bank NZA

Chase AMP has also been prominent with its presentations and invitations together with the old, established but new-look Bank of New Zealand. And other banks will certainly follow these examples, in one way or another.

## BARCLAYS BANK AUSTRALIA LIMITED

### INTEREST RATES FOR TERM DEPOSITS OF $5,000 TO LESS THAN $50,0000

| Term | Interest payable quarterly and on repayment | Interest payable monthly | Interest compounded quarterly |
|------|------|------|------|
| 30 days to 3 months | 11.00% | | |
| 3 months to 6 months | 17.50% | | |
| 7 months to 12 months | 15.50% | | 15.50% |
| 13 months to 24 months | 15.00% | 14.50% | 15.0% |
| 25 months to 36 months | 14.50% | 14.00% | 14.50% |
| 37 months to 48 months | 14.50% | 14.00% | 14.50% |
| 49 months to 60 months | 14.50% | 14.00% | 14.50% |

### CHALLENGE BANK

#### TERM DEPOSITS

| Term | | Interest per annum |
|------|------|------|
| 7 days | $1–999 | 6.5% |
| | $1000–4,999 | 13.64% |
| | $5,000–19,999 | 14.64% |
| | $20,000 and over | 15.64% |
| For deposits of $200 and over: | | |
| 30 days to 3 months | | 14.00% |
| 45 days | | 14.00% |
| 60 days | | 14.50% |
| 75 days | | 14.50% |
| 3 months | | 16.00% |
| 4 months | | 16.25% |
| 5 months | | 16.25% |
| 6 months | | 16.50% |
| 7 months | | 15.50% |
| 8 months | | 15.50% |
| 9 months | | 15.50% |
| 10 months | | 15.50% |
| 11 months | | 15.50% |
| 1 year | | 15.50% |
| 2 years | | 14.50% |
| 3 years | | 14.50% |

#### ACHIEVER ACCOUNT (at call)

| | |
|------|------|
| $500–2000 | 8.00% |
| $2000–10,000 | 10.50% |
| $10,000–20,000 | 11.00% |
| $20,000–50,000 | 13.00% |
| $50,000 and over | 14.00% |

Interest rates effective June 1989.
Interest rates subject to change without notice.

# Building Societies

During the past few years Building Societies have attract-ed millions of investors, and deposits are now usually classified as Trustee Investments. Funds are readily avail-able and interest rates are frequently far more attractive than those available elsewhere. These institutions also establish that second vital link for would-be home buyers and borrowers.

As with other investments couples should have sep-arate accounts — *not* joint accounts — and should each authorise the other to withdraw on their account.

Parents should encourage children to open accounts in their own names — at the earliest age possible, in other words as soon as they can sign their name. At the same time the child should authorise one or both parents to withdraw from the account in the event of illness or absence.

Some building society accounts calculate interest on a monthly basis while others calculate interest on a daily basis, so it can pay to shop around. Where interest is calculated on a monthly basis, 'timing' your withdrawal is essential otherwise you could miss out on some inter-est. In other words, make sure you withdraw on the first day of the month, not the last day. And this applies to other institutions as well.

A recent and welcome service has been the introduc-tion of *term deposits* generally ranging from 30 days to 24 months. The longer the term the higher the interest. (It should be noted that Building Society interest rates can vary from State to State.)

However, as with other fixed interest investments, it could pay to have a mixture of the various terms, then if interest rates do rise, the short term deposits can be reinvested at higher rates as they mature. If interest rates start to fall, then reverse the situation and select longer term investments.

Reinvestment of interest as it is received is a practice followed by many investors, and it would be helpful to open a separate building society 'Investment Account' for this purpose. When the interest has grown to a

9

reasonable size it can be withdrawn and reinvested, to earn higher interest, in another term deposit or in semi-governmental loans or debentures.

Children should have building society accounts as well as bank accounts. This is just in case the bank cannot or will not lend them money when they need it. In the meantime they are earning more in interest with a building society and the money is readily available if needed.

Remember, some building societies pay interest every six months, some every three.

## St George Building Society

Deposit from as little as $1000 up to a maximum of $100,000. Term Deposit rates.

| Term | Interest per annum | Interest payable |
|------|--------------------|------------------|
| 4 months | 14.50% | On maturity |
| 3 months to 6 months | 14.00% | On maturity |
| 7 months to 12 months | 15.75% | On maturity |
| 13 months to 60 months | 14.75% | On maturity |

Rates effective 1 July 1989

**Home Loans** The main objective of Building Societies is to provide money for housing and this they normally do very well. Even allowing for the upward and downward movements in interest rates Building Societies in some cases are much more competitive than banks, as can be seen from the following table of rates and terms available through St George Building Society.

### Monthly Repayments @ 16.75% P.A.

| Loan Amount $ | Term of Loan (Years) | | | |
|---------------|------|------|------|------|
| | 10 $ | 15 $ | 20 $ | 25 $ |
| 45,000 | 775 | 685 | 652 | 639 |
| 50,000 | 862 | 761 | 724 | 709 |
| 51,000 | 879 | 776 | 739 | 724 |
| 52,000 | 896 | 792 | 753 | 738 |
| 53,000 | 913 | 807 | 768 | 752 |
| 54,000 | 930 | 822 | 782 | 766 |
| 55,000 | 948 | 837 | 797 | 780 |
| 56,000 | 965 | 852 | 811 | 795 |
| 57,000 | 982 | 868 | 826 | 809 |
| 58,000 | 999 | 883 | 840 | 823 |
| 59,000 | 1017 | 898 | 855 | 837 |

| | | | |
|---|---|---|---|
| 60,000 | 1034 | 913 | 869 | 851 |
| 63,000 | 1085 | 959 | 913 | 894 |
| 65,000 | 1120 | 989 | 942 | 922 |
| 70,000 | 1206 | 1065 | 1014 | 993 |
| 75,000 | 1292 | 1141 | 1086 | 1064 |
| 80,000 | 1378 | 1218 | 1159 | 1135 |
| 85,000 | 1464 | 1294 | 1231 | 1206 |
| 90,000 | 1550 | 1370 | 1304 | 1277 |
| 95,000 | 1637 | 1446 | 1376 | 1348 |
| 100,000 | 1723 | 1522 | 1448 | 1418 |
| 105,000 | 1809 | 1598 | 1521 | 1489 |
| 110,000 | 1895 | 1674 | 1593 | 1560 |
| 115,000 | 1981 | 1750 | 1665 | 1631 |
| 120,000 | 2067 | 1826 | 1738 | 1702 |

Rates effective 1 July 1989

With a number of mergers and takeovers the Building Society movement is certainly undergoing a period of rationalisation. The trend is likely to continue and we could well see the Credit Unions playing an even greater role in providing 'people services', including greater lending for housing.

# Credit Unions

These days there are not many companies, local councils or government departments that do not have a credit union. Over the past few years they have become innovators as well as strong competitors of banks and building societies. They offer attractive rates of interest on savings and if you want to borrow money, it is far easier and usually a lot cheaper to borrow from your credit union than from a finance company. It is also frequently cheaper than some bank loans.

If your company does not have its own credit union or you are self-employed, you are likely to find a community credit union in your own district. So check your phone book or your local Credit Union Association for details.

As with banks and building societies funds can be deposited in a variety of investments which quite frequently offer higher returns than those available from banks and building societies. Interest rates will, of course, determine whether one utilises the facilities of a credit union, building society, bank or other institution. If it suits your purpose use them all.

But it is important to note that interest rates vary from one credit union to another and from state to state.

## FIXED TERM DEPOSITS
### (EFFECTIVE 19 JUNE 1989)

| Term | Minimum each deposit | Interest rate | Interest calculated daily and payable |
|------|----------------------|---------------|----------------------------------------|
| 30 days at call (Up to $9,999) ($10,000 and over) | $500 | 11.00% | Quarterly |
| | $500 | 12.00% | Quarterly |
| 60 days | $500 | 13.25% | On maturity |
| 190 days | $500 | 14.25% | On maturity |
| 100 days | $1000 | 17.00% | On maturity |
| 120 days | $500 | 15.00% | On maturity |
| 150 days | $2000 | 15.75% | On maturity |
| 180 days | $500 | 14.50% | On maturity |
| 1 year | $500 | 13.25% | Half yearly |
| Initially 1 year, then 30 days at call | $5000 | 14.00% | Fortnightly |
| 2 years | $500 | 12.75% | Half yearly |
| 3 years | $500 | 12.75% | Half yearly |

## Savings Accounts

Free counter cheques and postage. Access via ATMs, Visa cards and personal cheque books. Interest calculated daily on minimum monthly balance, credited quarterly:

| At Call and Future Savers | |
|---|---|
| Up to $1,999 | 7.00% |
| $2,000–$4,999 | 8.00% |
| $5,000–$19,999 | 10.00% |
| $20,000 and over | 11.00% |
| Christmas Club | |
| $1 and over | 10.00% |
| Target Savers | |
| up to $4,999 | 8.00% |
| $5,000 and over | 10.00% |

By way of example, if you obtain a line of credit of $10,000 at an interest rate of 19 per cent per annum and you use the full amount, the interest payable for the first month will be $161.37. In addition, each month you will probably be required to repay at least 5 per cent of the total outstanding balance ($500), but then you can again draw up to your original available credit of $10,000. The facility remains in place indefinitely, and you pay only for what you use.

# Taxation

**Your Financial and Investment Priorities**

These days, more than ever before, it is essential to place taxation high on your list of financial and investment priorities. And in view of the recent changes as well as the proposed changes to the taxation laws, you must have tax in mind at all times whether you are investing your lump sum superannuation payment, buying shares, investing in fixed interest securities such as Bonds, Debentures and Notes, Approved Deposit Funds, Deferred Annuities, Annuities, Managed Investment Bonds or Friendly Societies. Because the tax area is now a minefield you could get *blown up* or badly hurt — financially, as well as personally — if you receive the wrong advice or make the wrong decision. Once again it is back to basics.

**Personal Income Tax**

The 1989/90 scale rates for personal income tax are as follows:

Total Taxable Income

| Not less than $ | Not more than $ | Tax on total taxable income |
|---|---|---|
| 0 | 5100 | Nil |
| 5101 | 17,650 | Nil + 21¢ for each $1 in excess of $5100 |
| 17,651 | 20,600 | $2635.50 + 29¢ for each $1 in excess of $17,650 |
| 20,601 | 5,000 | $3491 + 39¢ for each $1 in excess of $20,600 |
| 35,001 | 0,000 | $9107 + 47¢ for each $1 in excess of $35,000 |
| 50,001 and over | | $16,157 + 48¢ for each $1 in excess of $50,000 |

**Investments for Children**

Tens of thousands of parents and grandparents continue to open and operate trust accounts or invest *in trust* with Credit Unions, Banks, Building Societies, Finance Companies and Cash Management Trusts on behalf of their children and grandchildren without realising the taxation implications.

Following a change of interpretation, the Taxation Department is now saying that taxpayers who have invested *in trust* (not family trusts) in reality control the investment and that being so they are obliged to include the interest earned in their own personal income tax returns.

So, what are the solutions?

- Once the children can sign their own names in *running writing* the children open the accounts in their own names.
- Where they are unable to do this, buy investments that will not involve parents etc. in a taxable situation.

This could include buying new and old Aussie Bonds, old Treasury Bonds, semi-Government loans and Debentures etc. It could also include the purchase of shares — contact a stockbroker — irrespective of the children's ages.

**Children's Threshold**

The children's investment tax-free threshold is $416 and it is essential that this figure is not exceeded. So if it is necessary to transfer investments into another name or sell them or cash them in to keep the income below this figure, you must act quickly.

**Resident Minors — Unearned Income**

NEW THRESHOLD

The Government has eliminated the incentive for splitting 'unearned' income with minor children and the rates of tax are as follows:

| | |
|---|---|
| $1 to $416 | Nil |
| $417 to $1525 | 66¢ |
| $1526 and above | 48¢ |

**Non Residents**

The same rates of tax apply to the unearned income of non-resident minor children except that income up to $416 is taxed at 29% from 1989/90 with appropriate shading-in arrangements above $416.

But there are several additional points on children's income that should not be ignored. If, for example, you run a business or farm, you can legitimately pay your child or children wages which will be tax deductible to you — the employer — and tax-free to the children up to the adult tax-free threshold of $5,100 and that also applies to their part or full time earnings. On top of that money earned from investment by the child or children will not be subject to the $416 threshold either. So all told they can earn up to $5,100 tax-free from these sources.

**Casual Workers**

These days many people work on a part time or casual basis. It might be from choice, it might be the only sort of work available. Whatever the reason, part time or casual workers have the same tax obligations as full time workers. If they earn more than the tax-free threshold they will pay tax. If they earn less than $5,100 no tax will be payable. Some casual or part time workers might be tempted into thinking they can ignore their tax obligations completely. They may have got away without paying tax in the past, but the scene is changing very quickly. Casual moonlighting might seem fun but if you evade your income tax obligations and you are caught the fines alone will make it a very expensive pastime.

**Omitted Income Blitz**

Widespread media coverage regarding the Taxation Department's blitz on omitted income from bank, building society and credit union investments etc. should not come as any surprise. Lists of interest earned have been going to the Taxation Department for years.

Be it petty tax evasion or massive tax evasion, the majority pay, particularly PAYE taxpayers. Tax minimisation is one thing but tax evasion is another. Despite the tightening of the rules over recent years, tax minimisation — within the law — is quite legal.

**Lodging Returns**

How quickly you lodge your income tax return will depend on whether you expect a refund or you expect to pay some extra tax.

Many employers go out of their way to provide group certificates and tax stamps well before the end of the financial year and this is a practice to be encouraged.

If, for one reason or another, the issuing of the group certificates etc. is delayed, and you are expecting a refund you may be very frustrated. But if you expect to pay some tax, then delay lodging your return till the last day possible, which is usually 31 August. But make sure your lodgement is no later unless an extension has been granted.

**Provisional Tax**

Each year thousands of Australian taxpayers receive an income tax assessment which includes a bill for provisional tax.

Provisional tax is the tax due to be paid when taxable income from any source exceeds $999 in the financial year when tax has not been deducted at the source. This tax, which, in the eyes of many people can only be described as obnoxious, hits people from all walks of life.

They include pensioners with savings invested in banks, building societies, credit unions, bonds and debentures; people with a second job; people who own income-producing property and, of course, retirees who live off their investment income.

The important considerations with regard to provisional tax are first to be aware of it, second to understand it and third to plan for it.

While paying tax in advance, so to speak, is certainly unfair, in principle it is not quite as bad as people make out. In the case of PAYE taxpayers, tax is deducted from the weekly, fortnightly or monthly pay packet but in the case of provisional tax in effect you have nine months grace before the tax is payable.

And this means that the money can be invested to earn interest/income over that nine month period.

Some people make it a regular practice to put money aside to meet the provisional tax bill. But it can be a major problem for those people in receipt of investment income of one kind or another and retirees, certainly in the first year, should be aware of the situation. Sad to say, on many occasions they are not and this is when the provisional tax bill comes as a shock.

Sometimes it can mean the forced sale of recently made investments — even at a loss — to find the tax money. So it is imperative that money is set aside in one form or another and ensuring that it is readily available around provisional tax time. Many people find it difficult to understand or know what their provisional tax bill is likely to be. However a phone call to the Taxation Department — you do not have to give your name — will usually solve the problem. In some cases provisional tax can be minimised or eliminated by legally changing, if only in part, from one type of investment to another. The immediate aim here should be to keep the investment income less than the threshold of $999.

An alternative might be to transfer investments to another member of the family. If, for example, you have $15,000 which you intend investing for 12 months at 10 per cent it would pay to choose an investment that will give you $750 this financial year and $750 in the next financial year. In this case you will not be up for provisional tax because the interest earned is less than $999.

**Capital Gains Tax**  While this tax applies from 20 September 1985, it is important to note it is not backdated, nor does it apply to the all-important family home.

Consequently we can expect to see more people investing in more expensive homes and also adding to their existing homes.

While the new tax is indexed for inflation — in other words you pay tax only on your real nett gain — it really is a classic case of negative thinking as the tax revenue to be gained will be nominal to say the least, certainly in the immediate future, and will be reduced by the cost of policing the tax.

It is even more surprising that there is not a tax-free threshold for nominal gains to reduce some administrative costs.

**Capital Gains Tax — The Old**

In all discussions heard since the tax reforms were announced one could be forgiven for thinking that capital gains tax only started from 20 September 1985.

These statements are misleading for under the old Tax Act we had a capital gains tax; for it still comes back to one's intention at the time the investment was made.

If you bought some shares to re-sell at a profit, it would not matter if you held the shares for 20 years — you would still be liable for tax on the gain made after you sold. And the same would apply to gold, silver and other commodities.

If, on the other hand, you bought some shares for investment purposes — as against resale — then in normal circumstances your capital gain would be tax-free, providing the shares had been held for at least 12 months and preferably longer. And the same would normally apply to real estate.

**Minimise Tax Bill**

As mentioned elsewhere, the timing of decisions in relation to ceasing work, retiring and the selling of investments can have an important bearing on your tax bill. And this certainly applies to the 'old rules' regarding superannuation and long service leave.

Despite constant reminders over the years, many retirees give little thought to their retirement date and this oversight can be a tax cost.

If, for example, you have the choice of retiring this financial year or the next, opt for the later date when your income from all sources is likely to be lower. So too will be your tax bill in relation to your lump sum superannuation payments.

**Old Tax Rules and Super**

A lot of people are still worried and confused as to the old rules and their application in relation to more recent tax changes. In reality there is nothing to worry about.

The old rules still apply in relation to superannuation benefits and this means that the lump sum will be subject to tax on only 5 per cent of the total 'earned' up to 30 June 1983. That is tax *on* 5 per cent not 5 per cent tax.

So in the case of a $100,000 lump sum you will pay tax on only $5,000. The same tax rules apply to long service leave 'earned' up to 15 August 1978.

**Include Interest on Borrowings**

Another problem for the majority of taxpayers concerns tax deductions. Surprising as it may seem, many people fail to include interest paid on borrowed money as an expense, be it for renting out the holiday home, buying a unit or running a business.

Whether it is an investment made before or after changes to the negative gearing rules in relation to real estate, interest paid on borrowed money which is used to produce income is partly or wholly tax deductible in normal circumstances.

On the other hand, any income received, be it by way of bank, building society, credit union, bond, debenture or note interest and dividends must be included in your return. If it is not included, and the Taxation Department finds out, the penalties could be horrendous, as is the case with other forms of evasion.

**Dividends Taxable**

Most company dividends are taxable and should be included in your tax return. Opening accounts in phoney names is foolhardy. So, too, is buying bonds and shares in fictitious names.

Under the old rules, capitalising your pending dividends can also save tax dollars. If, for example, you are about to sell some shares and there is a dividend coming up you might be tempted to wait till after the dividend is paid, but assuming you are a taxpayer you will then have to include the dividend in your return.

On the other hand, if you sell the shares just before the dividend is paid you will usually receive a higher selling price, which is classed as capital, and depending on how long the shares have been held and for what purpose they were purchased, then there is no income in the 'normal sense' of the word and therefore no tax to be paid.

**Late Returns**

Tax returns for the majority of people are due to be lodged by 31 August, but delays can occur. If you should find yourself in this situation, it would pay to protect yourself by writing to the Taxation Department and asking for an extension of time. They may grant an extension or they may not, depending upon the reasons given, but at the very least you have kept in touch with them. On the other hand, if you do not ask for an extension and you lodge your return weeks or months after the due date, then you are simply asking for a fine, so why throw away money?

**Use your Deductions?**

Would you lend someone money interest free for 12 months? Probably not. Then why lend it interest free to the Taxation Department? Every year tens of thousands of taxpayers use tax deductions as a form of compulsory saving and these excess payments run into millions of interest free dollars for the government. If it is difficult for you to save on a regular basis then go ahead with the present arrangement and collect your refund cheque at the end of the year. On the other hand, you could ask your employer to arrange for an extra five or 10 dollars per week to be automatically deducted from your pay packet through one of the payroll deduction schemes as a better form of compulsory saving.

**Invest your Refund**

At tax refund time millions of dollars flow back to many thousands of taxpayers. For some the refunds will be small but for others refunds will be quite substantial — in some cases running into thousands of dollars.

Whether the refund is big or small, tax refund time is a good time to start your own investment programme.

For many people there is a great temptation to rush out and spend the refund, but if you can hold off and invest it wisely instead, eventually you will have more money to spend.

And make sure you cash your refund cheque as soon as you get it, whatever your use for the money. Do not leave it lying around for days or weeks — an uncashed cheque earns no interest.

**Expenses**

Expenses incurred in earning a salary or wage must be substantiated. Expenses to be looked at in detail include:
- Subscriptions to trade, business and professional organisations
- Interest with borrowing and mortgage discharge expenses

- Lease payments and related expenses
- Tools of trade, trade journals and protective clothing
- Depreciation together with repairs to plant and equipment

The information to be disclosed should include:

- The date the expense was incurred
- The name of the provider of the goods and services
- Total expenditure
- The date of the invoice or receipt etc.

Taxpayers involved in overseas or extended domestic travel for business or professional purposes must maintain a diary of expenses including the following information:

- Activities conducted on the trip
- The place, date and time the activity began
- The nature and duration of the business activities
- All taxpayers should note that deductions will not be allowed for any business activities not properly recorded

In relation to substantiation requirements for employment-related expenses, two general exclusions apply:

- Claims of reasonable overtime, meal allowances under industrial awards or reasonable travel allowances for domestic travel
- Claims for employment-related expenses other than for the above which in total do not exceed $300

There are several ways of overcoming these difficulties, the first being to carefully maintain your own personal diary of expenses. Another way would be to take out an expense account Bankcard, Visa, Mastercard, American Express, Diners Club etc. and all business-related expenses will be automatically and formally recorded.

Strange as it may seem, expense account credit cards have been around since credit cards were first introduced but very few people have been aware of them, let alone made use of them.

On top of that, very few people in the credit card business have actively promoted the idea.

# Fixed Interest Investment

Success in the field of Fixed Interest Investment comes from:

- Knowing the various investment avenues available
- Selecting those appropriate to your needs and (MOST IMPORTANT OF ALL)
- Being able to anticipate or take advantage of INTEREST RATE CHANGES

As far as *interest rates* are concerned it is the market place and governments of the day which influence and help determine these levels. At the federal level it is the interest rates paid on Government Securities which are the generally accepted yardsticks. These rates determine what you will *earn* in interest when you invest money and what you will *pay* when borrowing money. Notwithstanding deregulation, these rates also influence other interest rates, including what you will earn from banks, bank bills, building societies, credit unions, cash management trusts, debentures, notes, Treasury notes, mortgages etc.

These days it is an economic fact of life that while interest rates can fall they can also rise, and the sooner this all-important fact is recognised and accepted the better. Without doubt the major fault of most fixed interest investors is that they tie up their money for long periods of time. When interest rates go up they find themselves in a 'locked in' situation.

If they sell their investments before maturity they will suffer a capital loss. On the other hand, if they keep their 'old' investments they will miss out on the higher interest rates.

To be fair to most fixed interest investors — certainly in the past — they usually got 'locked in' due to ignorance or ill-informed or downright biased advice from 'assumed' professional investment advisors.

**Australian Savings Bonds**

Series 29 was the last Australian Savings Bond to be issued, however old Savings Bonds can still be purchased as Bearer Bonds or inscribed stock.

**Bearer Bonds or Inscribed Stock**

Old Bearer Bonds are still available with interest coupons attached. When the interest falls due you simply clip the coupons from the bond and present them at *any* bank for payment. Some banks now make a charge for cashing interest coupons and, although this charge is only nominal, if your bank is in this category go to a bank which will not make a charge, preferably the Reserve Bank. Bearer Bonds must at all times be kept in a safe place such as a bank safety deposit box for, if lost or stolen, anyone can cash them. At the same time, make a list of the bond serial numbers as an added precaution. But do not put the list in the safety deposit box!

The alternative to Bearer Bonds is Inscribed Stock. For most people Inscribed Stock is the safest way to hold bonds. New bonds, as mentioned earlier, are no longer issued in Bearer form.

**Old Bonds**

Although Australian Savings Bonds are not 'officially' listed on Australian stock exchanges a very active secondary market can develop in some of the *old* series bonds. Before the recent increase in interest rates there was a very active market in Series 22 and Series 23 bonds.

These bonds which carry interest rates of 14.75 and 13.75 per cent respectively could have been purchased — at a premium — but even allowing for the extra cost and the buying brokerage, which incidentally is only 25 cents per $100, the returns (yields) were well above the returns available from later bond issues.

By the same token, if interest rates should drop, anyone holding high coupon Savings Bonds will probably find their bonds are worth more than they paid for them. If this situation should arise sell the bonds through a stockbroker rather than encash them.

**Bond Switch**

Whenever interest rates go up, *all* investors should immediately review their existing fixed interest investments with a view to 'switching' from the lower interest rates to higher interest rates.

This is particularly important to holders of Australian Savings Bonds. As previously mentioned one of the major attractions of these bonds is the ability to encash them at any time by giving one month's notice. Yet through ignorance or just plain laziness thousands of investors continue to hold millions of dollars worth of old bonds even though the interest rates they are receiving are less than the current rate. The following list details all Australian Savings Bond issues since they were first introduced.

## AUSTRALIAN SAVINGS BONDS

| Series | Interest Rate % | Maturity Date |
|--------|-----------------|---------------|
| 1 | 10.50 | Feb 1, 1983 |
| 2 | 9.50 | Nov 1, 1983 |
| 3 | 9.20 | Feb 1, 1984 |
| 4 | 9.20 | Apr 1, 1984 |
| 5 | 9.50 | Jun 1, 1984 |
| 6 | 9.80 | Jun 1, 1984 |
| 7 | 10.00 | Aug 1, 1984 |
| 8 | 10.00 | Dec 1, 1984 |
| 9 | 9.75 | Jul 1, 1985 |
| 10 | 9.35 | Jul 1, 1985 |
| 11 | 9.00 | Sep 1, 1985 |
| 12 | 9.00 | May 1, 1986 |
| 13 | 8.75 | Jun 1, 1986 |
| 14 | 9.25 | Dec 1, 1986 |
| 15 | 9.25 | Jul 1, 1987 |
| 16 | 9.75 | Dec 1, 1987 |
| 17 | 10.25 | Apr 1, 1988 |
| 18 | 11.50 | Aug 1, 1988 |
| 19 | 12.25 | Dec 1, 1988 |
| 20 | 12.25 | May 1, 1989 |
| 21 | 13.25 | Oct 1, 1989 |
| 22 | 14.75 | Dec 1, 1989 |
| 23 | 13.75 | Mar 1, 1990 |
| 24 | 12.25 | Aug 1, 1990 |
| 25 | 12.25 | Feb 1, 1991 |
| 26 | 11.75 | Jul 1, 1991 |
| 27 | 11.25 | Aug 1, 1991 |
| 28 | 11.25 | Subject to |
| 29 | 13.00 | date of purchase |

Investors holding any early issue bonds — with low interest rates — should give the required 30 days notice of encashment immediately and reinvest in higher interest savings bonds or elsewhere.

It is important to note that a new interest saving facility was introduced when Series 21 was announced. In essence it means that if you are transferring Series 20 Saving Bonds — and any subsequent series — into new savings bonds the higher interest rate will apply from the day you give notice not 30 days later.

**Early Redemption**

In the event of redemption before the first interest payment there is an interest rate penalty of 4 per cent meaning that instead of receiving an interest rate of 13 per cent on Series 29 bonds the return would be only 9 per cent. *However* it is also important to note that by giving the required 30 days notice say 29 days before the first interest payment you would '*qualify*' for the higher rate.

**Indexed Bonds**

Another long-overdue investment has been the introduction of *Indexed Bonds* which were launched in August 1985. The initial *minimum investment* is $1,000 and investors can buy up to $100,000 of each maturity. The type of Indexed Bonds you buy will of course be influenced by personal as well as financial considerations. If, for example, you need regular income then the Interest Indexed Bonds would be more appealing.

These bonds protect investors with an automatic adjustment of the interest rate in line with the rate of inflation. So these bonds should appeal to retirees and others wanting money to live on. They could also appeal to parents and grandparents seeking an appropriate investment for the education needs of their children and grandchildren along with other investments such as friendly societies and managed investment bonds subject of course to the tax considerations at the time the investments are made.

On the other hand *Capital Indexed Bonds* would well suit those not in immediate need of money to live on. These bonds protect investors with the *capital value* being adjusted every three months once again to compensate for inflation. At the same time fixed interest rates will apply on the adjusted capital and the interest (as is the case with the interest indexed bonds) will be paid every three months.

Arrangements can also be made to have the interest sent to you by cheque or credited to your bank account or, where appropriate, to a building society account. Once again, unlike Australian Savings Bonds, Indexed Bonds cannot be '*cashed in*' by giving 30 days notice. But like Treasury Bonds they will be *listed* on Australian stock exchanges ensuring hopefully a ready made market. Additionally up to $25,000 face value of a holding can be sold to the Reserve Bank — at the current market price — on any banking day.

By way of example it should be noted interest payments due in, say, November 1990 will be based on the *average change* in the Consumer Price Index over the March and June quarters, while February 1991 payments will be based on the June and September quarters of 1990. Income, whether in the form of real interest discounts or increases in the capital value of the Indexed

Bonds, will be taxable each year on the amount received or compounded over that year. So it would pay to buy these bonds in the name of the lower taxpayer or better still a non-taxpayer.

Another point to note is that if you are buying bonds as a part of your retirement investment portfolio buy a '*spread*' of bonds which will mature over a period of years.

**Treasury Notes**

These short term Commonwealth Government guaranteed investments are offered from time to time by *periodic tender* for terms of 13 or 26 weeks. The *minimum investment in Treasury Notes* is $100,000 *face value* and in multiples of $5,000 *face value* thereafter. Obviously Treasury Notes involve large sums of money and normally would not interest small investors. It is, however, interesting to note that over the past 12 months a number of financial institutions are offering access to Treasury Notes with sums ranging from $10,000 to $20,000 and the yields (returns) have been equal to or better than cash management trusts and bank bills and that has meant returns as high as 18 per cent per annum. Treasury Notes are frequently advertised and people looking for a short term government guaranteed investment offering higher returns than those available elsewhere would be well advised to take advantage of these offers when and where appropriate.

**Costs of Buying**

For direct applicants there are no costs in buying Treasury Notes and where investors are buying a 'part Treasury Note' 'brokerage costs' are allowed for in the sale price. So, in effect, if you are offered a return of say 16, 17 or 18 per cent per annum that return allows for any charges.

**Taxation**

The increase in the value of a Treasury Note from the date the notes are purchased or otherwise acquired and the date on which the notes are disposed of or redeemed will be assessable income for taxpaying investors. So once again it is a question of looking at your overall tax position as well as the returns available.

**Commonwealth Securities**

Although not Commonwealth Bonds in the normal sense Commonwealth Securities still enjoy the status of a Commonwealth Government guarantee. Some of the better known Commonwealth Securities would be

Northern Territory Bonds
Telecom Bonds (see Application sample —
Appendix 3)

The *minimum investment* varies from authority to authority but it is usually $100 to $1000 and thereafter in multiples of $100. But with certain issues such as Telecom's Monthly Interest Bond the initial minimum investment is $6,000 and thereafter in multiples of $100.

The maximum investment can also vary from one issue to another but could be $500,000. Interest payments can be — depending upon the authority — monthly, quarterly or compound (annually).

For some strange reason the bonds cannot be bought in the names of minors but in most cases they can be bought on the layby system by putting down a 10 per cent deposit and paying off the balance within a prescribed period usually two months. There are no charges in buying new bonds and they can be purchased through stockbrokers, banks, offices of the authority e.g. Telecom or through newspaper advertisements.

**Selling before Maturity**

These bonds can be sold before maturity either over the counter through a stock registry, through stockbrokers or privately, and the time taken is usually 24 hours to a few days.

**Private Issues**

In the case of Telecom Bonds existing investors can invest in private issues of new bonds even if a public issue is not available. So it can pay to enquire from time to time at Telecom offices as well as reading your mail.

**Semi-Government Loans**

As well as Commonwealth Bonds and Commonwealth securities, semi-governmental loans would also be classified as *gilt edged investments*. Although lacking a Commonwealth government guarantee they do have a State government guarantee. Some of the more popular semi-governmental loans would include:

State Energy Commission of WA (SECWA)
Premier State Bonds of NSW
Queensland Bonds
Queensland Electricity Trust
TAS Bonds
VIC Bonds
SAFA Bonds
(See Prospectus sample — Appendix 3.)

As with other government loans these bonds can usually be bought with just a few hundred dollars and in
most cases they can also be purchased on the 10 per cent
layby system with the balance again being payable within
say a two month period. And in a number of cases they
can also be used by parents as an investment for young
children in the same way as Aussie Bonds and the age
limit is sometimes higher than 14 years of age, e.g. 15 in
the case of Queensland Bonds.

Like *old* Treasury Bonds, *old* Semis (as they are called)
can also be bought and sold through the secondary
market.

## Debentures

Debentures are basically the same as mortgages and from
a security point of view they are one of the safest and
most rewarding forms of fixed interest investments because they usually have first call on the company's assets.

There are many types of debentures available, including ordinary debentures, flexible interest, compound
interest, deferred interest, just to name a few.

For the retired, ordinary and deferred interest debentures in particular, could be very important inclusions in
the investment programme.

Apart from debentures issued at call, debentures are
usually issued for fixed periods of time ranging from
three months to one, two, three, five, ten or even twenty
years.

These days, with high inflation and fluctuating interest
rates, you must be very careful not to tie up money for
long periods of time without adequate protection. At the
moment, most debenture investors are not going beyond
five years as a maximum term. However, when interest
rates appear to be coming down, the period of investment
could be extended to, say, up to 7 or 10 years in order to
'lock into' the high rates. The same advice would apply
to government bonds.

## Compound Debentures

In all forms of investment, there are always traps for the
unwary, and this would apply in the fixed interest field
also. The classic illustration would involve the purchase
of Compound Debentures.

When you invest in compound debentures, it means
that instead of receiving an interest cheque regularly each
month, quarter or half year, the interest is added to the
original sum invested. In other words, the interest is

automatically reinvested (compounded) to earn more interest.

For lazy investors or for those not in need of immediate income, this type of investment, at first glance, may seem attractive. However, with some companies, a closer look will uncover several major disadvantages.

First, interest can be credited annually. Second, the interest rates offered on some compound debentures are below the rates offered on ordinary debentures in the same company.

Based on current interest rates the following illustration clearly shows the substantial difference in returns.

### Five Year Compound Debenture

Capital $1,000
Rate of interest — 14 per cent
Interest added to capital (annually)........................ $140.00

### Five Year Ordinary Debenture

Capital $1,000
Rate of interest — 15 per cent
Interest (paid quarterly) ..................... $150.00 per annum
Difference in income $10 per annum
On $10,000 investment the income difference is $100 per annum.

But we do not stop there. Most finance companies for example pay interest on ordinary debentures monthly, quarterly or half-yearly. Those who invest in compound debentures with annual interest credits are lending their interest to the company — without interest — for twelve months. Providing it fits into your overall plan, it would be far better to buy ordinary debentures and then automatically reinvest the interest as it is received in additional debentures. In other words, *you* compound your interest on a regular basis.

**Deferred Interest Debentures**

Another type of fixed interest investment is the Deferred Interest Debenture. Investors subscribing to this type of investment will not receive any interest until the debenture matures or is redeemed.

Although this type of investment would not be suitable for those in need of *regular* income, for people without immediate income worries, deferred interest debentures could have a major tax attraction.

Deferred interest debentures should also be included in the investment programmes of those approaching retirement. For after retirement, when tax would normally be lower or non-existent, the investment can be withdrawn.

**Monthly Income Debentures**

Many finance companies have also introduced monthly interest paying debentures. Although this facility will certainly cater for the needs of retirees and those in need of regular income, it should not be ignored as an investment facility by those not in need of regular income, for regular reinvestment of the monthly interest cheque — over a 12 month period — would certainly increase the return to well over 17 per cent per annum. (See AGC debenture and/or unsecured note application and bond certificate sample — Appendix 3.)

**Partly Paid Debentures**

Although rare, with some new debenture issues, companies give applicants a choice. They can pay in full at the time of application, or they can pay a deposit and pay off the balance over a three, six or 12 month period, in one or more instalments. With some new debenture issues the deposit can be as low as 10 per cent.

Interest on Partly Paid Debentures is, of course, paid on the amount paid up. Surprisingly, very few investors, including 'professionals', elect to buy on a partly paid basis, yet at times they can be more rewarding than the 'fully paid securities', especially when interest rates are on the way down.

The following illustrations show what can be achieved by buying Partly Paid Debentures instead of Fully Paid Debentures.

| | | | |
|---|---|---|---|
| (i) | Fully Paid Debenture | Market Price | Capital Gain |
| Cost | $100 | $110 | 10 per cent |
| | Partly Paid Debenture | Market Price | Capital Gain |
| Cost | $10 | $14 | 40 per cent |
| | (Balance owing $90) | | |
| (ii) | Fully Paid Debenture | Market Price | Capital Gain |
| Cost | $100 | $106 | 6 per cent |
| | Partly Paid Debenture | Market Price | Capital Gain |
| Cost | $25 | $30 | 20 per cent |
| | (Balance owing $75) | | |

In the first illustration, the capital gain on a fully paid debenture is 10 per cent. But the capital gain on the partly paid debentures is 40 per cent. In the second illustration, the capital gain on the fully paids is 6 per cent while the capital gain on the partly paids is 20 per cent.

Strange as it may seem, the 'listed' partly paid debenture is a better buy than the fully paid. In the previous illustration, the partly paid debenture was selling for $14, with $90 still to pay — making a total cost of $104. The fully paid debenture, however, was selling for $110. Without forgetting the interest difference, there is still a considerable margin in favour of the partly paid debentures plus, of course, cheaper brokerage, when buying.

Although capital gains and price differences of these proportions are extremely rare, it is important to be aware of them. Of course, not everyone would be interested in buying, or, for that matter, trading in partly paid debentures. Even so, the partly paid debenture can serve the same purpose as the partly paid semi-governmental loan when funds are not immediately available to pay for them in full.

**New Issues: Debentures — Notes. Buying Procedures**

Like government bonds, semi-governmental loans, debentures and notes can be purchased in several ways:
1. In the case of a new issue, by direct application through stockbroker, bank, institution or company
2. In the case of a priority issue
   (a) by direct application to the company concerned
   (b) by the purchase of existing listed securities; and
3. Through the market

Before investing in a new debenture or note issue, it is essential to check the following:
- Calibre of company
- Terms of issue
- Asset backing
- Interest cover
- Date/s interest paid
- Early repayment provisions (if any)

**Priority Issues**

In the case of priority debenture and note issues, these are made to existing investors in the company — including share, debenture and note holders. Only on rare occasions will a portion of such an issue be open for public subscription.

Most priority issues are keenly sought, particularly when leading companies are involved and the interest rates offered are attractive.

However, even if you are not an existing investor in a

31

company making such an issue, a purchase of shares, old debentures, or old notes, even a nominal purchase and prompt registration into your name will entitle you to participate in the new issue.

Some companies when making priority, or 'family' issues, as they are sometimes called, pitch interest rates below the market rate and rely on the loyalty and support of existing investors to fill the issue.

Loyalty is admirable, but it should not be taken to extremes. If the interest rates offered in a priority issue are out of line with the market, invest your capital elsewhere.

**Implied Recommendation**

Many new investors automatically, and wrongly, think that because the debenture or note prospectus is on display in a bank or stockbroker's office, that firm or institution is 'recommending' the investment. While this is understandable, it is not the case. So, before investing in any company, seek a professional and unbiased opinion. If in doubt, get a second opinion, or invest your money elsewhere.

**Through the Market**

A third way — and in many cases the best way — to participate in fixed interest investment is to buy securities which are already listed.

Every week, millions of dollars worth of 'old' bonds, semi-governmental loans, debentures and notes change hands through the various stock exchanges.

In nearly every case they are a better investment than buying new loans or debentures.

It is not generally realised that the brokerage costs in buying through the secondary market (the stock exchange) are nominal to say the least, and range from 25 cents per $100 face value for Government bonds, semi-government loans and *short dated* (less than 12 months to maturity) debentures and notes. For debentures and notes which mature later than 12 months from the date of purchase, the brokerage is just $1 per $100.

To be fair to both would-be buyers and stockbrokers, buying 'through the market' would only be worthwhile if a sizeable sum of money was involved and 'sizeable' can vary from stockbroker to stockbroker. In the normal course of events, however, $10,000 would be a reasonable minimum to participate.

Apart from the financial press, information on the

secondary market can be obtained from any stockbroker or bank investment advisory service, and some private advisors.

**Debentures — Selling before Maturity**

Although debentures are usually issued for fixed periods of time, if you should ever need money you can nearly always sell them through a stockbroker before they mature. What you receive in selling price will be determined by the rate of interest and how long there is to go before the debenture is due for repayment.

If you are forced to sell before maturity and interest rates have gone up in the meantime, then you will probably lose money on the sale, and that is not a happy thought.

There is a simple way of avoiding these losses. It is called 'spreading' and will be explained later.

However, it should be noted that in a genuine financial emergency, most finance companies will give you some or all of your money back before the due date. They are not compelled to but if they do they will probably adjust the interest rate downwards. If you hold any medium or long term debentures or notes which pay a low interest rate, on rare occasions it could pay to sell them before they mature even if you do so at a loss and reinvest the proceeds at higher rates. This is very important when interest rates are at record levels. So always check out the situation with a stockbroker.

**Debentures and Security**

If a company strikes trouble and cannot pay what is owing to you, you have first call on the company's assets. If you hold first ranking debentures you are first in line, but if you have second ranking it will mean you are *second* in line as far as repayment is concerned.

Because second ranking debentures are not as safe, interest rates are usually higher and it is here many investors fall into 'the greedy trap'. Past experience suggests it always pays to accept a lower rate of interest and know your money is safe.

**Unsecured Notes**

Not unnaturally, many people are frightened by the word 'unsecured'. Consequently they pass up many attractive investment opportunities. In fact the word 'unsecured' is a misnomer.

While you would be classified as an unsecured creditor, in the event of a company going into liquidation you would still rank ahead of shareholders for payment of interest, and what is more important, repayment of capital.

Probably the best way to understand the situation is to look upon the debenture as the 'first mortgage' and the unsecured note as the 'second mortgage'.

Like debentures, unsecured notes are secured by a trust deed and trustees are appointed to ensure the note holders' interests are protected.

In fact from a security point of view, some unsecured notes would be a safer investment than some debentures, particularly second ranking debentures.

In buying unsecured notes, the calibre of the company should, as always, be the top priority and dozens of first class companies issue notes where security is virtually assured.

For example, if a company such as CSR or AGC issued unsecured notes, one would not hesitate to buy them. (See sample AGC unsecured note application and sample certificate — Appendix 3.) If, however, an unknown company issued unsecured notes it might be best to avoid them, no matter how attractive the interest rates offered.

**Speculating in Fixed Interest Investments**

To the average investor, fixed interest investment would not usually be considered as an avenue for speculation. But on occasions, it can be just that.

While fortunately few in number, some companies do get into financial difficulties and some will be placed in the hands of receivers. When this happens, the market price for the companies' securities usually drops in value — in some cases quite dramatically — including their debentures and notes as well as their shares.

Bearing in mind that from a security point of view debentures usually rank first for repayment, a calculated and objective purchase of first ranking debentures — not unsecured notes — could be a profitable exercise. However, in situations like these it must be remembered that there will always be an element of risk. The company may not recover, in which case it could take time for the debenture holders to be paid out in full or in part.

As with any form of speculation, the funds invested must be surplus to one's needs.

**Liquidity**

In the past, security and income have been considered the No. 1 priorities for most retiring people.

In these uncertain economic times, however, there is another priority of equal importance and that, of course, is 'liquidity'. Expressed simply, liquidity means the ability to convert assets and/or investments into cash when you want to, hopefully without loss of capital or income. For no matter how valuable the asset or investment, it loses its worth if it cannot be sold without sacrificing the price.

For retired people, in particular, liquidity is essential, not only to provide capital for personal needs, but also to be able to take advantage of upward movements in interest rates, or unexpected and advantageous investment opportunities.

A $10,000 investment in an 8 per cent ten, fifteen or twenty year bond or debenture or mortgage may be a safe investment. But if interest rates rise, as they have done in the past few years, to 15, 16 or 17 per cent, the holder of the 8 per cent investment is locked in and cannot take advantage of the higher rates of interest without selling the original investment at a considerable capital loss.

**Spreading Maturity Dates**

A simple way of overcoming this problem is to have bonds, debentures, notes and mortgages maturing in consecutive years, twice a year, four times a year or, going to extremes, even monthly.

Then as each investment matures, it can be reinvested by the 'roll over' process in the following way:

In 1991 $1,000 falls due for repayment. If not required for personal needs, the $1,000 is reinvested in bonds, debentures, notes or mortgages which will mature in 1996. Year after year this procedure is repeated thus providing automatic return of capital every twelve months.

Depending upon the issue and the institution or company concerned, interest on bonds, debentures and notes is frequently paid in different months of the year. This applies to dividends as well. Those to whom a regular and average monthly income is desirable can select investments which pay interest — dividends — in different months of the year.

**As Interest Falls, Debentures Attract**

From time to time, there are some very attractive returns offered, for short term deposits. And investors should rightly take advantage of the situation. However, it could pay to look ahead. If, 12 months from now, interest rates really fall, when your old short term investments mature then you will have to accept the current rate which might be 15 per cent or even less. But if you invest some of your money into, say, two or three year debentures, you could be looking at 17 per cent plus for the entire period.

**Debentures, Notes Deposits — Check before Renewing**

If you own any debentures, notes, or have money on deposit, do not automatically renew these investments without first checking with your stockbroker or financial advisor. First, the status of the company may have changed since the original investment was made and what may have been a safe investment then may not be so safe now.

Second, it may be possible to reinvest the money from the maturing investment into other companies which pay higher rates of interest. Of course, common sense must be used and you should never sacrifice security for the sake of earning a little more income. But it could pay handsome dividends in more ways than one to double check the situation before re-investing your money.

# Real Estate

Many people think real estate is the best investment and, for a comination of both financial and personal reasons, it probably is, certainly in the case of your own home.

Apart from being the biggest investment you will ever make, your home will normally increase in value and, upon resale, the profit is usually tax-free. And with 'the family home' exempt from the new capital gains tax, many families will upgrade their homes or extend them as a form of investment.

**First Home Owners' Assistance Scheme**

The First Home Owners' Assistance Scheme came into operation in October 1983. This scheme offers a range of tax-free benefits which, depending upon one's family situation, could be worth up to $6,000 for owner-occupier first home buyers.

To receive full benefits for a couple with two dependent children, taxable income must not exceed $26,000. But a taxable income in excess of this amount but below $34,000 would entitle you to a proportional benefit.

**Benefit Options**

With the first option of a subsidy only, a first home buying couple with no dependants would get $3,000, with one dependant $4,500 and with two or more dependants $5,000.

A 'couple' can be a married couple, a couple in a *de facto* relationship or two friends who live together or intend living together.

A single applicant, who can receive a maximum amount of $4,000, must have an income below $15,500 for a partial subsidy and below $11,500 for a full subsidy. The assessment of income is based on the financial year ending before the date of signing the assistance agreement.

The money can be paid in three other ways. Option one is for a monthly subsidy over a period of five years; option two is for a small lump sum (less than half) and the balance over five years; option three is for a larger lump sum (more than half) and the balance over five years. Actual sums are determined according to the size of the subsidy and particular needs.

In many cases the large lump sum option could help bridge the deposit gap which in itself could mean buying now — before values start to rise — rather than waiting.

**Watch for Pitfalls**

Recently two brothers joined together and bought their first home. They pooled their resources to comply with the lending authority's requirements as to the deposit and their capacity to meet the repayments.

As the property was purchased in joint names, naturally the incomes of both were taken into account and as their combined incomes exceeded $34,000, the scheme's original income threshold, they both missed out on the benefits of the First Home Owners' Assistance Scheme.

What they should have done was to have purchased the property in just one name with the other brother or someone else acting as guarantor. By buying in this fashion, both brothers could have purchased separate homes now and/or in the future and each could have been entitled to all or some of the benefits. To put it bluntly, they were badly advised.

**Anomalies**

Sad to say, the scheme makes no allowance for divorced people. And this is a gross social oversight.

Say, for example, in the previous marriage a marital home was purchased and one or both parties remarried people who had never owned real estate before. They cannot qualify, simply because one spouse has already owned real estate during the previous marriage.

Although it is very easy to oversimplify situations like these, in cases of remarriage the couple concerned should be entitled to half the benefits if one partner has not owned real estate before.

**Information Sources**

Banks, building societies, credit unions, real estate agents and builders should provided advice and assistance for people interested in the First Home Owners' Assistance Scheme. If they do not, then ask why not. Apart from these sources you can contact the Department of Housing and Construction in your own state.

**Wet Day Inspection**

Most prospective real estate buyers go house hunting on a nice sunny day. Buyers should, in fact, inspect the property twice at the very least. By all means on a sunny day, but also on a wet day and if convenient at night as well.

This wet day visit will allow you to check for a leaky roof, poor drainage, dampness, as well as damaged guttering and downpipes. This wet day visit could mean a saving of hundreds of dollars and, in extreme cases, it might even save thousands and in some cases it might show you the property is unsuitable. And the same might well apply with a night visit.

**Real Estate — Using Deposits**

In any real estate transaction there is a buyer and a seller. And frequently the obvious is overlooked, certainly in relation to investing deposits. If, for example, the property under consideration is worth $100,000, in normal circumstances a $10,000 deposit is required (10 per cent). What is not usually appreciated is that this deposit can — in some states and territories — be invested in the short term money market, or in other forms of investment providing both parties agree. In reality this should be an automatic suggestion by all involved in the transaction, especially the agent and solicitor. In this situation, the profits on settlement will be split down the middle so that both parties will benefit. And it could well mean earnings of hundreds of dollars, and in some cases thousands. So if the agent or solicitor fails to make this suggestion then ask why.

**Saving Time and Money**

Many people are now beginning to realise how important it is to live close to their place of employment, not only to save money, but also to save time. In fact prices for homes, home units and apartments near town centres have again started to rise.

So, if you are thinking of buying a home, home unit or apartment nearer your place of employment, do not delay it for too long, otherwise it could be a costly exercise. On top of that rents are rising dramatically as the accommodation shortage worsens.

**Home Loans — Higher Repayments or Longer Repayments**

If you have a mortgage and interest rates go up, you will probably be asked to increase your repayments. In some cases, however, your bank, building society or credit union may give you the alternatives of increasing your repayments or extending the life of the loan.

If you are given a choice then, subject to the interest rate being changed, extend the period of the loan. A low interest mortgage could be an asset for the simple reason that you are borrowing money today and repaying the loan over a 10, 15 or 20 year period. Some people are even fortunate enough to have 30 and 40 year mortgages. The same principle applies if you can extend your mortgage for an extra two or three years. Inflation will usually mean increased pay. This will make it easier to pay the same amount each month out of the extra dollars earned — 15 or 20 or more years from now.

But, as mentioned, your interest rate will be the deciding factor. With current interest rates of 15.5 per cent or more early repayment or increased repayments could save you a lot of money.

## Real Estate — Buying for Investment

Buying real estate as an investment has several major attractions. The most important is that, even if the rents you receive do not equal your mortgage repayments, the interest you pay can be claimed as a tax deduction in full or in part and offset against income from other sources. If you can borrow money at a reasonable rate of interest to buy some property, so much the better. In the meantime, if you have bought in the right area your property will be increasing in value. Any profit made on resale will be taxed subject to the rate of inflation. So buying a home, unit, town house, apartment or block of land as an investment could be a profitable exercise.

When property values rise, it can also pay to use the increased value of your own home to borrow enough money to put down a deposit on another property.

But, as always in situations like these, common sense should be used and you must be very careful not to overcommit yourself with regard to interest rates, repayments and, of course, the purchase price.

Another reason to invest in real estate is to *anticipate retirement*. By buying a home unit, town house or villa now, as an investment, and renting it out, you would also be catering for your own accommodation needs in the future when you are forced to leave your own home. Another point to remember is that in selling your own home the proceeds will be tax-free and when you eventually move into the unit, town house or villa that then will become your permanent place of residence.

## Interest Only Mortgages

Finance is often a problem when you are buying property for investment purposes, particularly if you are still paying off your own home.

One source of finance frequently ignored by many people is the 'interest only mortgage'. These mortgages, which are normally for three or five year terms, can be arranged through stockbrokers, solicitors or mortgage brokers. As the name implies, you do not pay off any principal, you just pay interest. When the mortgage is due for repayment, if you are short of capital and you have been a good payer, you can 'roll over' the mortgage or take out another one at the current rate of interest.

Depending upon the source of the money, interest rates for these loans do vary, but you would pay around 15.5 to 17 per cent. It is also possible to buy property this way with limited funds providing the value is there. In fact, it is possible with just a 10 per cent deposit. And interest only mortgages could also be used by first home buyers who are short of funds.

Recently a couple purchased a property — it was a bachelor apartment — and the purchase price, believe it or not, was $47,000. By using a three year interest only mortgage, they needed a cash deposit of only $7,000. And with lower repayments per month financing the property this gave the couple three years' grace to save extra money.

**Refinancing**

You could also refinance your old debts and mortgages by using an interest only mortgage. Without forgetting costs and charges in arranging a new loan or in paying out the old one, you could still be looking at an interest rate difference of five per cent per annum if not more. And, of course, with an interest only mortgage, your monthly repayments would be considerably lower than the repayments of an ordinary mortgage. Farmers, in particular, might well consider interest only mortgages as a new and cheaper source of finance to help them overcome current difficulties, particularly with relatively high interest rates being charged by way of overdrafts etc. But be sure to deal with reputable people and be extremely careful about borrowing offshore.

**Paying Off**

As previously mentioned if you are lucky enough to have a mortgage, then do not rush to pay it off. Subject to the interest rate being charged it could be one of your biggest assets. Some people may be fortunate enough to have an old war service loan with an interest rate of 3.75 per cent or other low interest loans.

If you let the mortgage continue rather than pay it off, you can use this money to buy more real estate or invest in managed investment bonds or friendly societies which can give you a much greater return — part or all of which could be tax-free. In other words, by not paying off your mortgage you are making more money.

Even if you are paying 13.5 per cent in interest, it could still be to your advantage to keep your mortgage going. If you spread your investments and make money

— then having a debt like a mortgage is not necessarily a bad thing if you have a favourable interest rate. Of course, not everyone is lucky enough to have low interest loans, but your mortgage could still be an asset particularly when inflation is high.

Assume your present income is $25,000 per year and your mortgage repayments including principal and interest amount to $5,000. This means that one-fifth of your income is being used to pay off the mortgage, but with salary and wage increases as well as inflation, your income in ten years time might be $50,000.

Without forgetting possible increases in mortgage interest rates, you are now paying only one-tenth of your income. In other words, inflation will help you pay off your mortgage. Also remember that after you have bought that all-important first home or unit, it might be very difficult to negotiate another mortgage under the same terms and conditions.

But, on the other hand if you are a worrier, pay it off. It is not worth the hassle.

**Unregistered Mortgage**

If you lend money to a member of the family, there are definite tax advantages in receiving a cash gift rather than interest.

But it is often difficult to know how *far* one should go, in relation to security, for a loan to a family member. Trust may be there now, but of course things can change and family splits do occur.

One way of overcoming the problem *where real estate is concerned*, is to arrange for an unregistered mortgage to be drawn up as security for the loan. This document can then be kept in a safe place until the loan is repaid or in case other action may be necessary.

**Mortgages**

Cautious investors and those inexperienced in stock exchange and other areas of investment frequently use mortgages as their major source of investment income. Like debentures, mortgage can play an important role in fixed interest portfolios, not only to provide security but also a high return. Most people, of course, would lend money only on first mortgage, and today the interest rate would be around 17 per cent per annum if not more.

As with any form of investment, it is important for the security to be first class. In the case of mortgages it is essential for the amount lent to be well below the market value of the property — in case of default by the borrower — and for the mortgage to be insured.

Interest on mortgages is normally paid half yearly or quarterly, but on occasions it can be monthly. Second mortgages, like second ranking debentures, offer a higher return — but the risk is obviously greater.

In the past most mortgages have been arranged through solicitors or mortgage brokers. These days, however, as with interest only mortgages and mortgage trusts, stockbrokers and others have entered the field. In some cases, after the mortgage has been arranged there is sometimes a lack of supervision as to the prompt payment of interest due. For those who need the income to live on, these delays can be frustrating as well as worrying.

With debentures and notes, interest must be paid on the due date and the same should apply to a mortgage. If there should be a delay in receipt of interest, contact the solicitor or broker concerned and ask for the matter to be rectified.

**Property — Watch your Tax Situation**

But a word of warning about taxation. Under the 'old rules' land does not produce any income, so it could mean that when you sell, if that is your intention, then the taxman will want his share. The same situation could apply in the case of flats or units.

By way of example, one investor purchased some units on the far north coast of New South Wales. His purpose was to hold them for 18 months or so and then sell them, which he did at a handsome profit. But the units had been left vacant so, as he did not receive any rents, he could not prove to the Taxation Department that they were bought for investment and not for re-sale. And he had to pay tax on his gains.

**Watch Hidden Costs**

When it comes to buying — and also selling — real estate, be it your first home or an investment property, you must always allow for extra costs and charges that most, if not all financial, institutions impose. Things like:

Loan application fees and charges
Survey fee
Stamp duty
Legal costs including cost of preparing a mortgage
Removal costs
Repairs and renovations
Furniture and carpets

When added together these costs can run into thousands of dollars so make sure you allow for them.

And watch out for transactions involving a purchase

and a sale with the same settlement date. Quite frequently there can be hold ups and delays which could mean borrowing the money for settlement — short term — at a much higher interest rate. It could also mean moving out of one property and 'boarding' until settlement of the new purchase has been completed.

**Interest Rate Risks**

While in one sense the increases in interest rates for first home buyers are disappointing, you should, providing you can service the loan, go ahead and borrow, even if it initially means an extra $30 to $40 per month in mortgage repayments. Rent in most cases is simply wasted money and it is more than likely that real estate values in most areas will continue to rise, as will the costs of building. Certainly in the first few years, there will be next to nothing being paid off the capital, so where possible pay off more than necessary, either by increasing the monthly repayments or by paying a lump sum. It is not going to be easy to do this, but once again with interest rates of around 17.5 per cent, if not more, it is in one's own interest to pay off as much as possible quickly.

**Strata Title or Company Title**

These days most home units, and a number of business premises, are sold under Strata Title which means that you have title to your own premises. Some home units however are still sold under Company Title and there are some advantages, as well as disadvantages, in purchasing real estate in this way. The advantages are that, subject to the availability of finance, Company Title Units are frequently cheaper to buy. But they are more difficult to finance through normal channels and you are subject to the rules laid down by the company.

**Buying Old Flats**

Subject to the purchase price, buying a block of flats under an old Torrens' Title could prove to be a worthwhile investment if the flats can be transferred into a Strata Title. Whilst this is not a cheap exercise it is worth considering, both by new buyers as well as existing owners. In many cases you could well have ready buyers in the existing tenants. If it is convenient, selling the unit to the tenants on favourable terms to both parties could make the transactions a lot easier and less costly.

**Renting Versus Buying**

Some people would suggest that it is better to rent a property rather than buy one, *but* overall there would be very few who would share this view. In *reality* rent is wasted money, and with rents rising rapidly nationwide the stage is being reached when many people will not be able to afford to rent. Even with the high interest rates currently being charged on home mortgages it could still pay you to buy your own house or flat. Whilst there may only be a nominal saving in this case in the first years of repayments, assuming you can meet them, the home is yours for as long as you wish. That may not always be the case with rented property.

**Land — Selling on Terms**

Over the years, many people have invested in land and you may be one of them. When you decide to sell this land, however, it may take time to get the price you want and if there is a credit squeeze or a slump you may not get any offers at all!

If you ever find yourself in this situation, do not despair and do not sacrifice your land at a lower price unless you are forced to. One way of overcoming this problem is to offer terms — vendor finance — to a would-be purchaser instead of waiting for a cash buyer. These terms can be flexible, but as a guide you might advertise the land on a 10, 15, 20 or 25 per cent deposit and let the purchaser pay off the balance in regular monthly instalments over a one, three or five year period.

The rate of interest you charge will, of course, be influenced by the rates prevailing at the time of the sale and just how desperately you want to sell. Offering land on terms may not always attract a buyer, but it is well worth trying.

**Auction or Private Sale?**

When it comes to selling real estate it is frequently suggested that it is best to sell by public auction as against a private sale or through one or more agents. In many cases auctions do indeed work out in the seller's favour, *but not always*. Quite frequently auctions can and do turn into disasters. The costs of auctioning can run into thousands of dollars on large properties, and auctions often result in a *no sale* because the bids are below the property's true value. On top of that sellers by auction are often talked into selling the property at below the reserve price. In reality auctions are only really worthwhile in a seller's market. In one sense the agents cannot lose, because you are paying for their advertising.

**Buying Property? Do not Rush in**

If you are selling one home to buy another, in most cases you will try to settle for the purchase and the sale on the same date.

At first glance, this may not be a problem, but if finance is involved — either in the sale or the purchase — make sure settlements will take place on the same day. Do not take everything for granted — and do not let your solicitor take you for granted.

Despite what you might be told initially, dates of settlement can be a major problem when more than one property is involved. It is up to your solicitor to make sure there are no last minute delays and it is also up to your solicitor to advise the bank or building society, well in advance, that settlement is requested on a specified date. If the bank or building society is not given reasonable notice, do not blame them if settlement does not take place as planned. So, when you are advised the date of settlement, confirm the advice in writing — it could save you a lot of time, money and frustration.

**Sell before you Buy**

If you are thinking of buying another home, there is a great temptation to sign the contract before you have sold your first home. This is understandable because property values are high, but if you cannot sell your own home, you might find you are forced to borrow at high rates of interest, by way of temporary finance. This may not matter for a month or so, but if it goes on indefinitely, it could be financially crippling. At times people are encouraged to sign the contract by so-called professional advisors and this is a very dangerous practice. By delaying, you could miss out on the purchase, but, by the some token, delaying could be to your advantage,

# The Sharemarket

It is probably fair to say that, without knowing it, two out of every three Australians invest indirectly in shares by way of superannuation schemes and life assurance premiums, etc. However, up to 1 July 1987, when the government changed the taxation law, personal investment in shares was less popular here than overseas because of the double taxation of share dividends.

**Small Investors**

While for some people the sharemarket is seen as a place for wheeling and dealing on a very large scale, it is important to note that the backbone of the sharemarket is in fact the small investor. A few dollars set aside and invested on a regular basis over the years could grow into a sizeable sum or even a small fortune.

Once you have made contact with a stockbroker, buying shares and other securities is really quite a simple procedure.

**Buying Procedures**

Suppose you decide to buy 500 shares in BHP. When the shares are purchased, you will be sent a contract note as your confirmation of purchase. After you have sent the stockbroker the money, he or she will arrange for the shares to be registered in your name and if you so desire you will receive a share certificate from the company. (See sample share certificate — Appendix 3.)

By the way there are a number of ways to place both buying and selling orders and they are as follows:

- at a firm limit
- at discretion
- close market
- at best

Unless the market is on the boil the normal way to place an order is *close market*, which is close to the last sale. But providing you have confidence in your broker leave the buying and selling to him or her — in other words buy or sell at *best*. However, if the market is overheated and stocks are moving up or down in price very quickly then it could pay to place a commonsense buying or selling limit on your order/s particularly if it is a mining stock. And in the case of mining stocks, and also industrial stocks, check your share certificates before placing a selling order so that you are selling the right stock, e.g. fully paid shares and not partly paid or contributing shares or for that matter other types of shares.

In the case of a sale, when you receive your contract return it to the brokers with your share certificate/s attached. Providing the paperwork is in order you will be paid immediately and that could mean on the same day as the sale and certainly the following day. This is another attraction about the sharemarket — it gives almost instant liquidity.

**Assessing the Market**

Before you invest in the sharemarket the first thing to consider is: What is the general state of the economy, locally and on a world scale? A correct assessment can mean much, and decide the question — whether to buy now, or wait.

A local assessment is not as difficult as it may seem if you read and absorb the information made available daily. Information concerning the state of savings bank deposits, bank overdraft levels, excessive amounts outstanding on hire purchase, unemployment and availability of jobs, interest rates, immigration, sudden population increases, new motor vehicle registrations, levels of taxation both individual and company, changes or popularity of governments, effects of controls on local industry, stability of salaries, wages and costs and the rate of inflation.

Collectively this information gives an invaluable picture of our immediate and long-term future.

On the international scene many of the above examples are equally important. Also to be considered is the nation's ability to produce and sell products on world markets and thus create favourable overseas balances.

The stock exchange is generally the mirror of economic tides, often in advance of general business reactions, and one of the best guides to the state of local sharemarkets is the list of daily sales. These are shown in the financial pages of your newspaper and tell you at a glance the condition of the market.

If, for example, 100 stocks increase in price and 10 stocks fall, this indicates that the market is strong because the number of buyers outnumbers the sellers by 10 to 1. (See sample listing of stock market rises and falls — Appendix 3.)

On the other hand, if 100 stocks fall in price and only 10 rise, this indicates a weak market.

There will, however, always be special situations like takeovers, where some stocks will continue to rise even though the market is falling.

By the way, do not judge the stock market on just one day's sales. You will have to watch the lists for weeks to see what the overall trend is. But here again your stockbroker can assist.

## Yield

Most newcomers to the sharemarket are puzzled and confused by the term *yield*. Expressed simply, this is the return you receive on your investment by way of interest or dividend.

If, for example, you invest $100 in Northern Territory Bonds and the interest rate is 15 per cent, then your yield is 15 per cent.

If on the other hand you bought some shares in an Australian company for a dollar, even though the company is paying a 12 per cent dividend your yield might be only 6 per cent. In Australia, shares are issued at a nominal value. These nominal, or par, values are determined by the company. Now, many shares have a par value of 50 cents, so when the company declares a 12 per cent dividend, it is 12 per cent on 50 cents not 12 per cent on the market value of a dollar, whereas savings bonds are normally purchased at face value. (See sample list with yield — Appendix 3.)

## Shares — Buying Partly Paid Shares

Partly paid, or contributing, shares (as they are sometimes called) are often cheaper to buy than fully paid shares.

Suppose a fully paid share is selling on the stock exchange for $1.00. A partly paid share in the same company is selling for 73 cents and there is still 25 cents owing on the partly paid share.

By buying the partly paid share instead of the fully paid one your total cost eventually will be 98 cents instead of $1.00 which means a saving of 2 cents per share. On a hundred shares this saving is $2.00, on a thousand the saving is $20.00.

Apart from saving 2 cents per share in purchase price, it is important to note that when you buy partly paid shares you also pay less brokerage.

**Buying
Shares —
Old or New**

If you look at the financial pages of your newspaper, you will sometimes see more than one class of share listed for the same company. They might be partly paid shares or they might be new shares.

New shares normally follow a new issue, bonus issue or a takeover. New shares may or may not receive the same dividend as the old shares, but even allowing for this, new shares, like partly paid shares, are normally cheaper to buy not only in purchase price but also brokerage.

Next time you decide to buy some shares and you have a choice, ask your broker to buy whatever is the cheapest. You may not save much by buying new shares. It might be only a cent or two, but every cent counts.

**No Liability**

Before you buy partly paid shares in a mining company, make sure you know what you are buying. Check to see how much is still owing on the shares and find out if it is a *no liability* company.

No liability, as the name implies, means you are not legally liable for any money or calls, as they are named, owing on the shares. This can be a wonderful protection if your shares should drop in price and end up being virtually worthless.

You will forfeit your shares by not paying the calls when due and you may lose most, if not all, of your original investment, but why throw away good money after bad when it is not necessary?

Next time you receive a call notice ask your stockbroker whether you should pay or forfeit the shares.

By the way, do not sell any of these shares unless you are sure all calls were paid on the due date.

Many shareholders do not realise they have forfeited their shares by not paying the calls and if they sell, they are selling shares they do not own and that is 'technically' illegal. Your stockbroker will also have to buy back the shares you sold at the market price which could be higher and you, the original seller, will be liable for any loss.

So, if you own any partly paid no liability mining shares, check with your stockbroker or the company before you sell. It could save you a lot of money.

**Tax-free
Dividends**

As mentioned earlier one of the most important and long overdue tax reforms is the abolition of double taxation of company dividends. On 1 July 1987, income from company dividends became to all intents and purposes tax-free. *And there are no upper limits.*

Dividend Imputation
Example:

|  | $ |
|---|---|
| Dividend | 51 |
| Assessable (dividend plus credit) | 100 |
| Tax on $100* | 39 |
| Less credit | 49 |
| Net credit | 10 |

*Based on marginal tax rate of 39 per cent.

Using the above example the $10.00 credit can also be used to offset income from other sources such as interest etc.

**Double Taxation**

Under the old rules, when companies made a profit they paid tax on their profit and when they paid a dividend, those shareholders who were taxpayers were also obliged to include the dividends in their own personal income tax returns, losing up to 60 per cent of that income in additional income tax.

The new rules have certainly encouraged thousands of new investors to take a fresh look at the sharemarket. And this in turn has caused yet another revolution of the local investment scene.

**Dividend Reinvestment Plans**

Under dividend reinvestment plans, shareholders not in need of ready cash may elect to have their dividends automatically reinvested in additional shares in the company.

But shareholders retain their right to reverse the arrangement at any time. So, should an investor's personal circumstances change, dividend payments in cash may again be requested.

It should be noted that taxpaying investors will not receive any tax advantages by participating in these schemes. However, most shares are issued at a discount on the market price, and these discounts range from 5 per cent to 10 per cent.

Some companies have also been offering 'employee share schemes' and it is obvious that these schemes could and should be encouraged to complement dividend reinvestment plans.

Looking ahead, schemes such as these will attract new shareholders to the company and thus widen the shareholder base and this should encourage greater shareholder loyalty.

Participation in one or more such plans would be an important step in planning for one's retirement years in advance. It would also be a great way to set money aside for children or grandchildren as a projected nest egg or simply to build up your investment portfolio.

But, as mentioned earlier, should circumstances change and you need the dividend income or interest to live on, then you can *elect* to change.

Looking at the attractiveness and success of dividend reinvestment schemes, there would appear to be a major oversight by Australia's finance houses in relation to interest on debentures and notes.

It is a feature that could also be looked at with regard to government and semi-government bond issues.

In the meantime, would-be shareholders should be looking at companies with existing schemes and existing shareholders in other companies without such a scheme should be encouraging their introduction.

The current list includes:

| | |
|---|---|
| Allied Mills | Lend Lease Corporation |
| Ampol Petroleum | Mayne Nickless |
| ATS Resources | National Australia Bank |
| BHP | OPSM |
| Brambles | Pacific Dunlop |
| CRA | Pioneer Concrete |
| CSR | Ralph McKay |
| General Property Trust | Stockland Trust |
| Goodman Fielder | Westpac |
| James Hardie | Whittakers |
| Leighton Holdings | Woolworths |

There are also advantages to companies — with these schemes the major advantage is the retention of funds within the company, which makes more than a meaningful contribution to cash flow.

Of the many schemes introduced, the CSR plan is one of the most impressive and the details are presented in Appendix I as an example. (See sample of Share Purchase Plan statement — Appendix 3.)

**Look for Bonus Patterns**

ANZ Bank's pattern of issues over the past nine years demonstrates the importance of investing in companies that also make regular bonus and cash issues.

The ANZ Bank position is as follows:

1979 one-for-four bonus
1981 one-for-four bonus

1982 one-for-five bonus
1984 one-for-ten bonus
1984 one-for-four cash
1985 one-for-ten bonus
1986 one-for-five cash
1987 one-for-two bonus
1988 one-for-six bonus

And there are many similar company situations. Boral Ltd was yet another company to make regular issues, many of them bonuses.

1979 one-for-five bonus
1981 one-for-five bonus
1982 one-for-five bonus
1984 one-for-five bonus
1985 one-for-five bonus
1986 one-for-four bonus
1987 one-for-ten cash
1988 one-for-five bonus
1989 one-for-ten bonus

The list of companies adopting the same approach would run into dozens. While not all companies would necessarily be as generous with their issues as those shown in the above examples, once a pattern has been established it should continue, providing the company continues to expand.

That is why it is important, when setting up a quality share portfolio, to choose companies such as these. Sources for information are stockbrokers and the research and publications departments of the various stock exchanges.

**Anticipate Bonuses**

If it is your birthday or anniversary you will probably celebrate in one way or another. Public companies also frequently celebrate an important event by making a bonus issue, or paying a bonus dividend, or both. Bonus issues are gifts of shares and no cash outlay on your part is involved.

The likelihood of birthday or anniversary issues can often be estimated by checking how long a particular company has been in business.

For example, a company has been operating for 49 years and it is performing well. Next year, the 50th year in business, a bonus issue could well be on the cards. This happens quite often — so check the dates — it could make you some money. Some recent examples have been the ANZ Bank and BHP. When one company in a particular industry announces a bonus issue, it is quite on the cards other companies in the same industry will do likewise so as not to be outdone by their competitors.

Of course these bonus issues may not be announced immediately; in fact, it may take 6 to 12 months for other companies to do the same.

**Takeovers**

If you own shares in a company, one day you might be involved in a takeover offer. Your company might want to take over another company or vice versa.

Either way, there are profits to be made providing you know what to do, and the profits can be substantial.

Suppose your shares are selling for $2.00 on the stock exchange and you suddenly receive a cash offer of $4.00 for each share you own.

Do you accept this offer or not? This depends on who is making it and whether the directors of your company recommend acceptance. If the offer is a good one, it could pay to sell some of your shares immediately and sit on the balance. But overall it usually pays to wait.

**Takeovers — Wait on News**

Most takeovers involve a share exchange, cash or a combination of both. If it is a straight out share exchange and quality companies are involved there should not be any problems. If you are happy with the offer you will accept it. But whenever a takeover offer involves a cash alternative it also pays to wait until just before the offer closes. If you rush in and accept the share exchange you might find — particularly in a falling market — that the shares fall in value and in the end it works out to be less than you would have received in taking the cash alternative. By waiting you can work out whether it is best to accept the share exchange or the cash.

**Takeovers — Trends**

Takeovers can be expected where one company owns shares in another, as has been the case with Westpac and AGC and the ANZ Bank and the ANZ Bank NZ.

After a takeover offer has been announced in a particular industry, shares in other companies in the same industry will often rise in expectation of other takeover offers. There is no guarantee that any of these companies will receive an offer. But once a trend starts it sometimes continues.

One final point: make sure the company in which you invest is a quality one, so that if a takeover does not eventuate, you will still be holding a first class investment.

**Convertible Notes**

If you are interested in the sharemarket, look out for convertible notes, for these investments frequently offer a cheap way into company shares and the prospect of larger capital gains. In simple terms, a convertible note is a security which is issued for a fixed period of time at a fixed rate of interest. (See sample convertible note certificate — Appendix 3.)

As the name implies, however, if you want to (and in most cases it is not compulsory), you can convert your notes into ordinary shares in the same company at specified dates in the future.

The right to convert into ordinary shares is an important attraction, but there are other advantages. If you own convertible notes, and the company makes a new issue of shares or a bonus issue, as a noteholder you will be entitled to participate in these issues in one way or another according to the number of notes you own.

At the same time, if the ordinary shares of the company move *up* in price, you can convert some or all of your notes into shares and sell them or keep them.

On the other hand, if the shares do not increase in value and it is not worthwhile converting, then in the majority of cases you simply keep the notes until they mature, when they will be repaid at face value. In the meantime, the notes will be earning regular interest.

Convertible note issues can also be a way of taking immediate profits. Say, for example, at the time of the note issue a company's shares were selling at one dollar, but the notes were being issued at 80¢ each. Large shareholders in the company could sell an equivalent number of old shares at $1.00 and come back into the company by way of the convertible notes. After allowing for brokerage and stamp duty on the sale of the shares, this would have resulted in an immediate profit of around 17¢ per share.

**Anomalies on Notes**

Also watch out for some worthwhile anomalies in relation to convertible notes. As mentioned earlier, convertible notes give you the opportunity to take up shares in the company and also bonus issues. However it is important to note bonus issues are usually credited to the owners of convertible notes rather than issued separately. Some companies have made more than one bonus during the life of their convertible notes, so if you buy some convertible notes you might well be buying some 'bonus share credits' as well, which would make the convertible notes a better buy than the shares in many cases.

**Watch out for Trends**

When a recently formed Sharemarket Trust was launched it was announced that it proposed to invest a substantial proportion of its funds in convertible notes, and 'substantial' means millions and millions of dollars. This being so, it will create a shortage of quality convertible notes and that is another reason to look at this area.

So, check the financial pages of your newspaper and make a list of all the convertible notes you can find. At the same time, ask your stockbroker for suggestions about which convertible notes are worth buying. (See sample convertible note list — Appendix 3.)

**Averaging**

If you are a shareholder in a publicly listed company, it is a frightening experience to see your shares suddenly drop in price. But do not worry, you will lose nothing unless you are forced to sell your shares while the price is down. These paper losses might last for a long time, however, and if you ever find yourself in this situation and you have some spare cash available, buy some more shares in the same company at the lower price. In effect, this will reduce the cost of your original shares.

If later on your shares continue to drop in price, then buy some more! This is called 'averaging' and can often prove a very profitable exercise.

| | |
|---|---|
| 200 MIM | $3.00 |
| 200 MIM | $2.50 |
| 200 MIM | $2.00 |
| 200 MIM | $1.50 |

Although the original purchase was at $3.00, by buying extra shares at lower prices the average cost per share is now reduced to $2.25.

But, a word of caution before you rush in and start buying. Do not average down unless the company is a quality one and has a long-term future, otherwise you might be throwing good money after bad.

**Trading in Shares**

If you buy shares and it is your intention to re-sell them quickly, do not forget to tell your stockbroker of your intentions. If you buy shares and pay for them within five days and then you re-sell them within 28 days, some brokers rebate half the normal selling brokerage, and that is an important saving.

Second, your broker will delay registering the shares in your name and this means you can be paid for the sale immediately. On the other hand, if your purchase is in the process of being registered, it could mean unnecessary delays in settlement of the sale.

If you ever find it is not profitable to re-sell within the 28 day period, then tell your broker to register the shares in your name.

**The Ground Floor**

If you read the stock market report you will sometimes see headings like 'Stags have a field day'. What does this mean?

When it comes to investing in shares, being in on the 'ground floor' can be a very profitable exercise. By way of example, the shares of a company called Hitech were offered to investors at their nominal value of 50 cents per share. The day these shares were listed on national stock exchanges, they came on the market at between 70 and 86 cents and around 13 per cent of the public issue was stagged.

'Stags' are investors who buy in at the 'ground floor', in other words in the original float. Their intention is to sell at a profit as soon as the shares are listed, and in Hitech's case the stag did very well, making capital gains from 40 per cent up to more than 70 per cent, and that was in a matter of weeks. While taxpaying stags will have to give the taxman his share, they are still left with a tidy profit, and non-taxpaying stags will enjoy seeing their profits tax-free. So, if you are lucky enough to participate in a quality new issue, it always pays to take a profit in at least part of the holding, if not the lot.

**Return of Capital**

From time to time, shareholders in some companies will be offered a return of capital. This simply means the company is returning part of its capital and this, in effect, becomes a tax-free gift.

Assume you own some shares which have a nominal or par value of $1.00 and these shares are selling on the stock exchange for $2.00. Now the company decides to return 50 cents per share. Just because half the capital is to be repaid does not mean that the value of your shares will drop by half. On the contrary, the shares should be worth at the very least $1.50 and possibly a lot more.

Next time you see a company announce a return of capital, contact a stockbroker for advice. The company's shares could be worth buying, particularly if you can do so before the capital repayment is made.

**Tips and Rumours**

Whenever there is a sharemarket boom, thousands of so-called new investors are tempted to have a flutter.

Having been told about the fabulous deals and profits — *but never the losses* — made by friends and workmates, they too want to make their fortune overnight.

Tips from amateurs on what shares to buy can pay off occasionally, but in the majority of cases, these new investors will end up losing most, if not all, of their money and they will be the first to complain. They are not investing, they are gambling.

If you fit into this category, do not blame anyone but yourself. For listening to tips and following rumours is usually one of the quickest ways to lose money.

Having been warned of the dangers, if you still want to 'play' the sharemarket, make sure it is money you can afford to lose if the worst should happen.

**Delays on Scrip**

When you buy shares, providing you pay for them promptly, your broker will automatically send the documents of purchase to the company concerned for registration in your name. These days signatures are not normally required as far as purchases are concerned.

Once the documents are received by the company, in normal circumstances the new share certificate (scrip) should be issued within 10 days.

On occasions however, delays can occur and they can be annoying. So, if you have been waiting a long time for your share certificates, check out the situation with your stockbroker.

By the way, even if it does take time for the documents to be processed any dividends or new or bonus issue entitlements are still yours, so do not forget to remind your broker about these as well.

**Mining Shares — Metal Prices**

Prices for mining shares can go up and down quite dramatically, so it is important to know when to buy and when to sell. One of the best guides apart from your broker, is to watch world metal and commodity prices.

These are published daily in the financial pages of your newspapers and mentioned on radio and television and tell you in advance what the company in which you want to invest can expect in the future.

If, for example, the price of copper goes up by a hundred dollars a tonne and continues to increase in price, this will naturally mean bigger profits for the copper producer and its share price should rise. If the price of copper falls, this will mean smaller profits or no profit and a lower share price on the stock market.

**Stockbrokers — Not Accepting New Clients**

When the stock market is booming, many would-be-investors experience difficulty in finding a broker, particularly if the amount they have to invest is relatively small.

In some cases, you will need $5,000 or more to get a foot in the door and for many people this is a lot of money. For on such occasions it is physically impossible for brokers to handle the needs of their existing clients, let alone take on new ones.

Even so, there will normally be some brokers who will accept new clients and the best way to find one is to contact the Advisory Department of your local Stock Exchange and ask for an introduction to such a stockbroker.

**Lost Share Certificates**

Every year, thousands of share certificates (debenture certificates etc.) are accidentally destroyed or lost. They might even be stolen.

On many occasions the loss may not be noticed for months or even years. These certificates are, of course, valuable documents and should never be left lying around or tucked away in a drawer.

Immediately they are received make a note of the details, particularly the certificate numbers, and then put them in your safety deposit box. If you cannot find any of your certificates, or if you lose any in the future, notify the company concerned immediately and ask for a replacement certificate. This is doubly important in the case of elderly people, so be forewarned and check the situation now. It could save a lot of problems and money later.

**Shares for Children**

You might think about buying shares in the names of children — not only to save tax, but also to encourage them to invest at the earliest possible age. Although there is no 'real' age limit to investment, it would be preferable for the children to be able to sign their names legibly, in case you or they want to sell the shares at a later date.

However, there is one exception to children buying shares before they are of age, and this applies to contributing or partly paid shares. By law, children (minors) would not be liable for the money owing on a contributing share if they did not pay the call on the due date, so companies insist on a declaration of age and liability being signed at the time of purchase. To avoid any problems or unnecessary costs, do not buy partly paid shares for your children — buy only fully paid ones.

**Review Portfolios Regularly**

When the stock market is booming, most sharemarket investors take an active interest in what is going on. Even so, there are thousands of shareholders who fail to take advantage of sudden price increases simply because they do not review their portfolios regularly.

These days taking profits is the name of the game and it applies to holdings of blue chip stocks as well as others. Providing you have a reasonable shareholding, sell some and wait to see what happens. If your shares continue to increase in price then sell some more. Later on, if the market falls, you can buy back what you sold at a lower price.

Of course, you must always consider your tax position but even so it pays to turn paper profits into real profits. By the way, if you do sell and the shares continue to go up, do not start fretting. The recipe for successful share-market investing is to leave something for someone else.

**Orders and Brokerage**

Since deregulation of the Securities industry stockbrokers can and do impose their own rules in relation to *minimum orders* and *brokerage*. As far as minimum broker-age is concerned this might average at around $40 ir-respective of the amount invested so that in buying say 100 shares at $1 the cost would be as follows:

| | |
|---|---|
| 100 at $1.00 | $100.00 |
| Stamp Duty | 30¢ |
| BROKERAGE | 40.00 |
| TOTAL | $140.30¢ |

For small investors this charge is, of course, totally absurd. It is important to find a broker who does not impose a minimum brokerage charge and there are still some around. So in this situation the charges would be as follows:

| | |
|---|---|
| 100 at $1.00 | $100.00 |
| Stamp Duty | 30¢ |
| BROKERAGE | 2.50 |
| TOTAL | $102.89¢ |

In reality, you should be looking at a charge of around 2.5 per cent on the total value of the order, *but* some brokers do impose a $5 order fee in addition to the brokerage charge.

In the case of other advisors the costs and charges vary considerably. It may be, as is the case with some bank advisory services, that the first consultation is free and then if the portfolio is prepared a flat fee of $75 or $100 might be charged. In many cases however, where commissions are involved, excesses are refunded to the clients. In the case of salespersons their commissions can be as high as 4 per cent and in some cases even more. It is essential to check out the costs well in advance.

**Rights to New Issues**

To profitably benefit from 'rights' to new issues of shares, convertible notes, options etc., it is essential to know what they are, how they come about and, most important of all, what to do with them.

The term 'right' is really self descriptive. When a company decides to increase its capital (raise more money) it will usually announce a new issue — usually of ordinary shares. The shares to be issued may be fully paid or partly paid.

They can be issued at par (the unit value assigned to a share by the issuing company), or at premium (above par value).

Normally they are made to existing shareholders based on a ratio decided by the company.

If, for example, you hold 1,000 50 cent shares and your company announces a new issue at par (50 cents) on the basis of 1 × 5, as an existing shareholder you have the first right to apply for 200 extra shares in the company at 50 cents per share.

If, however, you do not wish to increase your shareholding from 1,000 to 1,200 shares or you lack the funds to do so, you can usually sell your rights (entitlement) to the 200 shares through the market and still retain your original holding of 1,000 shares.

Alternatively, you may keep some and sell some.

Proceeds from the sale of rights will, of course, reduce the cost of the original holding and can be reinvested elsewhere if the money is not required for personal needs.

Any new issue will obviously increase the number of shares available and the market will adjust prices accordingly. This price adjustment is based on what is called 'theoretical value'. Here is an example of how to work out these values.

**Calculating Theoretical Values**

A company has an issued capital, say, of $500,000 in $1 shares. Their market value is $3. The company decides it needs additional capital and plans to make an issue of ordinary shares on the basis of one new share for every three shares held. The issue is to be at par. To calculate theoretical value of the shares and rights, the following procedure is adopted:

| | |
|---|---|
| Three shares at $3.00 | $ 9.00 |
| Add application money | $ 1.00 |
| Four shares now cost | $10.00 |
| Average price per share | $ 2.50 |
| Deduct application money | $ 1.00 |
| | $ 1.50 |
| Theoretical value of shares ex rights | $ 2.50 |
| Theoretical value of rights | $ 1.50 |

In assessing the theoretical value, one must remember that quite often the new shares to be issued will not receive the same dividend as that due on the old shares and allowance must be made for this dividend difference in your calculations.

As a price guide, the importance of theoretical values cannot be over-emphasised. In fact, many 'professional' investors calculate these values twice before rights trading begins.

The first calculation is based on the market price of the share the day before the issue is announced. The second is based on the market price of the share the day before 'rights' trading commences.

This information is extremely valuable when issues are announced months in advance. For the tone of the market can change quite dramatically between the announcement of an issue and the commencement of rights trading.

By comparing the values, it is easy to pinpoint any extreme variation in prices that may have occurred and take appropriate action.

**Sequence of Events**

While it is essential to know how to work out theoretical values, it is doubly essential to know the sequence of events followed in new issues.

When properly used, this information can mean the difference between buying or selling well, and between marginal or large profits or no profits at all.

The sequence is usually as follows:

- Formal announcement by company of issue together with details
- Rights trading commences
- Letters of entitlement sent to shareholders
- Rights trading ceases and applications close
- Renunciations close

**Announce-ment of Issue**

Whenever a company announces a new issue, details are forwarded to the stock exchange and released to the financial press.

In addition, the *Australian Financial Review* and other financial journals publish a complete list of all new issues current and pending.

The details contained in these lists are invaluable and should be studied in conjunction with the patterns of price movements mentioned later.

Points to look for include:

- Size and terms of each issue
- Date rights trading begins
- Date applications close
- Total number of new cases current or pending
- Total amount of money involved in all issues

This information should also be related to the overall tone of the market.

Of equal importance is the ability to work out your own entitlements immediately new issues are announced. This early calculation is extremely valuable, particularly if it is your intention to sell the rights. For, contrary to popular belief, rights can be sold on the first day of trading without formal documents being to hand.

If in doubt, or if the issue is an involved one, check the details and calculations with your broker.

**Quotation of Rights**

Every new issue announcement will state a 'books closing' date to determine those shareholders entitled to participate in the issue. It should be noted, however, stock exchanges in Australia always quote the rights five business days before the date stipulated by the company. This five days grace is to assist brokers to lodge last minute transfers.

Buying or selling shares just before a new issue can be

a little confusing for some investors, particularly when protections and claims are involved.

With some last minute transactions it is physically impossible to finalise documentation.

In the case of purchases, if there is not sufficient time to register the shares in the buyer's name, the stockbroker will protect you for your entitlement by claiming on the selling broker.

In the case of sales, a claim will be made on the seller to deliver the rights involved in the issue.

Some investors become a little irate at receiving claims. It is, however, the correct procedure. The important thing to remember is shares bought or sold before rights trading begins are on a cum rights basis. Shares bought or sold after the rights are listed are on an ex-rights basis.

While in most cases these protections and claims are automatic, there are several important exceptions. These are:

> Priority Issues
> Non-renounceable Issues
> No Liability Mining Company Issues.

In these cases it is up to the buyer to ask for protection.

When an issue involves rights to prepaid shares, or a choice between paying in full or on a partly paid basis, the buyer is required to advise the broker as to the basis of payment desired.

In view of these exceptions, it would be well worthwhile checking with your broker regarding any issue to ensure your interests will be totally protected.

## Letters of Entitlement

Letters of Entitlement play a major role in determining future price movements. Very few investors, however, appreciate their importance and value. So much so, that in every new issue, small and large sums of money are thrown away and the main reason for this is, yet again, ignorance of procedures.

All companies will formally advise shareholders by mail as to their entitlements.

Depending on the size of the company and the size of the issue, it can take from a few days to a few weeks or even longer for the new issue documents to be prepared and posted to shareholders. In most issues, these letters are posted after the rights have been listed. It is here most money is lost.

Expressed simply, the weight of selling orders increases dramatically just after letters of entitlement are received. Therefore, those shareholders who work out their own entitlement as soon as the issue is announced and who sell early will often receive a better price than those who wait for formal advice from the company and then sell.

**Closing of Applications**

Another important detail in new issue announcements is the closing date for applications.

This means shareholders taking up rights must forward completed acceptance forms together with application money, at the very latest by that date so it is essential not to be late, otherwise your application could be rejected. Bearing in mind the time it can take for mail to be delivered, the wisest course would be to allow a minimum of three to four days for delivery.

If the application involves a sizeable investment, it would also pay to forward the documents by registered or certified mail.

Alternatively, documents can be handed or forwarded to your broker who will lodge the application on your behalf at no extra cost.

**Listing of New Shares**

Once rights trading ceases, the 'new' shares arising from the issue are listed and quoted the following day on a 'del' basis.

'Del' is the abbreviation of 'delivery not enforceable'.

This separate listing remains until the new share certificates have been issued and posted to shareholders. If there happens to be a dividend difference, the shares will then be quoted on a 'new' basis until the old and the new shares rank equally.

Thereafter only one class of share is quoted.

In the case of partly paid shares, there will, of course, be a separate listing until they become fully paid and rank equally.

**Renunciations**

When a shareholder sells all or part of his entitlement, he signs a document renouncing his claim to the rights (new shares).

This document is then forwarded to the broker who will then remit the proceeds of the sale to his client.

The renunciation form is then handed to the buying broker who completes the acceptance section on behalf of his client and forwards it to the company for registration.

While applications for new issues close on the same

day as rights trading ceases, brokers are allowed 10 business days grace to lodge renunciations.

This is to give brokers time to finalise documents with those clients who may have been dealing in rights in the last few days of trading.

If you are running late with an application, or applications have already closed, contact your broker immediately. For it may still be possible to participate in the issue by renouncing your entitlement.

While this is not a practice to be encouraged, and it could involve you in extra charges, you would at least be participating in the issue.

## Patterns of Price Movements

'Rights' and also old shares will normally follow one of three patterns before and during a new issue. These patterns are as follows:

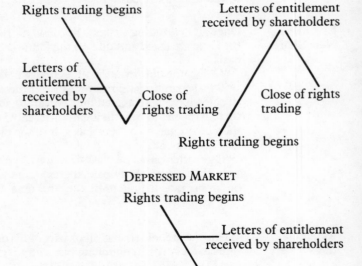

As can be seen in the first example, opening prices are high and then progressively fall to their lowest levels just after letters of entitlement are received by shareholders.

Bearing in mind thousands and, in some cases, tens of thousands of shareholders are involved, it should not be surprising to find prices falling, due to the weight of selling orders. Again it is a question of supply and demand.

In a normal market, the falling prices attract more buyers who then absorb the weight of selling.

Once the wave of selling passes, prices will usually start to rise again. In many cases the recovery can be quite substantial.

In a weak market, opening prices are high and then progressively fall. The weight of selling which follows receipt of letters of entitlement, however, accentuates the fall and with little buying support prices will continue to drop with little likelihood of recovery.

If the market is very depressed, the fall in prices can be dramatic. During one rights issue, the rights opened at 35 cents and progressively fell to a cent.

In a strong market, the pattern of price movements is usually the reverse of that followed in a normal market, providing the issue is not too large.

For example, a 1 × 10 or 1 × 20 new issue would not impose too much of a financial strain and most shareholders would take up their entitlements. On the other hand, a 1 × 2 issue would be a severe strain on shareholders' funds and many would be forced to sell.

With fewer rights on the market, prices would tend to rise and any selling orders following receipt of letters of entitlement would be quickly absorbed and the fall in prices would be marginal.

The patterns outlined are, of course, guides and there will be occasions when they will vary. In the majority of cases, however, they are repeated again and again and it is here success can often be achieved.

**Timing Important**

Providing purchases are well timed, buying rights can be a very profitable exercise. New investors will find they are an excellent way to begin an investment portfolio which can be progressively built up in subsequent rights issues. Existing shareholders have the opportunity of adding to their holdings at favourable prices, not only through their own entitlements, but also by buying additional rights.

Traders, and that can include everyone, have the opportunity of making profits in many cases on a relatively small outlay, sometimes more than once, and in just one issue.

Success will largely depend upon when you buy and what you buy — either rights or old shares.

Rights, like shares, are normally bought and sold in marketable parcels. The parcels are not identical, however, and it is important to note the differences.

**Marketable Parcels**

RIGHTS

100 where the price does not exceed $5
  50 where the price exceeds   $5 but does not exceed $10
  20 where the price exceeds $10 but does not exceed $25
  10 where the price exceeds $25 but does not exceed $50
   5 where the price exceeds $50

SHARES

2000 shares — 1 cent to 25 cents
1000 shares — 26 cents to 50 cents
 500 shares — 51 cents to $1.00
 100 shares — $1.01 to $10.00
  50 shares — $10.01 and over

Bearing this information in mind, we must again go back to the patterns of trading.

Having established that in a normal market prices are often at their lowest level just after letters of entitlement have been acted upon, this then is the best time to buy.

At the same time, the market price of the shares must also be related to the market price of the rights. For they usually move up and down in sympathy.

Even if you are not a shareholder, you can still ascertain when the letters of entitlement will be posted by contacting your broker, or the company making the issue. This one phone call could mean the difference between a small or a large profit.

**Brokerage**

The financial pages of newspapers and some financial journals have separate sections detailing current 'rights' issues. They tell at a glance whether the old shares or the 'rights' are the better buy. Not only from the point of view of price, but also brokerage and stamp duty. The figures speak for themselves. (See sample Rights listing — Appendix 3.)

**Money in Advance**

In an endeavour to eliminate unnecessary correspondence, most brokers automatically include application money on the contract note when rights are purchased.

While, technically speaking, application money is not due until the date stipulated by the company, for buyers who do not intend to trade, this procedure is advantageous to both parties.

In mentioning contract notes, it is well to remember that the processing these days is frequently done by computers. But even so, mistakes still occur. Therefore it is always advisable to check each contract note to ensure the correct security (and the correct quantity) has been purchased.

Also check prices, stamp duty, and brokerage. If there should be an error, advise your broker immediately, no matter who is at fault. It can save you money.

**Selling Rights**

In any renounceable issue shareholders normally have three options. They can:
- Take up their entitlement in full
- Sell their entitlement in full
- Sell a sufficient number of rights to provide the wherewithal to take up the balance of their entitlement.

The decision will, of course, be influenced by money. If money is plentiful, shareholders will be inclined to take up their rights. If there is a shortage of money (credit squeeze) shareholders will be forced to sell their entitlements in full or in part.

When the market is very depressed and a number of issues are current or pending, any additional new issue announcement will bring about an immediate, and in some cases a substantial, fall in the price of the shares long before rights trading begins.

If this situation should arise, there is a fourth option which many experienced investors choose.

They immediately sell part or all of their holding. The intention is to buy back what they sold, either just before rights trading begins or after. On many occasions they can show a handsome profit.

Be it rights or shares, again it is a question of supply and demand which determines prices.

As previously mentioned, most shareholders do nothing about their rights until after they receive formal advice from the company. It is then most will decide to 'take up' or sell.

With one exception, this is not the time to sell.

The times to sell, if that is your intention, are as follows:

| | |
|---|---|
| NORMAL MARKET | As soon as trading begins: an alternative is towards the end of trading. |
| DEPRESSED MARKET | Immediately trading begins. |
| STRONG MARKET | Immediately after letters of entitlement are received or at the end of trading. |

Irrespective of the market price of the rights, there is another option, which few investors appreciate or value.

This involves selling the old shares and taking up the rights.

Reference to the list of rights illustrated shows there is normally a price difference in favour of the old shares, as far as selling is concerned, even after allowing for the brokerage involved in selling and dividend difference, if any. By selling old shares, the proceeds of the sale can be used to take up the rights.

On occasions this approach can be extended further. For, in some issues, the price disparity between the old shares and rights can be quite substantial. In this situation, you can sell not only the equivalent of your entitlement, but also part or all of your entire holding.

Then, with the proceeds of the sale, you buy additional rights through the market, with payment and application money being again provided from the sale of old shares. In market terminology this is called 'switching'.

If you should ever decide to switch, remember to instruct your broker to buy and sell concurrently. Otherwise, you could find yourself in the position of selling and not being able to buy, or the reverse.

At the same time, should your broker be unable to switch or the price difference between the shares and rights narrows to such a degree that it is not worthwhile, do not give up watching the stock. Quite frequently, the margin necessary to switch may reassert itself before rights trading ceases.

**Taking up Rights**

Not everyone wants to sell or trade in rights. A large proportion of shareholders automatically take up their entitlements and send the application money to the company as soon as the documents are received.

In principle, this is the correct procedure. There will, however, be occasions when it pays to wait. Rights can have an unexpected rally and prices could move up dramatically.

While it may not have been your original intention, a sale might be warranted. By the same token, prices can also drop and the rights may end up being worthless. In this case it may pay to forgo your entitlement.

The decision must, of course, be influenced by the calibre of the company and the overall state of the market. If the issue involves a very large company, rights trading can cover a period of 2 or 3 months.

In lodging your application early, you are lending money to the company without interest. By deferring lodgement until nearer the closing date, the money can be invested (safely) for a month or so to earn at least some interest.

If you should decide to delay lodgement of your application, don't go to extremes and leave it till the last day.

In any new issue there will always be a number of people who fail to take up or who sell their entitlements.

The reasons for not doing so are many and varied:
- Ignorance of procedures
- Lack of money
- Extended absence from home or business
- Lost mail
- Change of address

Failure to act can be a costly exercise. For although some companies automatically collate the rights not applied for, sell them and distribute the proceeds to the shareholders involved, many companies do not. The rights revert back to the underwriters of the issue, or the company, and the shareholders miss out. If in doubt, contact your stockbroker or other financial advisor before the issue closes.

If you are likely to be absent from home for an extended period, leave authority — with someone you can trust — to act on your behalf. Once again your broker can help.

While mail can, and does, go astray, shareholders are given advance notice of new issues in the financial press and journals. Even if the documents are lost in the mail, it is still the shareholder's responsibility, not the company's.

Finally, do not forget to advise of any change of address.

Remarkable as it may seem, this is one of the major reasons so many investors miss out on their entitlements.

**Evening up — Odd Lots**

Every issue will also leave some shareholders with an uneven holding.

For example, a 1 × 3 new issue would mean an entitlement of 33 rights on a hundred shares. On a holding of 200 shares the entitlement would be either 66 or 67 rights, depending upon the terms announced by the company concerned.

Normally it would not pay to sell such a small number of rights because of the brokerage and stamp duty involved. For the same reason it would not pay to buy just 67 rights.

If, however, it is the intention to invest additional capital in the company, subject to the market price of the rights, it could pay to buy, say, 367 rights which would leave you with the following:

| | |
|---|---|
| Original holding | 100 shares |
| Entitlement | 33 rights |
| Purchase | 367 rights |
| Total holding | 500 |

The purchase or sale of odd lots normally involves an 'odd lot margin'. During a new issue, however, other shareholders will be in a similar situation and it is sometimes possible to buy or sell odd lots through your broker without any margin being involved.

**Trading in Rights**

For existing shareholders in companies making new share issues, there are many opportunities to trade profitably. And, as suggested earlier, with the right timing profits can be made several times during the currency of just one rights issue.

For example, by selling the rights as soon as they are listed, it is frequently possible to repurchase the rights at lower prices after the letters of entitlement have been issued.

If you have bought well and the market goes up you can then re-sell the same rights and again make a profit. The following illustrations clearly show the type of profits that can be made from trading in rights.

| EXAMPLE A: | Opening price | 35 cents |
|---|---|---|
| | Low price | 17 cents |
| | Closing price | 32 cents |

|          |               |          |
|----------|---------------|----------|
| EXAMPLE B: | Opening price | 90 cents |
|          | Low price     | 65 cents |
|          | Closing price | 85 cents |
| EXAMPLE C: | Opening price | 90 cents |
|          | Low price     | 55 cents |
|          | Closing price | 85 cents |

In each case the pattern is clear. Prices are high at the opening and then gradually fall and later recover, if only in part.

Even if you are not an existing shareholder, you can still trade. By recognising the trading patterns, you can buy rights and then re-sell before the issue closes.

As the amount of money involved in the purchase of rights is usually much less than that involved in the purchase of shares, proportionately the profits can be greater. This, together with the rebates in brokerage, adds to one's profits.

This type of trading is also possible with old shares. The costs of buying and selling, however, will, of course, be greater.

By the same token, if the pattern of trading should go against you, always have enough money in reserve to take up the rights purchased, for investment or resale at a later date. Of course, there will always be exceptions to the rule, but it is remarkable how often these patterns are repeated.

Any taxpaying investor who trades in rights and makes profits will be liable for capital gains tax, which might deter many investors from taking advantage of these price variations. But a profit is a profit only when it is taken, and these days profits should be taken at every opportunity. Common sense, however, must always be used and one should not go to extremes just for the sake of a cent or two.

**Non-Renounce-able Issues**

Occasionally, shareholders in companies will be offered rights which they cannot renounce (sell). If the offer is not accepted, then it will lapse.

Although infrequent, non-renounceable issues and/or special sales do crop up from time to time, and it is essential to know how to deal with them.

Shareholders in a well known Australian company were offered the right to buy additional shares. The terms of the offer were one new share at $2.00 for every 11 shares held.

Through ignorance, most shareholders without funds let the offer lapse. A stupid and costly decision, as the following illustration shows:

| | |
|---|---|
| Market price — old shares | $2.35 |
| Offer price — new shares | $2.00 |

Using a holding of 1,100 shares to simplify the example, it would have paid to sell 100 old shares at $2.35. From the proceeds of the sale you now accept the offer at $2.00 to restore the holding to 1,100 (the original number). After allowing for brokerage and stamp duty, shareholders would have saved around $25.00.

Another recent non-renounceable issue of shares was made on the basis of one share at par (50 cents) for every 5 shares held. The old shares were selling for 80 cents.

Using a shareholding of 2,500 as an illustration, you now sell 500 old shares at 80 cents and accept the new shares at 50 cents. The holding is still 2,500 shares. Plus a profit.

One word of caution. In these situations, make sure the old shares are quoted ex priority or ex entitlement. If they are not, you are not selling just the old shares but also your entitlement to the new shares.

**Priority Issues of Shares**

During the mining boom, priority issues were quite common. Today they are relatively rare.

Priority issues normally arise when a company decides to float one of its subsidiaries, or to form a new company.

In these situations, existing shareholders are given first priority to apply for shares in the new venture. On occasions, such an investment can be extremely rewarding. Profits are not always automatic, however, and care must be exercised before committing your capital.

Profits to look for include:

- Calibre of company making issue
- Type of venture
- Estimates of profits and dividends if any
- General tone of the market

While most priority issues are made on a fixed ratio basis, occasionally they are made without any specific entitlement. This means that a nominal holding of shares — even one share — would entitle you to apply for shares in the new company.

Providing there is sufficient time for you to be registered on the company's books, it can pay to buy into the company making the issue, as soon as details are announced.

That is, providing you buy early. For, with some issues, there is such a rush to buy shares of the promoting company, prices are pushed up to absurd levels. If this should happen, do not chase the stock. Wait for the new company's shares to be listed.

In the case of existing shareholders, it would pay to take the unexpected profit, if only in part. The proceeds of the sale can then be used to buy into the new company after its shares are listed and then to buy back the old shares.

# Trusts

**What is a 'Trust'?**

A trust enables investors to *pool* their money to invest in real estate, bank bills and government securities, shares, both local and overseas, mortgages etc. depending upon the type of trusts you are investing in, and hopefully — but by no means always — you will enjoy the rewards provided by professional managers.

Every year sizeable sums of money are invested in the various trusts which are available and once again you have a wide choice including

CASH MANAGEMENT TRUSTS
PROPERTY TRUSTS
EQUITY TRUSTS
INTERNATIONAL TRUSTS
MORTGAGE TRUSTS

The popularity of these investments will be influenced by a number of factors including

- Their performance
- Tax benefits if any
- The returns, capital gain — income or both
- Social security benefits

**Cash Management Trusts**

These highly popular trusts which were introduced a few years ago enable investors — particularly small investors — to take advantage of the high returns available from time to time in the short term money market. *Most important of all* your money is available at 24 hour or daily call depending upon the trust/s in which you invest. And many trusts also provide you with telephone redemption facilities. The initial minimum investment varies from trust to trust but with at least one trust you can invest as little as $500. Since their introduction many trusts have shown short term returns as high as 20 per cent but, as the returns fluctuate depending upon the levels of interest rates, a reasonable average annual return — at the moment — would be around 14 to 15 per cent.

**Security**

From a security point of view most if not all cash management trusts are extremely safe, with many restricting their investments to government securities and bank bills. And there are several trusts which invest only in government securities.

76

Cash management trusts are an ideal investment for
- SHORT TERM INVESTORS
- BUSINESS CASH FLOWS
- RETIREES (LONG SERVICE LEAVE PAYMENTS)

By way of example, you might have sold your home and be waiting to buy another. By investing at least part of the proceeds — say 10 per cent — to cover your future deposit needs, you will ensure that your money is readily available and at the same time earning a good return. Another example, without ignoring the importance of bank links and accommodation, is to use a cash management trust as a short term business investment to maintain that all-important *cash flow*. Retirees could also use cash management trusts for funds which are not eligible to be parked in *roll-over funds*. Although there has been some rationalisation within the cash management trust industry you still have more than a dozen from which to choose.

## Property Trusts

A few years ago property trusts were the number one investment but due to some disappointing performances and the collapse of some trusts many of the unlisted property trusts, in particular, have lost a lot of their appeal. On the other hand the listed property trusts like GPT-General Property Trust, Stockland and Capital Property Trust have performed extremely well, among others, and being listed on the Stock Exchange, investors have the added advantage of instant liquidity and a day-to-day market value for their investment/s.

As can be seen from the list in Appendix 3 you have literally hundreds of trusts to choose from and once again this is where the problem lies. Which trust or trusts do you choose? This is not an easy question to answer and shows — yet again — why it is essential to seek professional advice, and that does not mean a super salesperson representing their own product or products. (See sample Trust & Fund Market list — Appendix 3.)

With new trusts still being announced, the stage has now been reached where, quite frankly, there appear to be far too many trusts. And we could well see some long overdue rationalisation within the property trust industry, as has been happening in the case of cash management trusts.

The fee structures of a number of trusts appear to be excessive and so too are the commissions offered. Both should be reviewed, as should the sales tactics adopted by some of their representatives, and it is painfully obvious that investment advisors' licences are still too easy to obtain.

On this point it is interesting to note that rarely, if ever, do you see a *listed* property trust in the investment recommendations of so-called independent advisors. And the reasons are more than obvious: little or no commission.

Another survey on the performance of most of Australia's property trusts should be compulsory reading for everyone. The survey was again conducted by Norths, a leading stockbroking firm, and covered most of the property trusts of Australia. It was the listed property trusts that, in most cases, again led the field. Some unlisted property trusts did perform well, but not as many as the property trust industry or the promoters would like. A highlighted feature of the property trust survey was the high costs involved, not only in investing in a trust but also in getting out. So if you are interested in investing in property trusts make sure that you are getting value for money from the investment. According to one of our leading advisors, that usually means a proven track record of at least five years. Make sure also that you get a second, independent opinion before making a final decision.

**Other Trusts**  Fixed interest trusts are aimed at a high return through both local and overseas fixed interest securities, including government securities.

National resources trusts, as the name implies, will invest mainly in Australia's natural resources.

International trusts invest in securities listed on stock exchanges in North America, Europe, Japan etc. and minimum investments vary from trust to trust.

Apart from cash management trusts, equity trusts are designed for medium to long term investors — certainly for five years and preferably more.

Depending upon the type of trust in which you invest, income can be paid by cheque in the normal way, but some trusts also have interest reinvestment plans which allow investors to automatically invest in more units.

As with dividend reinvestment plans, this is a good way to build up the investment for people not needing 'money to live on'.

Personal preferences and performances, as well as professional advice, will determine the type of trust or trusts in which you invest.

It will take time for some trusts to perform and a few

might well disappoint, but they could still be ideal investments for lazy or inexperienced investors, and in certain cases would meet the needs of those planning for retirement, or who have just retired.

**Mortgage Trusts**

The security appeal of 'bricks and mortar' type investments is a major reason for conservative investors opting for investing some of their money in mortgages of one kind or another. One way of doing this is to invest in a mortgage trust or fund. Over the past few years high interest rates have meant that investors in mortgage trusts have enjoyed attractive returns, in some cases exceeding 17 per cent per annum. In many cases mortgage trusts are a better investment than other fixed interest investments such as bond, debentures and unsecured notes. And even when interest rates fall the returns from mortgage trusts are maintained for a longer period of time. As more and more trusts are introduced investors have a much wider choice and that includes trusts established by many of Australia's banks.

**Costs**

With the majority of trusts or funds there are no entry fees or costs at the time the investment is made, but early withdrawal (sale) could involve a fee. So it is essential to check out these facts (including the costs of running the trust) before you invest.

**Minimum Investment**

The minimum investment required again varies, but you could start with as little as $500 and usually you can add to your investment at any time, subject of course to the rules of the trust.

**Interest**

Interest can be paid monthly or quarterly, again depending upon the trust you invest in. A number offer automatic reinvestment of income in additional units, similar to dividend reinvestment plans. So for safety conscious investors a spread of mortgage trusts should provide some worry-free investments. As always seek a second opinion before you invest and do not put all your money into just one trust.

**Taxation**

It should be noted that capital gains tax could pose problems for some unit trust investments so once again investors face difficulties and anomalies due in the main to hastily introduced legislation. Hopefully commonsense and equity will prevail in the long run but until that happens it is essential that the current situation be fully explained to *all* potential investors. (See sample Macquarie Investment Bond Fund — Appendix 3.)

**Friendly Societies**

For investors not requiring regular income but still seeking security, Friendly Societies — together with Managed Investment Bonds (Insurance Bonds) offer attractive returns which can be *'tax free'* subject to how long the investment is held and a person's marginal tax rate.

It should be noted that, unlike Insurance Bonds, Friendly Societies are controlled and supervised by State legislation not Commonwealth so rules can and do vary from State to State.

In the main Friendly Society investments are 10 year *single premium* policies, but in some situations the policy can be for 10 or 40 years.

**Types of Investments**

Usually the funds can only be invested in 'approved investments' such as
> Government Securities
> Semi Governmental loans
> Bank Bills

There are a number of well-managed Friendly Societies in which you can invest including the following:

| SOCIETY | FEES (Initial) | MINIMUM INVESTMENT |
|---|---|---|
| I.O.O.F. | 3.6% | $500 |
| Macquarie Bank (Over 50s) | 3.5 | $5000 |
| Manchester Unity | 3.6 | $500 |
| O.S.T. | 3.6 | $1000 |

**Withdrawal of Funds**

You may surrender or partially surrender the policy or policies but in the case of full surrender before the annual bonus rate has been declared an interim bonus *may be paid*.

**Taxation**

TAX RATE ON GAINS
(FRIENDLY SOCIETIES)

| | Years 0 to 8 | 8–9 | 9–10 | 10 Years |
|---|---|---|---|---|
| 21% | Nil | Nil | Nil | Nil |
| 29% | Nil | Nil | Nil | Nil |
| 39% | 9 | 6 | 3 | Nil |
| 47% | 17 | 11 | 6 | Nil |
| 48% | 18 | 12 | 6 | Nil |

**Social Security**

In the case of social security benefits any maturity or surrender will mean that the excess over cost will be deemed to be income under the income test for the next 12 months, whilst under the assets test the capital plus the accrued profit is treated as an asset.

**Emergencies**

In the case of accident, financial hardship or illness any profits which are withdrawn are not taxable, and the same situation applies in the case of death.

Maximum investments vary from state to state, but could well range from $7,000 up to $50,000 and in certain cases even more. The minimum age for investment is 14 years.

**Insurance or Managed Investment Bonds**

Tax-free or partly tax-free investments are not easy to find so it is little wonder that investment in insurance bonds and Friendly Societies has grown at an incredible rate and providing the taxation rules are not changed these products will continue to attract billions of dollars every year.

TAX RATE ON GAINS
(INSURANCE COMPANIES)

|       | Years 0 to 8 | 8–9 | 9–10 | 10 Years |
|-------|--------------|-----|------|----------|
| 21%   | Nil          | Nil | Nil  | Nil      |
| 29%   | Nil          | Nil | Nil  | Nil      |
| 39%   | Nil          | Nil | Nil  | Nil      |
| 47%   | 8            | 5   | 3    | Nil      |
| 48%   | 9            | 6   | 3    | Nil      |

In reality Managed Investment Bonds are 10 year and sometimes longer single-premium life assurance policies and as with many life company promoted products there are usually sizeable up-front charges of around five per cent. Another point to note is that size does not determine market performance. In view of the fee and cost structures, which vary from company to company, potential investors would be well advised to take as long a view as possible to enable the managers to perform. Other points to note before investing would include

• Quality of management
• Past performance
• Type of investment portfolio/s
• Cashability

In mentioning the type of investment portfolio some companies have an above average proportion of their funds in shares and if the sharemarket should drop this would obviously be reflected in the returns to bond holders. (See sample application for Investments Bonds — Appendix 3.)

A survey by stockbrokers Norths revealed that the returns on Managed Investment Bonds ranged from around 8 per cent up to around 80 per cent. And as with Approved Deposit Funds and Deferred Annuities you have dozens of products to choose from under various names and combinations. (See sample Insurance Bonds list — Appendix 3.)

**Taxation Aspects**

As with Friendly Societies, for 30-cents-in-the-dollar taxpayers, profits can be cashed in at any time without any tax liability because there is a 30 per cent tax rebate on investments such as these. For higher taxpayers early 'taking of profits' would result in the following:

|  | TAX RATE | TAX PAYABLE |
|---|---|---|
| Up to eight years | 39% less 30% REBATE | 9% |
|  | 48% less 30% REBATE | 18% |

After eight years the tax liability is further reduced and after 10 years the profits will be free of tax to all taxpayers.

# Retirement

Many people seem to think retirement is the end of their life. But if properly planned, retirement can be the beginning of a new life. Unfortunately, very few people plan for their retirement until just before the big day and this is much too late. Even if you are under 40, the sooner you start planning the better.

Apart from mental and physical activity, which are essential, a number of important financial decisions must be made. For example, if you are given a choice do you accept a pension or a lump sum? Do you sell the family home and buy a unit? Do you pay off all your debts? Can you qualify for any social security payments?

**Timing Saves Money**

As mentioned earlier, it can be costly if you elect to retire on or just before 30 June. The addition of a superannuation lump sum payment to the yearly income will usually mean increased tax. By postponing retirement until just into the next financial year, income will normally be lower and so will be the tax bill.

Of course it is not always possible to postpone the big day. There is, however, no harm in asking and it could save you money.

**Enforced Retirement**

These days a number of people are being forced into early retirement. This might be because of government legislation, changes in company policy, some kind of accident, or ill-health. Whatever the reasons, to be retrenched or forced to retire at an early age, and when you are not expecting it, can be quite a traumatic experience. It can bring mental as well as financial problems, especially if you are still raising a family and have financial commitments.

It is essential then to know your rights as far as superannuation, long service leave, and holiday pay are concerned.

Whenever you join a superannuation scheme, ask for a copy of the trust deed. It will explain what you get if you are retrenched and it will tell you what you are entitled to in all situations. It is also a good idea to obtain a copy of the information booklet on long service leave.

**Retrench-
ment**

Depending on your award, the superannuation fund you belong to and the state in which you live, it can be to your financial advantage not to resign but to be sacked.

If you resign you could be missing out on your long service leave and some of your superannuation. On the other hand, if you are retrenched or fired you will probably receive all your entitlements.

Further, if you are retrenched you automatically qualify for social service benefits, but if you resign you will probably have to wait six weeks before you qualify.

Even if you do receive unemployment benefits after you are retrenched, it might be difficult to meet your commitments until you find a new job. So you will have to take a close look at the family's financial position. What do you need to live and meet your everyday costs, such as food bills, electricity, gas, rent, rates, telephone, etc.?

Apart from these items, one of your main worries will be meeting your mortgage repayments, hire purchase bills and other debts. If you cannot meet them, face the facts. Contact the people concerned and explain the situation. Most financial institutions will appreciate your honesty and try to assist.

If you live in your own home, taking in a boarder or two could also help. But you must carefully check the background of the people before you take them in. On the other hand, it might pay you to move to a smaller house and rent out your own home. It may mean only a few extra dollars, but it could prevent you from losing all you have worked for.

**Paying off
Debts**

It has generally been regarded that one should eliminate as many debts as possible either before or on retirement.

Depending upon the attitude of the person/s concerned, this can frequently be taken to extremes, proving to be a costly exercise.

In many cases it can be advantageous to owe money, certainly in times of high inflation.

Of course, with some people, advancing age brings the added burden of worry and for those in this category it would be advisable to pay off the mortgage and other debts and sleep peacefully.

For others who owe only a nominal amount on their mortgage (excluding those with War Service loans) consideration could be given to paying off the existing mortgage well before retirement and negotiating a new mortgage for the longest period of time possible and at the most advantageous rate. This, however, should not be left until the last moment. The sooner it is done the greater the likelihood of more favourable terms from the lending body concerned. But remember the timing of the negotiations will be of paramount importance, certainly as far as interest rates are concerned.

**Retirement — Country Style**

On retirement, some people may, and do, find it appropriate to move to country areas where living costs in certain categories are lower than in the city. There can be quite considerable savings in housing, depending on the area chosen.

During the past decade, many people have become disenchanted with city living and the quest for material things and we have seen an exodus back to the land. This exodus involves not only the retired but young people as well.

For those accustomed to country life, the change in living styles can be smooth, but for those born and bred in the cities the lure of living 'country style' may seem very attractive in the beginning but can frequently lose its appeal after a period of time.

Social life in country areas is frequently better. Costs of membership of golf, bowls and social clubs are often less than in city or suburban areas and new friendships easier to create.

Depending upon one's place of residence, transportation costs may be more expensive. On the other hand, if there are a few surplus acres for the growing of vegetables, running of stock, poultry etc. there is always the advantage of being able to live off the land. However, there are dangers.

**Dangers**

From time to time one sees full page advertisements offering five, ten, twenty-five, fifty or one hundred acre properties near major country towns at seemingly low prices when compared to city real estate values. Unfortunately, the lure of the advertisements often tempts people to buy without proper investigation. For example, with smaller farms the acreage may not be adequate for compliance with local council regulations for the erection of a home. There may be a lack of other facilities, such as electricity, telephone, water etc. and the provision of these services could be costly.

So before rushing in, it would be advisable to spend time in visiting the various country areas to acquaint oneself with the facilities offered and find an area that is personally appealing.

**Retirement — Overseas Style**

Travel is one of the major joys of retirement, particularly when money is not a problem. Providing one enjoys good health, these days there is an ever increasing trend to spend extended periods of time travelling to, and in some cases, living in, overseas countries. From a financial point of view this can be accomplished in several ways. For example, if one is prepared to let the family home, the income received, together with any pension and investment income would be more than enough to live in reasonable comfort in some countries.

It is also important to remember that retired people can elect to travel at any time and the travel industry today is a very competitive one. Those who can arrange to travel 'off season' can save quite considerable amounts in transportation and accommodation costs.

For those people with ancestral links with the countries concerned travel can be an added pleasure.

Before such a 'holiday' is contemplated quite obviously health would be a prime factor, and it would be essential to take out insurance to cover illness or accident, which can be very expensive items in some countries. The political and economic stability of the country chosen must also be looked at carefully, not forgetting the value of the Australian dollar as well as other currencies.

People whose income is derived mainly from investments and who undertake extended, or frequent, trips either locally or overseas, should appoint someone to manage their affairs during their absence. This may be under 'Power of Attorney' (as will be mentioned later) or general instructions to one's stockbroker, accountant, solicitor, banker or family.

In the local sense, we have already seen evidence of the problems of four weeks annual leave, let alone extended absences from home — with telephone, gas and/or electricity being cut off because the relevant bills have not been met on time.

Looking from afar, retiring to a foreign country may seem very appealing. For some people, however, the different customs, language and food can turn an expected joy into an anti-climax — or even a nightmare.

It would, therefore, be advisable to avoid long term rentals of units, apartments and villas until one is certain one can cope with the change in life style in the adopted country.

**Retirement — City Style**

On retirement, the majority of people, quite naturally, elect to maintain the style of living they have created over their working years.

For some no change of scene is necessary. For others, however, it can often mean a change of residence. Over the years real estate values have increased dramatically and — allowing for the peaks and the troughs — will continue to do so, even if at a reduced rate.

The family home, generally purchased many years before, has now acquired a value beyond expectations. Not surprisingly, when the children have grown up, this home now appears too large and too costly to maintain. Frequently, in these situations and without too much thought, the decision is made to sell, take the profit and move into a home unit or smaller dwelling. While such a move can be successful for some, it may be a very costly exercise for others, and not only in the financial sense.

Before deciding to sell the family home, one should consider other alternatives. For example, it might pay to try out unit living by renting one for six or twelve months — if you can obtain an option to buy, so much the better.

If this style of living is satisfactory, then by all means sell the family home and buy the unit. If not, then no harm has been done and you can return to the former home.

If there is no objection to letting the family home, income to cover the rental of the unit can come in part or in full from the rents received and income from other investments.

Providing the necessary capital is available, another solution to the problem of the over-large home could involve the creation of a separate flat or apartment. This would provide not only additional income, but also company without too much loss of privacy.

Such a move would involve obtaining local council approval. But the end result could be extremely satisfactory in a number of ways and eliminate the need to sell the family home. One cannot and should not ignore or underestimate the value in comfort or contentment the family home can provide and it can never be expressed just in financial terms.

Even with advancing age, one should not leave the family home unless forced to do so by financial circumstances, ill-health or incapacity. But anticipating this years ahead could be a very wise move.

**Hobbies and Interests**

For some people retirement is a joy, and the days are active — for others retirement is a bore with time always seeming to drag.

For the sports minded, retirement will provide many hours of enjoyment — be it on the golf course, bowling green, tennis court or in fishing, sailing or boating. For some, however, after the initial wave of enthusiasm, sporting activities can lose their appeal.

As previously mentioned, mental as well as physical activity is essential for the retired. This can be approached in two ways — income producing or non-income producing. Whatever way is chosen will largely be determined by one's financial situation and interests.

Some may seek to obtain part or full-time employment in a new or complementary field. Others may turn a part-time hobby into a full-time occupation.

There are, however, some activities which will obviously provide great satisfaction and involve many hours of enjoyment. The keen gardener for example may decide to concentrate on growing roses, carnations, geraniums etc. for exhibition, sale or both. The handyman may decide to buy secondhand furniture and restore it. For those interested in art, endless hours can be spent in painting, sketching or drawing and visiting the numerous galleries and exhibitions. Music and reading can also provide hours of pleasure. Philately can be not only a stimulating hobby but also a source of capital gains. So too can managing your own share investment portfolio.

The same comments, of course, would apply to collecting coins, notes, china, silver, antiques — in fact anything — providing, of course, you have the necessary skills.

**A New Education**

Many of the older generation, who are about to retire or have retired, were forced to leave school at an early age.

These days more and more schools, colleges of advanced education, technical colleges and universities are providing a variety of educational programmes covering many fields, occupations and interests.

With time no longer a problem, participation in one or more of these educational programmes could be well worthwhile.

One could, of course, go on and on giving similar illustrations of retirement activities and the list would indeed be endless.

For investors, there are many ways of maintaining an active interest that will prove not only interesting but, on occasions, rewarding in several unusual ways. For example, a number of companies distribute gifts of their products to those shareholders attending the meeting. Some companies put on luncheons, wine tastings etc.

Apart from the handouts, attending company meetings can also be financially rewarding. On occasions, information may be given at the meeting which can influence the price of the company's securities. Reference may be made to possible new or bonus issues of shares, losses or setbacks which the company may be facing. Those present at the meeting can, of course, take advantage of this information.

## Voluntary Work

While for some retired people added sources of income are very necessary, for others this is not the case. For people in this category, there is a crying need for help by the various charity committees and voluntary help organisations. Quite often a wrong impression is gained of involvement in these areas, that is, one of an attempt to gain social recognition only.

Over the years many willing workers have been lost because of this image and a number of people have missed out on an interest which could have given an enormous amount of personal satisfaction and stimulus.

Last, and by no means least, there is the social contact with people of similar interests, which is so important in later years, particularly for single people, widows and widowers as well as couples.

## Holidays

Work and/or activity of one kind or another is, of course, a necessary therapy — even in retirement.

Unfortunately, some people think retirement is the beginning of one long, happy holiday and this is not necessarily the case.

For those who continue to lead an active life after retirement, regular holidays are just as important as for those in regular employment.

## Start Early

Common sense suggests that everyone should make a will long before retirement. Unfortunately, this is often not the case.

In reality, everyone should make a will the day they turn eighteen. For a variety of reasons, however, this is not done and, notwithstanding the best of intentions, is frequently ignored, or forgotten, year after year until it is too late.

Having made a will, it is important to review it from time to time according to changes within the family circle and/or government legislation. The appointment of executors to administer one's estate requires careful consideration and, of course, professional guidance.

In normal circumstances, the husband makes the wife the chief executrix, and the reverse applies as far as the wife's will is concerned. It is, however, always advisable to have more than one executor.

Depending upon the terms of the will, in certain cases it would be advisable to include the widest powers possible in relation to the investment of the estate's funds.

Once made, it is essential to ensure the will is kept in a safe place, and its whereabouts known by several members of the family, as well as the family solicitor.

Apart from making a will it is essential to keep and maintain up to date and accurate records of all investments and documents held including life assurance policies, mortgages, deeds, stocks, shares, debentures, surveys, etc., in fact, anything of importance.

Although it is also important for these documents to be kept in a safe place, it is essential for these records to be duplicated in the event of theft, fire, or loss etc., and for the duplicate list to be kept in a safe place as well.

It is also essential for a trusted member of the family (or even two) to be advised of the whereabouts of these documents and, where appropriate, a duplicate list of the records could be kept by the person/persons concerned.

It would also be prudent for those concerned to be made conversant with the overall financial situation.

**Power of Attorney**

Apart from your will, one of your most important documents will be a Power of Attorney. A Power of Attorney simply means you are legally appointing someone else to act on your behalf in the event of your absence or incapacity.

For elderly people, a Power of Attorney is a *must*. Unfortunately, it is rarely thought about until it is too late. Granting a Power of Attorney will certainly save you and your family a lot of worry. It could also save you money.

One final point. There must be complete trust in the person or persons being given this privilege, otherwise the Power could be abused. But do consult a solicitor in relation to wills as well as Power of Attorney. Alternatively you could use the service of a trustee company.

**The Retirement Home**

One solution to the problem of the retirement home involves buying or building a holiday home, week-ender or buying a block of land, well before retirement.

In fact, more and more people are already doing this to escape the rat-race of city living. Providing the second property is bought well in advance, over the years it can provide a place for holidays, a part or full-time investment and, of course, a new interest. If bought in early middle age, or sooner, improvements and additions can be progressively made so that, on retirement, the change of home can be a looked-forward-to event and not a traumatic experience.

The original family home could then be sold, to provide additional capital for investment, or let to provide additional income. Alternatively, if money is not a problem, both properties could be lived in at different times of the year.

Of course, the decision to keep both properties will depend upon a number of factors including income, be it private, social security pension, or both, plus, of course, the value of your assets.

These will include:
- Availability of funds
- State of health
- Rates, upkeep etc.
- Land Tax
- Income Tax
- Eligibility for pension
- Value of assets

In purchasing a second home, consideration should also be given to buying the property in the other partner's name.

# Social Security

Your eligibility for a social security pension is subject to an *assets test* and an *income test* which are detailed in the following pages. Over the years, many retirees have not utilised their savings to the best advantage, the aim being *maximum pension at all costs*. Another point to be noted is the question of *fringe benefits*. While their importance to some pensioners, particularly those on low or fixed incomes, is appreciated, it is important to realise that on average the fringe benefits would be worth around $1,500 to $2,000 per year. So, without ignoring taxation, if your investments can bring in an extra $4,000 a year, financially you would still be better off without fringe benefits.

**Taxation**

With certain exceptions, a *special pensioner tax-free threshold* applies and this is usually adjusted in line with the CPI. However following the 1989 Federal Budget the new figures are as follows.

### REBATE THRESHOLD

A special rebate is currently allowable to Australian taxpayers in receipt of an Australian social security or repatriation pension.

The maximum rebate for 1988/89 remained at $430. However, to allow eligible pensioners to take full advantage of the $430 rebate following the reduction in personal tax rates, the income level above which the maximum rebate begins to shade out *increased from $6,143 to $6,892 in 1988/89*. The rebate reduced by 12.5 cents for each dollar of taxable income in excess of $6,892 until fully extinguished at $10,332.

**Look Ahead**

When it comes to social security you must look ahead in terms of arranging your affairs to the best advantage. This includes selecting the right investments to *maximise* your pension entitlement in full or in part, but the Departments of Social Security and Veterans' Affairs have been and are still trying to change the rules regarding certain assets and income and this should be kept constantly in mind.

**Accrued Benefits are Income**

In relation to Capital Guaranteed Managed Investment Bonds and similar investments the Department of Social Security is now saying that the benefits whether *cashed in or not* are deemed to be income and will therefore influence the pension you receive.

By the same token if your circumstances should change the other way — say by reinvesting at a lower rate of interest, if a company reduces or passes its dividend — then you are fully entitled to apply to the Department of Social Security for your pension entitlements to be adjusted upwards — *immediately*.

**Gifts and Loans**

Under the existing rules pensioner couples can make cash gifts or loans of up to $4,000 per year without penalty. And in the case of single pensioners they can make cash gifts or loans of up to $2,000 per year. These gifts or loans apply to any 12 month period so it is not financial year or calendar year. While this arrangement may provide only nominal benefits in the first year or two, the benefits could prove to be quite substantial pension-wise over a longer term.

**The Assets Test**

The assets test applies to — age pension, invalid pension, wife's pension, widow's pension, carer's pension, supporting parent's benefit, rehabilitation allowance, sheltered employment allowance and repatriation service pension paid by the Department of Veterans' Affairs.

The assets test does not apply to pensions paid to blind people or to war and defence widow's pensions or repatriation disability pensions paid by the Department of Veterans' Affairs.

Payments for more than one child or dependent student of a blind pensioner do depend on income and assets.

WHAT ASSETS AFFECT YOUR PENSION

THESE DON'T COUNT
Some assets don't affect your pension, *no matter what their value*.

These include:
- Your home and the land around it which is used mainly for domestic purposes

- Proceeds from the sale of your home from which you intend to buy or build another home
- Special aids for disabled people
- Pre-paid funeral and cemetery expenses
- An interest in a deceased person's estate not able to be received
- The capital value of a life interest, for example the right to income from an estate
- Awards for valour not kept as an investment or hobby
- A gift car provided by the Department of Veterans' Affairs
- The value of a contingent or reversionary interest not established by you

### THESE DO COUNT

All other assets are taken into account. These are called *'assessable assets'*.

Examples of 'assessable assets':

- Money in bank accounts, building societies, credit unions, non-interest bearing accounts, and fixed deposits etc.
- Real estate apart from your home, e.g. holiday home
- Loans to family trusts, family, organisations, etc.
- Investments such as shares, bonds and debentures
- Cars (including antique cars)
- Caravans, boats and trailers, etc.
- Investments in property trusts, friendly societies and family trusts
- Businesses and farms
- Large amounts disposed of without adequate financial return, including gifts to family, etc.
- Household contents and personal effects

**Pensioner Couples**

The assets test will not affect you at all if the total net market value of your assessable assets is not more than these amounts:

- IF YOU ARE A HOMEOWNER
  $137,000 for a married couple (combined)
- IF YOU ARE A NON-HOMEOWNER
  $205,500 for a married couple (combined)

These amounts are increased each year with the cost of living adjustments.

## PENSION RATES UNDER THE ASSETS TEST

### HOMEOWNER

| Value of assets combined $ | No children combined $pf | One child* combined $pf | Two children* combined $pf |
|---|---|---|---|
| 137,000 | 430.80 | 478.80 | 526.80 |
| 140,000 | 418.80 | 466.80 | 514.80 |
| 150,000 | 378.80 | 426.80 | 474.80 |
| 160,000 | 338.80 | 386.80 | 434.80 |
| 170,000 | 298.80 | 346.80 | 394.80 |
| 180,000 | 258.80 | 306.80 | 354.80 |
| 190,000 | 218.80 | 266.80 | 314.80 |
| 200,000 | 178.80 | 226.80 | 274.80 |
| 220,000 | 98.80 | 146.80 | 194.80 |
| 240,000 | 18.80 | 66.80 | 114.80 |
| 245,000 | nil | 46.80 | 94.80 |
| 250,000 | | 26.80 | 74.80 |
| 257,000 | | nil | 46.80 |
| 269,000 | | | nil |

### NON-HOMEOWNER

| Value of assets combined $ | No children combined $pf | One child* combined $pf | Two children* combined $pf |
|---|---|---|---|
| 205,500 | 430.80 | 478.80 | 526.80 |
| 210,000 | 412.80 | 460.80 | 508.80 |
| 220,000 | 372.80 | 420.80 | 468.80 |
| 230,000 | 332.80 | 380.80 | 428.80 |
| 240,000 | 292.80 | 340.80 | 388.80 |
| 250,000 | 252.80 | 300.80 | 348.80 |
| 260,000 | 212.80 | 260.80 | 308.80 |
| 280,000 | 132.80 | 180.80 | 228.80 |
| 300,000 | 52.80 | 100.80 | 148.80 |
| 313,500 | nil | 46.80 | 94.80 |
| 325,500 | | nil | 46.80 |
| 337,500 | | | nil |

*Children under 13 years.
Children 13 to 15 years add an extra $20.20 a fortnight for each child.
Dependent students 16 and older, see your local Social Security office.
Concessions cut out when assets reach:
$157,000 for a homeowner;
$225,500 for a non-homeowner.

**Single
Pensioners**

The assets test will not affect you at all if the total net market value of your assessable assets is not more than these amounts:

- IF YOU ARE A HOMEOWNER
  $96,000 for a single person
- IF YOU ARE A NON-HOMEOWNER
  $164,500 for a single person

These amounts are increased each year with the cost of living adjustments.

PENSION RATES UNDER THE ASSETS TEST

| HOMEOWNER | | | |
|---|---|---|---|
| Value of assets $ | No children $pf | One child* $pf | Two children* $pf |
| 96,000 | 258.40 | 330.40 | 378.40 |
| 100,000 | 242.40 | 314.40 | 362.40 |
| 110,000 | 202.40 | 274.40 | 322.40 |
| 120,000 | 162.40 | 234.40 | 282.40 |
| 130,000 | 122.40 | 194.40 | 242.40 |
| 140,000 | 82.40 | 154.40 | 202.40 |
| 150,000 | 42.40 | 114.40 | 162.40 |
| 160,750 | nil | 71.40 | 119.40 |
| 170,000 | | 34.40 | 82.40 |
| 178,750 | | nil | 47.40 |
| 180,000 | | | 42.40 |
| 190,750 | | | nil |

| NON-HOMEOWNER | | | |
|---|---|---|---|
| Value of assets $ | No children $pf | One child* $pf | Two children* $pf |
| 164,500 | 258.40 | 330.40 | 378.40 |
| 170,000 | 236.40 | 308.40 | 356.40 |
| 180,000 | 196.40 | 268.40 | 316.40 |
| 190,000 | 156.40 | 228.40 | 276.40 |
| 200,000 | 116.40 | 188.40 | 236.40 |
| 210,000 | 76.40 | 148.40 | 196.40 |
| 220,000 | 36.40 | 108.40 | 156.40 |
| 229,250 | nil | 71.40 | 119.40 |
| 240,000 | | 28.40 | 76.40 |
| 247,250 | | nil | 47.40 |
| 259,250 | | | nil |

*Children under 13 years.
Children 13 to 15 years add an extra $20.20 a fortnight for each child.
Dependent students 16 and older, see your local Social Security office.
Concessions cut out when assets reach:
$109,500 for a homeowner;
$178,000 for a non-homeowner.

Additionally the permissible assets limits for fringe benefit exemption are
> *For Fringe Benefits*
> Single homeowners $101,750
> Single non-homeowners $165,750
> Married homeowners (combined) $146,000
> Married non-homeowners (combined) $210,000

**Income
Test for
Pensioners
Under 70**

MARRIED PENSIONERS
INCOME TEST

| Gross income combined $pf | No children combined $pf | One child* combined $pf | Two children* combined $pf |
|---|---|---|---|
| 140.00 | 430.80 | 478.80 | 526.80 |
| 160.00 | 420.80 | 478.80 | 526.80 |
| 180.00 | 410.80 | 470.80 | 526.80 |
| 200.00 | 400.80 | 460.80 | 520.80 |
| 220.00 | 390.80 | 450.80 | 510.80 |
| 240.00 | 380.80 | 440.80 | 500.80 |
| 260.00 | 370.80 | 430.80 | 490.80 |
| 280.00 | 360.80 | 420.80 | 480.80 |
| 300.00 | 350.80 | 410.80 | 470.80 |
| 340.00 | 330.80 | 390.80 | 450.80 |
| 380.00 | 310.80 | 370.80 | 430.80 |
| 420.00 | 290.80 | 350.80 | 410.80 |
| 460.00 | 270.80 | 330.80 | 390.80 |
| 500.00 | 250.80 | 310.80 | 370.80 |
| 540.00 | 230.80 | 290.80 | 350.80 |
| 580.00 | 210.80 | 270.80 | 330.80 |
| 640.00 | 180.80 | 240.80 | 300.80 |
| 700.00 | 150.80 | 210.80 | 270.80 |
| 760.00 | 120.80 | 180.80 | 240.80 |
| 820.00 | 90.80 | 150.80 | 210.80 |
| 880.00 | 60.80 | 120.80 | 180.80 |
| 940.00 | 30.80 | 90.80 | 150.80 |
| 1001.60 | nil | 60.00 | 120.80 |
| 1060.00 | | 30.80 | 90.80 |
| 1121.60 | | nil | 60.00 |
| 1180.00 | | | 30.80 |
| 1241.60 | | | nil |

*Children under 13 years.
Children 13 to 15 years add an extra $20.20 a fortnight for each child.
Dependent students 16 and older, see your local Social Security office.
Concessions cut out when income reaches $300.00 a fortnight. Add
$40 to this figure for each child.

## SINGLE PENSIONERS
## INCOME TEST

| Gross income $pf | No children $pf | One child* $pf | Two children* $pf |
|---|---|---|---|
| 80.00 | 258.40 | 330.40 | 378.40 |
| 100.00 | 248.40 | 330.40 | 378.40 |
| 120.00 | 238.40 | 322.40 | 378.40 |
| 140.00 | 228.40 | 312.40 | 372.40 |
| 160.00 | 218.40 | 302.40 | 362.40 |
| 180.00 | 208.40 | 292.40 | 352.40 |
| 200.00 | 198.40 | 282.40 | 342.40 |
| 220.00 | 188.40 | 272.40 | 332.40 |
| 240.00 | 178.40 | 262.40 | 322.40 |
| 260.00 | 168.40 | 252.40 | 312.40 |
| 280.00 | 158.40 | 242.40 | 302.40 |
| 300.00 | 148.40 | 232.40 | 292.40 |
| 340.00 | 128.40 | 212.40 | 272.40 |
| 380.00 | 108.40 | 192.40 | 252.40 |
| 420.00 | 88.40 | 172.40 | 232.40 |
| 460.00 | 68.40 | 152.40 | 212.40 |
| 500.00 | 48.40 | 132.40 | 192.40 |
| 540.00 | 28.40 | 112.40 | 172.40 |
| 580.00 | 8.40 | 92.40 | 152.40 |
| 596.80 | nil | 84.00 | 144.00 |
| 620.00 | | 72.40 | 132.40 |
| 660.00 | | 52.40 | 112.40 |
| 700.00 | | 32.40 | 92.40 |
| 740.00 | | 12.40 | 72.40 |
| 764.80 | | nil | 60.00 |
| 780.00 | | | 52.40 |
| 820.00 | | | 32.40 |
| 860.00 | | | 12.40 |
| 884.80 | | | nil |

*Children under 13 years.
Children 13 to 15 years add an extra $20.20 a fortnight for each child. Dependent students 16 and older, see your local Social Security office. Concessions cut out when income reaches $176.00 a fortnight. Add $40 to this figure for each child.

**Age Pension for the Over 70s**

If you are single and 70 or over you can have average fortnightly income of up to $80 (gross) and still get the full pension.

If you have income of $200 a fortnight or less, pension will be at least $198.40 a fortnight. As your income rises above $200 a fortnight, pension comes down.

Married pensioner couples, both 70 or over, can have a combined average fortnightly income of $80 (gross) and still get the full pension of $215.40 a fortnight each ($430.80 combined fortnightly pension).

If a married couple has combined income of $605.80 a fortnight or less, pension will be at least $99 a fortnight each ($198 combined fortnightly pension). As combined income rises above $605.80 a fortnight, the pension comes down and the table shows how this works.

### 70 OR OLDER
### SINGLE AND COUPLE INCOME TEST

| Gross income* combined $pf | Single Over 70 $pf | Married both over 70 combined $pf |
|---|---|---|
| 80.00 | 258.40 | 430.80 |
| 100.00 | 248.40 | 430.80 |
| 120.00 | 238.40 | 430.80 |
| 140.00 | 228.40 | 430.80 |
| 160.00 | 218.40 | 420.80 |
| 180.00 | 208.40 | 410.80 |
| 200.00 | 198.40 | 400.80 |
| 240.00 | 178.40 | 380.80 |
| 280.00 | 158.40 | 360.80 |
| 320.00 | 138.40 | 340.80 |
| 360.00 | 118.40 | 320.80 |
| 391.00 | 102.90 | 305.30 |
| 400.00 | 102.90 | 300.80 |
| 440.00 | 82.90 | 280.80 |
| 480.00 | 62.90 | 260.80 |
| 520.00 | 42.90 | 240.80 |
| 560.00 | 22.90 | 220.80 |
| 600.00 | 2.90 | 200.80 |
| 605.80 | nil | 198.00 |
| 640.00 | | 180.80 |
| 658.40 | | 171.60 |
| 666.00 | | 171.60 |
| 680.00 | | 164.60 |
| 720.00 | | 144.60 |
| 760.00 | | 124.60 |
| 800.00 | | 104.60 |
| 840.00 | | 84.60 |
| 880.00 | | 64.60 |
| 920.00 | | 44.60 |
| 960.00 | | 24.60 |
| 1000.00 | | 4.60 |
| 1009.20 | | nil |

*Income limits are higher if you have dependent children/students. See your local Social Security office. Concessions cut out when income reaches: Single $176 a fortnight; Couple $300 a fortnight combined. Add $40 to these figures for each child.

*Note:* If you are 70 or over and your wife or husband is under 70, you can still claim. Pension rates are as follows:

## COUPLE
### ONE UNDER 70, ONE 70 OR OLDER
### INCOME TEST

| Combined gross income $pf* | Married partner 70 or older $pf | Married partner under 70 $pf |
|---|---|---|
| 140.00 | 215.40 | 215.40 |
| 160.00 | 210.40 | 210.40 |
| 180.00 | 205.40 | 205.40 |
| 200.00 | 200.40 | 200.40 |
| 220.00 | 195.40 | 195.40 |
| 240.00 | 190.40 | 190.40 |
| 260.00 | 185.40 | 185.40 |
| 280.00 | 180.40 | 180.40 |
| 300.00 | 175.40 | 175.40 |
| 320.00 | 170.40 | 170.40 |
| 340.00 | 165.40 | 165.40 |
| 360.00 | 160.40 | 160.40 |
| 400.00 | 150.40 | 150.40 |
| 420.00 | 145.40 | 145.40 |
| 460.00 | 135.40 | 135.40 |
| 500.00 | 125.40 | 125.40 |
| 540.00 | 115.40 | 115.40 |
| 580.00 | 105.40 | 105.40 |
| 620.80 | 95.40 | 95.40 |
| 658.40 | 85.80 | 85.80 |
| 666.00 | 85.80 | 83.90 |
| 700.00 | 77.30 | 75.40 |
| 740.00 | 67.30 | 65.40 |
| 780.00 | 57.30 | 55.40 |
| 820.00 | 47.30 | 45.40 |
| 860.00 | 37.30 | 35.40 |
| 900.00 | 27.30 | 25.40 |
| 940.00 | 17.30 | 15.80 |
| 1001.60 | 1.90 | nil |
| 1009.20* | nil | |

*Income limits are higher if you have dependent children/students. See your local Social Security office.
Concessions cut out when income reaches $300.00.
Add $40 to these figures for each child.

# Superannuation

In these days of high inflation it is difficult to know what a reasonable retirement income would be. One's lifestyle will, of course, be a major influence. Assuming there are no major commitments, like mortgage repayments, a net weekly income of $200 would be more than enough for some single people, while for others it would be far too little.

In the case of a couple, and again assuming there are no major financial commitments, $250 to $350 per week could be regarded as a reasonable average.

These sums, of course, do not allow for future rates of inflation, so what may be an adequate income in 1989 or 1990 could be totally inadequate in five or ten years time.

To provide such an income today it would be necessary to have a capital sum of around $100,000 invested in bonds, debentures, mortgages, notes and the like. If shares are included the capital sum required would need to be greater.

Superannuation fund benefits will vary from company to company and from Government body to Government body. As far as retirement benefits are concerned, not all superannuation funds give employees a choice — they must take either a lump sum or a pension. However, a number of funds do give a choice of taking a lump sum, part lump sum and part pension or full pension.

When a choice is given, pending retirees face one of the most difficult and important decisions of all and a number of considerations must be carefully thought about before the final decision is made.

First, one's overall financial situation must be assessed with special attention being given to the advantages and/or disadvantages of the various options.

In times of high inflation, pensions which are linked to some form of indexation may seem to have certain advantages. One must, however, also consider the weekly income provided by the pension and relate it to the income considered necessary to maintain a reasonable standard of living. In the case of the husband, does the pension automatically pass to the wife if the husband dies first, and does the pension pass on at the same rate, a reduced rate or cease entirely? What happens to the pension if both husband and wife are killed in an accident or both should die shortly after retirement? In the majority of cases the funds will be lost forever.

**Timing Important**

Alternatively, a lump sum suitably invested might provide a greater weekly income. At the same time, by electing to retire on 1 July or later in the new financial year, instead of 30 June, there could be additional tax savings.

Then again, those taking a lump sum might be inclined to fritter it away, or make bad investment decisions, particularly if they are not used to handling large sums of money.

While the final decision will vary from couple to couple and individual to individual, where a choice is allowed, experience has shown a lump sum or part lump sum and part pension as the most popular decision in the majority of cases.

**Bad Management**

As with a number of deceased estates, the supervision and management of some superannuation funds also leaves a lot to be desired. For example, many but not all companies allow superannuation funds to withdraw up to 10 per cent of their debenture/note holdings each year at face value — sometimes with and sometimes without adjustment of interest, depending upon the company concerned — yet we find some superannuation funds still selling their debentures and notes at market value.

At the same time, some superannuation funds have found themselves financially embarrassed due to the current levels of inflation and bad investment decisions. This again must reflect on the management.

Members of a superannuation fund should be aware of these problems and ensure their interests are being fully protected and that the fund is, in fact, being properly managed.

**Super Options**

Employees should check the pros and cons of joining a superannuation fund or of establishing their own. For the self-employed, establishing and managing one's own scheme is very important.

Let us look at just one example. In 1978, a family started their own business. At the same time they also established their own private superannuation fund with the approval of the Taxation Department.

Once approved, thousands of dollars of private investments were formally and officially transferred to the fund.

Over the years and following guidelines relating to the ages of and the salaries paid to the members of the scheme, the company contributions were tax-deductible and the fund's income/profits were tax-free, providing the rules were strictly followed. And that is still the situation.

**Private
Funds**

Since the abolition of the 30/20 rule which required a proportion of funds to be invested in government and semi-government securities, many private superannuation funds still continue to waste money.

Many private, and some not-so-private, superannuation funds continue to hold on to old investments unnecessarily. They may have old Savings Bonds paying low rates of interest and old debentures etc. which should have been cashed in years ago.

Many superannuation funds hold finance company debentures which were purchased when interest rates were very much below current rates.

In many cases superannuation funds are allowed to cash in 10 per cent of their investment each year, frequently without any adjustment in interest.

So, apart from using this facility to pay out a retiring or job-changing member of your superannuation fund, a fund manager should use this facility as an investment medium. In other words, it is possible to cash in 10 per cent of your old investments which are paying lower than present rates of interest and, where appropriate, invest the money received in higher interest paying investments, either with the same company or other companies.

**Super as an
Asset**

On some occasions, you might be able to use your superannuation fund to advantage before you retire. Even by today's standards the superannuation lump sum benefits many people are receiving are mind boggling to say the least. Lump sum superannuation payments of $500,000 and more are now becoming quite common. But is this substantial asset being used to advantage in advance? The answer in most cases is no. Suppose you are coming up for retirement five years from now and would like to buy a home unit, or town house as an investment. Your greatest asset, apart from your own home, is your superannuation fund, and it is worth, let us say, $100,000. This asset could be used as security or as additional security to borrow money by way of an interest only mortgage. As mentioned earlier, you will be paying only the interest on the loan not the capital, or better still the tenants will be paying it. When you retire and take your lump sum superannuation payment, you can then pay off the interest only mortgage.

**Many Still not Covered**

At the moment, the great majority of the workforce do not enjoy any superannuation benefits whatsoever and it is one of the reasons for the ever increasing social security bill. Until we see a national superannuation scheme, wise people should try to provide for their own retirement needs and in doing so they will enjoy substantial tax savings. By way of example, joining a superannuation fund could mean a total tax deduction, not a rebate, of up to $1,500 and this will apply even if you join a superannuation fund on the last day of the financial year. But once again, shop around for the best deal.

Apart from these significant tax advantages on your retirement, you could be looking at a small fortune, depending of course on the age you joined and the performance of the fund. Joining an outside fund has a major advantage — portability — so if you change jobs you do not miss out on any of the benefits. There are a number of funds to choose from and it could well and truly pay to make some enquiries.

**Threshold Lift**

Subject to proposed legislation, the lump sum superannuation threshold for people 55 years of age and over has been increased to $64,500, which means that, from 1 July 1992, no tax is payable on this amount, while the remainder is taxed at 15 per cent. However, these rules will mean very little to most people in the foreseeable future. The reason for this is that the bulk of their lump sum will be taxed under the old rules — that is, at their marginal rate on 5 per cent of superannuation earned up to 30 June 1983.

**Tax Exempt Money**

There is one point about superannuation that continues to be overlooked year after year, and these comments unfortunately apply to the Taxation Office as well. I am referring to the fact that people change jobs and withdraw from old superannuation schemes without any profits or benefits whatsoever. When this happens many are not obliged to include any amount in their income tax return for the simple reason that they are only receiving back their own contributions. Not so many people would now be involved in these old type superannuation schemes, but even so the Taxation Office should not be excused for taking tax when it is not necessary. Worse still, no mention is made of this fact in the income tax forms or instruction sheets. So the message is if you withdraw from a superannuation scheme and you do not receive any contribution from your employer, and you do not receive any interest, then do not include any amount in your income tax return.

# Roll-over Funds

A roll-over fund is set up and operated under the terms of the *Income Tax Assessment Act*. Any person who receives an eligible termination payment can lodge such funds within a 90 day period of receipt of the monies into a roll-over fund. Approved Deposit Funds and Deferred Annuities are acceptable for lodgement of eligible termination payments.

Funds lodged in an Approved Deposit Fund can remain in the fund up to a maximum of age 65. Funds lodged in a Deferred Annuity Fund can remain in the fund indefinitely.

Funds can be withdrawn in part or in total at any time subject to the required notice of withdrawal period being adhered to.

**Interest**

Funds which invest for an 'interest only' return, normally calculate interest daily and credit interest to the sum invested quarterly or half-yearly.

Funds offering a more diversified investment portfolio are usually unit linked. These funds are re-valued on a weekly basis with the return reflected in the unit price.

**Costs and Charges**

A considerable number of roll-over funds attract an annual management fee of between 1 and 1.5 per cent as the only charge.

The unit linked funds normally attract a fee on either entry or exit from the fund — approximately 5 per cent on average. But in some cases the fee could be higher so check it out.

**Taxation**

Tax is payable on any amounts withdrawn from a roll-over fund at the time of withdrawal, unless the amount is being rolled over into another approved roll-over institution. The exception is on death, where funds payable to a dependent are not taxed when held in an Approved Deposit Fund.

1. 5 per cent of the pre-1/7/83 component is taxed at the client's marginal tax rate
2. The post 30/6/83 component is taxed at the following rates:

(a) Up to age 55 amounts are taxed at 31.25¢ in the dollar (including Medicare levy)

(b) At age in excess of 55 and for amounts up to $55,000 the rate is 16.25¢ in the dollar (including Medicare levy), on amounts in excess of $55,000 the rate is 31.25¢ in the dollar

**Supporting Information**

To lodge funds into a roll-over fund you will need

- A statement of termination payment from your employer (photocopy only) (see sample — Appendix 3)
- Completion of a roll-over payment notification form (triplicate) (see sample — Appendix 3)
- Completion of a deposit application form (see sample — Appendix 3)
- Cheque

**Benefits of Roll-over Funds**

They provide a haven for eligible funds when:

- Changing employment and a qualifying period is required before becoming eligible for a new superannuation scheme
- A person wishes to defer taxation on retirement until their marginal tax rate reduces
- A person wishes to defer payment of tax until age 55 to become eligible for the concessional rate of the post 30/6/83 component, i.e. 16.25¢ in the dollar in lieu of 31.25¢ in the dollar

The amount of money invested in ADFs and Deferred Annuities is increasing rapidly as more and more people take advantage of their benefits. But the number of funds and annuities currently available is mind boggling, and includes

FIXED INTEREST FUNDS

EQUITY AND FIXED INTEREST

CAPITAL GUARANTEED FUNDS

UNIT LINKED FUNDS

PLUS

IMMEDIATE ANNUITIES

One of the most professional and regular summaries of these investments is produced by TPF & C — actuaries and management consultants — as detailed in Appendix 2 at the back of the book.

# Investment Advisors

Now, more than ever before, it is so important to seek unbiased advice from professional advisors. Mostly they would be people with many years of practical experience in the world of finance and investment.

They should not be people pushing their own products under one guise or another. They should be people who put clients and customers first, not just their commissions.

Far too many so-called investment advisors rely on the commissions they charge or receive through the front door, as well as the back door, and customers would not have the faintest idea that they are being taken for a financial ride.

Despite the apparent aloofness of some stockbrokers, overall they must still be regarded as the professionals and their advice is usually free and without obligation.

While it would be fair to say some stockbrokers are a little inclined to push equities (shares), their advice is still based on sound fundamentals backed up with experience, qualifications and a very strict code of ethics as well as conduct.

A number of stockbroking firms have established — along with other institutions — investment advisory and retirement planning services and these services should be utilised at every opportunity. But if necessary, seek a second or third opinion, even from within the broking community. Remember it is your money.

**Finding a Stockbroker**

There are a number of ways of being introduced to a stockbroker including

- A personal introduction through a friend or business associate — probably the best way
- By contacting the stock exchange advisory service in your state
- Through your bank
- By looking in the yellow pages of the telephone book

However, it is essential to find a broker who is interested in personal clients and this should be clarified at the first contact or discussed at the time an introduction is being arranged through an advisory service or your bank. In mentioning banks it is important to note that a number have established formal associations with stock-broking firms and it is now possible to place buying and selling orders through a bank. But for a number of reasons a personal association is preferable.

**Private Advisors**

These days there are dozens of media invitations urging you — and retirees in particular — to put your faith in such and such a product or such and such a firm. And for some it is very easy to be overwhelmed by over-zealous salespersons when they are representing reputable, or so-called reputable, firms.

Accordingly, every person — and this means you — should ask a number of important questions. Questions like:

- Do you have a licence to advise?
- What type of licence is it?
- What practical experience have you had in the field of investment? It should be years not months. (Academic qualifications could mean little or nothing.)
- What commission will be received?
- How quickly can one convert the investments into cash and at what cost?
- If they are employed by, say, a bank, building society or credit union, how and why are they involved in an outside association (many of whom could be classified as competitors)?
- Are the products, or is the range of products, being offered controlled under one roof? If so — be careful.
- Is there an after-sales service and at what cost?
- Will the advice be put in writing? This is essential.

Even if the above questions seem to be answered in a satisfactory fashion, it will still be advisable to seek at least one or two other outside opinions before making any major investment decisions.

**Check Licences**

We are hearing a lot of announcements by financial institutions that they are going into or expanding their investment advisory business. So, as suggested earlier, in your check on the professionalism of the advisor/s you should find out if they have a general licence or a restricted licence. If it is a restricted licence, then it is important to note that they can advise only on their own product or products, not on competitive products. An extension of this restriction is that they cannot advise you to sell other products in order to invest in their own. But regrettably many advisors do this very thing.

The general licence is hard to come by, and rightly so, for there are hundreds of new advisors starting with very little experience. Some new advisors may be well qualified and have a general licence, but logic suggests that a large number are in the restricted category, and many cannot be classed as 'unbiased'.

**'Churning'**

Another danger area lies in the area of churning, which, in simple language, means that you will be advised to switch out of one or more investments into other investments mainly for commission reasons. Some private advisors and salespersons are notorious for this practice, so be warned.

The after-sales service — or lack of it — can be a key guide to the quality of the advisor and the product/s. By way of example, unreturned phone calls would suggest a quick exit from that particular scene. It should also suggest a call to an investigative authority such as the Corporate Affairs Department in your State.

The old saying — let the buyer beware — is more relevant today than ever before and that means using common sense and caution before signing on the dotted line. And that means never signing unless you have a thorough understanding of your commitments and the commitments of the other party. That advice applies to dealings with any financial institution and some of the top ones are criticised in a publication of the Trade Practices Commission on the Advertising of Deposits and Loans, the major highlights of which are as follows.

**Checklist — Deposits and Investments**

Interest rates:
- Check interest rate figures, e.g. 'minimum monthly balance', 'daily balance', etc.
- Where interest rates in an account are variable, and where rates may be varied without notice it must be made known
- If the account being promoted has a fluctuating interest rate, a qualification to the effect that 'the rate quoted may bear no relationship to future yields' is included

Fees and charges:
- The existence of fees and charges that apply to accounts should always be disclosed
- Care should be taken in using the word 'free'

At call:
- Check 'at call' to mean 'available on demand'

Penalties:
- Be aware of penalties on early withdrawal

Cheque clearance:
- Check on the institution's policy on clearing cheques

Security of investment:
- Check that promotional material does not misrepresent the types of security in which the institution invests
- Check that promotional material and application forms correctly describe the nature of the investment
- Check ambiguous references to security

Taxation benefits:
- When promoting taxation benefits as an incentive, ensure you are made aware of any matters which may affect those benefits being available

Investment advisory services should:
- Ensure you are aware of any qualifications that apply to the advice
- Maintain adequate organisation and office procedures to guard against mistakes and outdated information
- Avoid extravagant performance claims
- Claims as to independence should be capable of substantiation
- Disclose the existence of commission and of pecuniary interest

**Loans and Consumer Credit**

Interest rates:
- Check unqualified interest rates
- Ask whether interest rates are fixed or variable

Fees and repayments:
- Check information on repayment frequency and duration of loan well before the loan agreement is signed
- Check promotional material referring to the existence (and, if possible, nature and likely amount) of any additional charges, e.g. loan service fees

Penalties:
- Check, well before the loan agreement is signed, penalties that apply to early termination of loan and to late payments

Extravagant claims:
- Check any extravagant claims about the cost of the loan

Eligibility requirements:
- Ensure that promotional material makes reference to eligibility requirements

Security on loan:
- Be aware of fees and conditions in relation to secured loans

Insurance:
- Borrowers should have access to an insurer of their choice

**Legal Advice**

Legal matters, in relation to things like wills and Powers of Attorney, trusts or partnerships, often crop up in financial counselling. Some financial institutions such as credit unions are now offering free legal advice for a first interview and then on-going advice, if needed, at a reduced cost. This is certainly a move in the right direction and you might ask your credit union to introduce a similar service if it has not already done so.

It is essential that you deal with a solicitor or trustee company in relation to *wills* and *Powers of Attorney*. And *never* ever draw up your own will. Home-made wills are usually a disaster. But when it comes to investment advice many solicitors are not really qualified or experienced to give advice on the wide range of investments available and this is yet another reason to shop around. In fact any solicitor worth his salt would advise you to do that very thing. A solicitor is more than likely to suggest investing in one or more mortgages and if mortgages are appropriate to your needs then by all means invest in them *but* remember fee-wise it is to the solicitor's advantage as well.

**Move for Integrity**

Some of the most professional and unbiased advisory services have been recently established by Australia's State Banks, such as the State Bank of New South Wales and the State Bank of Victoria. Unlike some advisory services, these banks in particular put the needs of their customers first and that includes recommending a range of opposition products so it is little wonder that other organisations are thinking about following their example.

But no matter how good the product/s, do not put all your eggs in the one investment basket. That applies to all forms of investment. Many advisors suggest that no more than 10 to 15 per cent of your available funds should be invested in the one place. Had investors followed this rule over recent years, many would not have suffered major losses, certainly in the case of some property trusts.

In some States the Department of Corporate Affairs publishes a booklet giving advice on investment procedures and safeguards.

# Personal Points of Finance

**Do Not Hide Facts**

If you are applying for a loan or credit make sure you do not hide the facts.

Getting into financial difficulty is not a crime, but failing to live up to one's obligations is a serious matter, and so too is cheating by hiding the facts. These days it is very easy to find out if a person is a good or a bad payer or if a person has been in financial difficulty. This being so, it is frequently to one's advantage to disclose this when applying for a loan or credit. All the more so if you paid off your original debt or debts — even with some difficulty — for it is a sign that you have recognised your responsibilities. If, on the other hand, you hide the fact that you have experienced financial problems in the past, when your loan or credit application is checked and found to be incorrect, your application is quite likely to be rejected. It is not easy to admit to a past mistake, but laying your cards on the table could mean the difference between your application being accepted or rejected.

**Shop Around on Interest**

Recently the purchaser of a new car was quoted an interest rate of about 30 per cent per annum for hire purchase finance.

Realising that 30 per cent was somewhat excessive, he shopped around and was able to arrange the finance by way of a personal loan at around 19 per cent per annum.

When he advised the motor car dealer of the arrangement, he was told they could match that rate. This episode again emphasises the need to shop around when it comes to borrowing money, whether the amount required is $500 or $5,000, and even when the borrowing is from a bank or building society.

Apart from saving about 11 per cent per annum in interest on the original quote, buying the car for *cash* instead of under a hire purchase agreement also meant substantial savings in insurance premiums.

Another problem for borrowers is that many do not appreciate the difference between simple interest and flat interest. Do not be misled. A flat interest rate of 9.5 per cent is really a true interest rate of close to 18 per cent per annum. And a flat interest rate of 15 per cent is really a true or effective interest rate of around 30 per cent per annum. When borrowing money always ask if the interest rate quoted is simple or flat.

## Car Loans — Know Your Rates

A leading finance company recently asked six competitors to quote for an $8,000 loan to be repaid over 36 months in equal monthly instalments. The lowest repayment quoted was around $297 and the highest was $340.

But of even greater importance was the wide variation in the effective interest rates which ranged from 20 per cent to over 30 per cent at the top end of the scale.

Taking the highest rate first, the $8,000 loan would involve total repayments of around $12,240. And the total interest bill would be $4,240 over the three-year period.

The total interest bill at the lower end was around $2,702, again over a three-year period. The difference in interest came to a huge $1,538, which is a lot of money in anyone's book.

A bank personal loan for the same amount over the same period would involve monthly repayments of $288 with a total interest bill of $2,376.

Credit union rates vary from State to State and between the various credit unions. But an $8,000 loan would involve a total interest bill of about $2,440 with the effective interest rate being between 17 and 20 per cent. And loan protection insurance is usually an automatic inclusion.

## Other Sources of Finance

When it comes to borrowing money it might well be that you are overlooking other sources such as borrowing on existing life assurance policies where once again the interest rate would be much cheaper than loans from other sources.

So with interest savings like these, anyone with an existing finance company loan would be well advised to check out the effective rate of interest they are being charged. And find out if, in refinancing the loan, any early repayment penalties will be involved and, if so, to what degree.

Depending upon the interest rate currently being charged and at what rate you can borrow through competing sources, it will probably pay to refinance — even if there is a penalty to be paid.

If you are buying a car, a boat, caravan, washing machine, TV set or furniture and you can arrange cheaper finance through another source, such as a credit union, building society or bank personal loan, Visa, Mastercard, Bankcard or a finance company credit card, then you would be *foolish* not to do so.

**Inflation**

In times of high inflation or recession when the going gets tough, a lot of people are inclined to save their money rather than spend it.

Saving money for a rainy day might seem the right thing to do but you must remember your money is losing value every day and at the present rate of inflation, your dollar will be worth around 92¢ in 12 months. If this inflation rate continues, in five years your dollar will probably be worth around 60¢ and it could be worth a lot less if inflation should get out of hand.

If you want to add an extra room, refurnish the house or buy a new car, do it now. The longer you wait the more it will cost you.

**Timely Advice**

'It takes a lifetime to save money. But it may only take a second to sign it away.' That is the front page slogan on a brochure released by the NSW Corporate Affairs Commission on reducing investment risk.

The publication is certainly *timely* in view of what has been happening in some areas of investment and investment advice over the past few years.

The brochure should be compulsory reading for everyone and, as a matter of principle, should be made available to all school students, and not just in NSW.

*Some of the basic rules* highlighted in the brochure include what, in reality, should be obvious. And they are well worth repeating in principle again.

- Do not put all your money into one investment, no matter how good the product might seem
- Be wary of advertisements offering exceptionally high returns. Determine the level of risk, if any, that you are prepared to take
- Supervise and monitor your investments. Know your rights and available protections, and seek independent advice and not just from one source
- Spread your investment over at least six areas, with no more than 10 to 15 per cent in high risk areas

**Investment Advisors**

As mentioned on more than one occasion part of the problem, of course, lies with smooth-talking, hard-selling salespersons, and it is here a number of important points are again emphasised.

- Avoid people selling products with an over-emphasis on taxation or social security benefits
- Ask what experience the salesperson has had, in what areas and for how long
- Ask who the employer is. Also ask what commission is being earned and do not ask anyone to call on you at home unless it is a special situation and, remember, door-to-door selling of securities is illegal
- While people might be licensed to sell investments, it must be remembered that a piece of paper does not in any way guarantee the quality of the advice or the practical experience of the advisor
- The same situation would apply in the case of investment newsletters, where advice can vary from being sensible and professional to merely touting for business. Before subscribing, try to obtain some back copies of the newsletter
- Attending seminars is another way of teaching yourself some of the basics. But do not attend one only, but sufficient to give you an understanding of the quality of advice. And watch out for seminars where only the host company's products are being presented

Mention is also made of the role of other 'assumed' investment advisors, such as solicitors, accountants and bank managers. While they may be professional in their own areas, they may not be professional in the area of investment advice, and they should say so if that is the case.

There are a number of other points including your rights and protections, types of investment, plus that all important reminder of not signing anything until you are sure you know what you are doing.

**Discrimination**

It is sometimes very distressing to hear the difficulties being experienced by some people in borrowing money, and by women in particular. So let us take a look at one recent case. The lady concerned approached her bank for a loan. She was 55 years of age, held a very senior position with job security and could more than meet the bank's lending requirements. She was knocked back. When pressure was brought to bear on the bank manager from a more senior level, the loan was eventually approved. If you are a woman and your application for a loan is refused, write a letter of complaint to the General Manager of the financial institution concerned and ask why. Keep a copy of the letter and wait for the reply. If the reply does not appear to be satisfactory, complain to the Anti-discrimination Board or similar body.

**Unemployed can Borrow**

Although there has been a reduction in the number of unemployed, it still remains one of our biggest problems. Apart from the difficulties of finding a job, unemployed people might think they would not be in a position to borrow money. Providing you have people behind the scenes who will guarantee a loan you *can* borrow money. One case involved a bank and another case involved a credit union. In the case of the bank loan, the money was required to start a business. The bank manager approved the loan, the business is doing well and the loan has already been repaid. While not every lending institution will come to the party, do not be put off by a rejection. Keep trying, but whatever you do avoid 'loan shark' money lenders charging impossible rates of interest.

**Know your Terms**

Over the past few years we have certainly seen a number of innovators in relation to money and investment. As just one example, Beneficial Finance Corporation (the finance company which is wholly owned by the State Bank of South Australia) has along with other finance companies, a number of concessions when it comes to early repayment of investments, but with one important extra. If, for instance, you are a primary producer and the area in which you operate is declared a drought area or a disaster area, then Beneficial Finance Corporation will allow you to cash in part or all of your investment before the due date and there will be no adjustment in interest. So, when making an investment decision, do not look just for the highest return — look for other features as well.

**Family Loans**

After closing the schoolyard gate for the last time, or even before this many young people are looking for 'wheels' of one kind or another. Depending upon the family's financial situation, parents frequently come to the party by way of a loan.

Whether the amount involved is large or small, whether it is a short-term loan or a long-term loan, this loan should be arranged on a business-like basis and not quietly forgotten. Whether interest is to be charged is, once again, a personal matter. But all involved should do the right thing.

**Bargaining Power**

These days we live in a competitive world — and that applies to borrowing money, investing money and buying goods and services.

In the case of investors, you might have a bank, building society or credit union investment and you suddenly find out that a competitor is offering a much better return.

This being the case, it is important to note that you will not always have to close out your investment and transfer it elsewhere — for a mere mention of the funds being transferred or the account closed will often bring the response 'we can match that' or, in some cases, 'we can better that'.

On some occasions there may not be any response from the financial institution concerned and in situations such as these you may have to transfer your investment/ account elsewhere. On other occasions a little pressure, or more than a little pressure, frequently has the desired results.

In the case of borrowers, it is much the same situation. Shopping around can work wonders and save a mint. As mentioned earlier the interest rates being charged by some financial institutions are out of touch with reality — certainly as far as their clients and customers are concerned.

Buying or leasing goods can also mean a saving in money if you are prepared to bargain. And that is not just with those companies which publicly advertise that they, too, can match or better a competitor's price.

Many companies do not advertise this fact, so a few advance enquiries could save valuable dollars or involve a product of higher quality for the same price.

**Budgeting**

It is pretty difficult these days to make ends meet and all the more so if you have a family. However, many of the financial difficulties facing some people could be avoided if they learnt how to budget. Unfortunately, a lot of people start off with the best of intentions, but after a few months the budget is forgotten and their financial problems start all over again.

**Payroll Deductions**

The key to successful financial budgeting is disciplined saving. One way to do this is to arrange with your employer to have a certain sum deducted from your pay packet each week or fortnight and paid into a credit union, building society or bank account.

There are always certain months of the year when bills are heavier than usual and it is here careful budgeting can help overcome the problem.

**Keep the Family Informed**

Far too many men are inclined to keep the family's financial affairs to themselves. Many women, believe it or not, cannot even write a cheque or fill in a deposit slip, let alone make any financial decisions on their own.

Of course, there are faults on both sides in situations like these, but keeping the rest of the family in the dark financially can be a very costly exercise in the event of serious illness or death.

It is essential to inform your partner and also your children about the whereabouts of bank and building society accounts, what money you owe and to whom.

Also, the location of your will and other important documents, including a list of your investments, when you bought them and what you paid for them. So, if you are in this situation, you had better do something about it right now.

**Transferring Investments**

For a variety of reasons many people have investments in joint names. Apart from tax considerations (and they could be considerable) — in the event of death — many joint investments could be frozen until legal formalities have been complied with.

One way of overcoming this problem is to transfer the investments out of joint names into separate names. In the case of Government or semi-Government securities, this is really a simple procedure. Just contact the authority concerned, ask for the necessary transfer forms to be sent to you, and return the completed forms to the authority together with any certificates. It should also be noted that transferring Government securities does not *normally* involve any stamp duty or other charges.

This same procedure can, and should, be followed in the case of debentures and shares. Contact the companies concerned and ask what *their* procedures are.

Subject to laws of the various States, a statutory declaration may or may not be required. Again, subject to local requirements, stamp duty may or may not be payable.

Having obtained the necessary information, send the completed transfer forms — stamped if necessary — to the company concerned together with your debenture or share certificates. Another alternative would be to ask your stockbroker for assistance.

**Forgotten Money**

It is essential to notify your bank, building society, credit union and the companies in which you own shares or other investments of your change of address, so that they know where to send your statements, interest dividend cheques or new issue entitlements. If, for example, a company in which you have shares is making a new issue and you cannot be located, you could lose your 'benefits'.

Also, if you own partly paid shares and a call falls due you could forfeit your shares for non-payment of the call. Failure to receive a call notice is no excuse. It is your responsibility to keep track of these things.

There is also another problem, and, believe it or not, this relates to people not banking their cheques when they receive them. These days it is difficult enough to make money without throwing it away. So next time you receive a cheque, whatever the amount, put it in your credit union, building society or bank account immediately.

**Administering Estates**

Experience has shown the administration and supervision of many deceased estates leaves a lot to be desired.

Illustrations of mismanagement would include:

- Continued holding of old Savings Bonds at low rates of interest
- Delays in reinvesting proceeds from maturing bonds, debentures and notes
- Advantage not being taken of high interest rates to improve income.
- Unwarranted sale of debentures and notes through the market. For example, in the case of deceased estates, many — but not all — companies will repay debentures and notes at face value irrespective of their market value.

Many of the above problems can be avoided if the executors are informed. Where solicitors and trustee companies are involved, the executors should keep in constant touch to ensure the estate is being handled in a professional manner and there are no unnecessary and costly delays.

**Holiday Cash**

The floating of the Australian dollar now means that to all intents and purposes market forces — supply and demand — and not the authorities will determine its value. The move to float was essential and in the main it is to be applauded for, had we not done so, once again we would have been at the mercy of the overseas speculators. And we may still be.

Its day-to-day value will, of course, influence the cost of overseas imports and the returns from our exports of manufactured products, primary production and minerals.

But, depending on whether the dollar rises or falls in value against the US dollar and other currencies, it could mean more spending money for overseas travellers. Or it could mean a lot less should it continue to fall.

However, whether the dollar rises or falls, remember money is only worth the pleasure it gives you.

**The Holiday Dollar**

Every year, many thousands of people take their annual holidays. And for the lucky ones that will mean an overseas trip.

Whether it is an overseas trip or a local one, it is essential to use some advance common sense to ensure the holiday is not spoiled.

This means an adequate supply of money and usually much more than you expect to spend. So make sure your credit cards have a good balance.

If an overseas trip is involved, make sure you have the right travellers' cheques as well as a supply of local currency for the countries you will be visiting, particularly on arrival. And do not forget to ask for your travellers' cheques to be issued in two or more separate wallets and carry them separately. This should ensure that, if one wallet is lost or stolen, you will have another wallet of cheques to fall back on until the lost cheques are replaced. Also make a note of their serial numbers, a note of your passport number, and obtain telephone numbers and addresses of Australian Consuls in the countries you will be visiting.

**Changing Currency**

Overseas travellers should always check the best place to exchange their currencies and apart from local dealers — and here one must be very careful — the best place mostly will be the local banks.

Certainly do not change your money in the hotels in which you will be staying. The difference in the exchange rate offered by hotels as against banks runs to a small fortune.

And if the overseas visits involve more than one country, do not keep re-exchanging your left-over currency back into US or Australian dollars. Keep it until you arrive in the next country and then change it over to the local currency.

**Hidden
Travel Costs**

If you are travelling overseas or, for that matter, inter-state, you frequently find you are up for some extra charges — charges you were not told about or did not know about, things like free drinks one way and charges for drinks the other way. It is annoying to say the least and not very good PR as far as the companies are concerned.

The same thing applies in changing money at airports etc. The money exchangers already make a poultice with the exchange rates and on top of that they want extra dollars for the privilege of changing your money.

But most important of all, check those travel tickets, particularly if you are travelling by plane. Tickets are issued under a variety of terms and conditions and your ticket should be stamped to indicate this. If, for example, you wish to change your travel plans and you do not do it under the rules of the ticket, then you could be up for a thousand dollars or more. Remember to ask the airline or your travel agent under what terms and conditions your ticket is issued, and get a full explanation.

**Travel
Protection**

Wise people will always ensure that they are properly insured and this should also apply to travellers.

Make sure you have baggage insurance and, if you are visiting a foreign country, make sure you have more than enough health insurance or even additional health insurance.

In some countries, a day in hospital, let alone a week or more, can cost a small fortune, so extra cover would be money well spent.

In mentioning baggage, never forget that it can be left behind or lost. In situations like these it would be wise to take a change of clothing in, say, your overnight bag just to be on the safe side.

**Leave
Instructions**

If you are away overseas, your business and private affairs will still have to be looked after. Arrange for mail to be collected, cheques to be processed and, most important of all, bills to be paid. These days most workers enjoy at least four weeks leave and a lot can happen within this period. Telephones have been cut off because the bill has not been paid, and absence on holidays is not really an acceptable excuse. And the same has happened with electricity accounts. And do not forget about Bankcard. What you should be doing is to give people you can trust authority to act on your behalf. If it is to be an extended holiday, this could be in the form of a Power of Attorney. Apart from paying the bills, do not forget to cancel the papers and the milk!

**Insurance — General**

Wise people will always make certain they are properly insured. That means covering yourself in every possible way — ranging from proper insurance on your car, boat, house to week-enders, furniture and effects, personal accident and sickness insurance, and workers compensation both for full time as well as part time employees. Wise insurance should also include Public Risk cover. Valued possessions such as jewellery etc. should also be covered and as another form of insurance these items should also be photographed for identification, as well as replacement reasons.

**Insurance — Life**

Life assurance of one kind or another is a must for most people certainly in the sense of 'protection'. And you have a variety of choices including
- Whole of Life (payable on death or maturity of policy)
- Endowment (payable at a specified age or on death)
- Term Insurance (payable on death within a defined period)

One of the problems with the 'old fashioned' forms of life assurance was that as 'an investment' they really could not compete with other investments, as many people have found over the years. On top of that the commissions paid, certainly in the early years, would usually mean a loss situation if for one reason or another the policy was cashed in.

A few years ago the tax concessions were a major consideration in making life assurance appear to be attractive, but today that scene has changed. Young couples in particular should take out *term assurance* on each other's life so that in the event of premature death the survivors are protected from economic difficulties, such as meeting mortgage repayments etc.

A number of financial institutions now offer this type of cover with or without cost and it would be unwise to ignore the importance of such protection. And that advice would also apply in the case of personal loans, when the debt would die with the person.

**Insurance — Borrowing**

Whilst the old forms of life assurance may not have a competitive investment appeal premiums paid over the years together with bonuses can and do build into substantial sums of money. This *asset* is frequently ignored,

123

for the policy/ies can be used to borrow money at rates of interest well below those available through other sources.

For example banks will usually lend money by way of overdraft based on the surrender value of the policy, or you can borrow in similar fashion from the life company direct. Bearing in mind the cost factor this is probably the best way. Repayment of any money borrowed is entirely in the hands of the borrower, so you are not committed to any fixed repayments which might be the case with a bank overdraft. So if you're paying interest of 25 per cent or 30 per cent and you can borrow on your life policy to pay out the loan, then do so for you will save a lot of money.

People holding whole of life or endowment policies should as a matter of course obtain both surrender and loan values annually. Whether you need to borrow or not it is nice to know how much is available if you should ever need it.

**Are You Really Insured?**

Very few people know the details of their insurance cover. Let us take a look at motor vehicles as just one example. Suppose you have a business or farm vehicle and that an accident puts the vehicle off the road for some weeks. You might be excused for thinking that you will 'automatically' be provided with a vehicle whilst the repairs are being effected. The situation might well be that you will be provided with one, *but* only for the time the vehicle is actually being repaired. If it is estimated the time it will take is say 96 hours then you will only be allowed to hire a vehicle for this time even though you are' inconvenienced for a much longer time.

**Insure for Full Value**

The Ash Wednesday bushfires tragically brought home the message of *no insurance* and *under insurance*. For it is a pointless exercise to insure a $100,000 home for just $50,000 from two points of view.

- The replacement cost
- The insurance cover

In the latter case as the property is only insured for half its true value you will only receive $25,000. Apart from ensuring you are fully covered make sure you automatically update your cover in line with inflation, at the very least every 12 months.

**Find a Professional**

As with investing money and borrowing money it will pay to shop around, for 'premiums' as well as 'cover' can vary from company to company. This can be done personally or you can use the services of a reputable insurance broker. But remember that the cheapest insurance is not always the best insurance.

**Other Bonuses**

Investors in a number of companies are entitled to a range of benefits including discounts on insurance premiums, etc. as is the case with AGC investors to name just one company.

# Case Histories

**Case for Conservatism**

I have always advocated that people should spread their investments — not to put all their money into just one investment. The wisdom of that approach has been emphasised on many occasions, but I was recently reminded that on some occasions it *can pay* to put most of your eggs in one basket. One illustration might be that of an elderly or young investor who does not have the capability of managing investments. That being so, the wisest course could very well be to have the money invested with a bank, building society, credit union or in Aussie Bonds. Providing the investments are safe, I would not criticise the decision for a moment and I am indebted to the person concerned for reminding me that there can be exceptions.

**Do What *You* Want**

Recently I received a call from a lady who had just sold her home. She was seeking my advice about the investment of the proceeds which, incidentally, amounted to a considerable sum of money. As we chatted, I sensed she was a little depressed and when I asked what she proposed in the future, she said she would be moving into a retirement home. When I asked if she was happy about the move she said no, not really, but her family was.

Bearing in mind this lady enjoyed good health, I suggested that she should buy a unit of her own. Judging from her response, I think she might do that very thing, and rightly so. In a different situation, the family might be right in suggesting a move to a retirement home, but in this particular case I think they were wrong and so did a number of other listeners.

**Interest — Flat or Simple**

Recently, I received a phone call from a young man regarding a personal loan he was arranging through his bank.

He was very excited because he said he was being charged only 9 per cent in interest, or so he thought. I then explained to him that he was not paying 9 per cent but around 18 per cent. In other words, the interest rate quoted was flat interest. This means he was paying interest on the whole amount whereas simple interest means he would have paid interest only on what sum of money was outstanding.

If you want to borrow money, ask if the interest rate quoted is flat or simple. If it is flat interest, double it and this will give you roughly the true rate of interest payable. This means in general terms that 10 per cent becomes 20, 12 per cent becomes 24 and 15 per cent becomes 30.

Not knowing the difference between simple and flat interest can be a costly mistake.

**Do not Bank on it**

Some investment documents were delivered to a bank late on a Friday afternoon. Due to the incompetence of the staff of this particular bank, the documents were not processed until the following Tuesday. When confronted by the annoyed customer, the bank officer concerned admitted it was a bank error and a letter of apology would be sent to him.

When the letter of apology failed to arrive, the customer again contacted the bank and this time was told in no uncertain terms the bank could not make such an error and the documents had not been received until the Tuesday.

Well, knowing the background to the story, quite frankly I question that particular bank's integrity and I also question the honesty of some of the staff. Unfortunately the customer concerned did not obtain a receipt or acknowledgement of delivery, so the point I am making is the next time you deliver anything of value to a bank, building society, credit union, solicitor, accountant or stockbroker make sure you obtain a receipt.

**Bad Advice can be Costly**

Recently a pastoralist received quite a large cheque. He asked his bank manager how this money should be invested and was told to place it in an interest bearing deposit. A few days later he was told by another bank manager that he could have invested his money in a commercial bill for three months and received 3 per cent more interest. By this time the customer was hopping mad and confronted his bank manager about the matter. As calmly as you please he was told the bank could arrange a similar transaction — when his interest bearing deposit matured. This he did rather grudgingly.

When the customer came to renew his commercial bill for a second time he was told he would earn only 12 per cent on his money. By this time the customer knew the going rate and told the manager he would transfer the money to a bank around the corner. Within five minutes his bank had increased the interest to that being offered by their competitor, which again proves you cannot always 'bank' on receiving the right advice.

## Accounts in False Names

Do you keep a bank, building society or credit union account in a false name? Well, if you do you are asking for trouble and not only from the tax collector or social security department.

I know why you are doing it. But do you really know what you are getting yourself into? Do your know that there are millions of dollars going into Government coffers because of unclaimed money?

What happens if you have one of these accounts and die. Unless you have left signed a withdrawal slip with someone you can trust, your money may be lost forever.

You decide if gaining a few dollars illegally is worth the money or the worry. Personally, I doubt it and you may end up robbing yourself or your family.

## Joint Cheque Accounts? Use Common Sense

During a holiday break we stayed with some friends and, as is usually the case, the subject of investment was raised on more than one occasion. Out of the conversations I was told something of their financial situation and, once again, there were a number of basic oversights. First, both husband and wife had separate cheque accounts. There is nothing wrong with that, but only one person could sign the cheques and one of the accounts was a business account. Where people have their own accounts by design, that is fine, but this time the separate accounts had been opened as a matter of course and no one, not even their accountant, had suggested the importance of a second signature which would allow someone else to sign in the case of illness, accident or absence. It could be your wife, husband, or your children, and of course there must be complete trust, but it is certainly a point not to be overlooked.

## Find a Caring Manager

Do bank managers really care about people? Well, from my experience some do and some do not. Recently I was informed that a lady with savings in excess of $20,000 had been unable to obtain a housing loan from any bank. This unfortunate circumstance had occurred in the ACT. I mentioned this during a recent seminar and within a matter of days, to my surprise and pleasure, the regional manager of one of the banks contacted me saying he was appalled to hear of this lady's difficulties and if I would put her in touch with him he would do all he could to ensure she received a loan. It is calls like these that really please me and, without being over-confident, I think the lady will be given a housing loan.

**Slow Transfers**

One would expect the process of transferring money through the banking system to be simple, but this is not always the case.

Recently, a friend of mine showed me some of his bank statements to point out just how long it was taking for money to be transferred to his account. From time to time he would deposit money into a local branch for transfer to his branch in the city. In this age of computers one would expect the transfer to go through on the same day or at least the next day, but this has not been so. On more than a dozen occasions it has taken four or more days for the money to travel, so to speak, 25 miles. To say this is a very poor service is the understatement of the year and a formal letter has been sent to the bank concerned demanding a full explanation. Quite frankly, my friend should have complained months ago. So, when it comes to transferring money from one bank to another make sure it is done immediately. If it is not, then you too should complain.

**Annoying Delays**

These days we are being offered the choice of receiving our interest and dividend payments by cheque or having them credited to a bank, a building society or, in some cases, a credit union account. The purpose is to speed up payments and to avoid those annoying delays.

Well, there is something wrong with some of the systems, for in some cases it is taking up to two weeks or even more for the credits to go through the banking system. To make matters worse, the notifications of the credits arrive on the due date but the payments do not. Interest and for that matter repayment of capital is due on a certain date, not two days later or two weeks later. If this is still happening to you, complain in no uncertain terms to the companies involved and at the same time ask for interest on the money from the due date until the time it is credited to your account. As I have said on more than one occasion, computers are not always as good as they are made out to be.

**Bank, Building Society Accounts for Children**

Not unnaturally many parents and grandparents have savings bank and building society accounts in trust for their children or grandchildren, and I would not criticise that for one moment.

What is not generally realised, however, is that children can open and operate savings accounts in their own names from around the age of eight. If you feel your children are wise enough and old enough to operate an account, let them go ahead. The sooner they can learn about money management the better, but as a precaution it would be advisable for one or both parents to be authorised to operate on these accounts in case of illness or accident.

Of course, common sense must be used and sometimes separate accounts would not be warranted at an early age. By the way, separate accounts could also mean fewer tax problems.

**Some Customer Comments:**

CALL NO. 1: A customer overdrew his account without reference to the bank and his cheques were returned. The customer realised he was in the wrong but was somewhat puzzled when he was charged interest on money he had not really borrowed.

CALL NO. 2: A customer with a private company account which had never been overdrawn was charged interest. At the time the account was in credit to the tune of thousands of dollars.

CALL NO. 3: A lady approached her bank with an application to invest money on behalf of her son. The young man had signed the debenture application in his own right. Yet according to the bank officer, the only way he could have any investments was for the mother to open an account in trust for the boy — naturally with that particular bank.

CALL NO. 4: A bank customer paid his Bankcard account days in advance of the due date. On receiving his statement he was puzzled to see a debit for interest. Rather than make a telephone enquiry he very wisely called personally in order to ascertain the situation. To his utter disbelief, he found that while his payments had been recorded on the master computer printout, days in advance of the due date, a computer malfunction had meant it took around a week for the payment to be processed.

That was why he was slugged with interest!

It was only by personal persistence that he won out.

On this point it is worth noting that one particular Bankcard operation has indeed had computer problems.

Not unnaturally, no announcement has been made to the cardholders so hundreds if not thousands of Bankcard holders will be up for unnecessary interest. The remedy is to check the date of payment on your Bankcard statement and if it has taken more than a day or two to be processed — particularly if the payment was made through a bank — demand an explanation.

CALL NO. 5: A customer had arranged for interest on his Government Bonds to be automatically credited to his bank account.

As a weekend was not involved, he was rather intrigued to find that the credit did not go through until the day after the due date.

On checking out the situation with the Reserve Bank he was informed the details of interest payments had been forwarded to the nominated bank — as is the usual practice — days in advance. This happened not once but twice.

The banks of Australia are spending millions of dollars every year in moves to attract new customers — but quite frankly, many are just wasting their money.

What they should be doing is getting back to the basics, and most important of all, putting their customers' needs first. And that means looking after existing customers. They should also introduce practical, down-to-earth staff training programmes.

**Education — The Best Investment**

It concerns me that there is a lack of 'compulsory' practical down-to-earth advice on money management, finance and investment in our school courses. There is no doubt in my mind that many of the financial problems encountered by young people are due to ignorance. And there is ample evidence to suggest that many marriage breakdowns initially start through financial worries. I am certain many of these problems could be avoided with the right education. Some students cover these topics at school, but the question I ask the education authorities is why are all students not included? They will all be involved with money at some time in the future, so the sooner common-sense money management is included as a compulsory subject in the school curriculum the better. In the meantime, you can play an important role by giving your children a bit of private tuition. It is not as difficult as you think. To begin with if you have some spare money and there is a birthday around the corner, why do you not buy some bonds, or better still, some shares. Not in your name, but in your child's name. I cannot think of a better way to involve them and you might be surprised at what you will all learn at the same time.

I know many young people these days have a different outlook on money. But, even so, I still maintain that learning how to manage and invest their money at the earliest age possible is more important than ever. And when the children are old enough they should be encouraged to open bank, credit union and building society accounts as soon as possible.

## Victory for Customers

A few years ago two of Australia's banks introduced what might best be described as loan service fees on 'old' home mortgages. At the time I, along with others, suggested that the fees were outrageous. They were nothing more than a *de facto* increase in interest rates. It did not take long for the banks to get the message — the proposed fees have been dropped. Those already imposed will be refunded.

This exercise again demonstrates what can still be achieved if enough people stand up to be counted. It is a victory for the customers and for common sense. It should also be a lesson to all financial institutions — that there is a limit to how far you can go in increasing charges. As a public relations exercise it was an absolute disaster.

## Cheque Accounts

I think it is true to say that some banks have lost that old fashioned service-with-a-smile attitude, but it is also true to say that some customers do not do the right thing by their banks. When this happens, it could cause a great deal of embarrassment. In the case of our bank accounts we sometimes work on overdrafts.

It is only on rare occasions we seek additional accommodation, but when we want to exceed our limit we always make a point of phoning the manager and explaining the situation and, where the extra accommodation is required for only a short period of time, there has never been a problem and there are no extra formalities to go through. This being so, I was horrified to see that we had recently exceeded our overdraft limit by $1,000 and I did not pick up the mistake (which I must admit was mine) until a week later. When I rang the bank to apologise, they said 'not to worry'.

We'd always conducted our affairs in a business-like manner and they knew a mistake had been made. They could have dishonoured the cheque but, because we run a good account, they did not. So next time you wish to exceed your limit, phone your bank in advance.

**Cheque Account Interest**

Banks are now allowed to offer interest on cheque accounts. And we have already seen announcements from a number of banks on the interest they are prepared to offer their customers and this will be one of the key issues in deciding which bank to go to. And I am not just talking about the interest rate being offered. I am also talking about whether the interest is calculated on a daily basis or a monthly basis.

If the interest is calculated on daily balances, fine. But if the interest is calculated on a monthly basis, watch out, for it means you will earn interest only on your minimum monthly balance. Suppose you deposit $1,000 in your cheque account, you keep it there until, say, the last day of the month and on that day you withdraw $999. You will earn interest just on the remaining $1. So check to see whether it is daily interest or monthly interest.

**Bad Bank Practice**

A few months ago a bank customer wanted to draw some money from one of his accounts. The amount was less than $1,000, but the customer's passbook had been lost, mislaid or stolen.

The customer's family had banked with that particular bank for decades, and specimen signatures of all family members were on file.

After an hour's verbal battle, the customer was informed there was no way he could withdraw money until a replacement passbook was issued — and that would take 15 days. There must be something wrong with that bank's system.

Checks with building societies and credit unions suggest that it would take seconds for a depositor to establish his identity. The bank concerned is about to lose not just one account but a number of accounts.

In another situation, a 15-year-old girl had saved $500 over 12 months and initially placed the money in a bank account. The money was earning 9 per cent interest but the young lady felt she should be earning a lot more.

But when she asked the bank about other investments

she was told 9 per cent was the best she could expect. No mention was made of interest-bearing deposits, Aussie Bonds, debentures or other investments.

Yet another instance is that of a farmer who was about to retire and wanted to invest a sum of $200,000. His bank manager advised him to place it all in an interest-bearing deposit. As I have said on many occasions there is nothing wrong with an interest-bearing deposit in the appropriate circumstances, but in this particular case there was no need for the entire sum to be invested in this way — as the customer found out a few months later.

No mention was made of bank bills, cash management trusts, Treasury notes or finance company debentures — let alone other investments.

While this particular bank had captured the entire $200,000 for a short period, they eventually lost the lot and also a long-standing customer simply by being greedy. When it comes to customer services, make sure you really are being served. If not, go elsewhere.

Incidentally, if you are expecting the repayment of a large sum of money or a large lump sum superannuation cheque, do not let the cheques be posted. Even if it means a special trip into town, go and pick up the cheque personally and bank it straight away or make other arrangements for it to be processed and cleared the same day.

**Wasted Charity Dollars**

During a recent trip to the country, I heard a request on a local radio station for the cash that had been collected on behalf of a local charity to be lodged at the end of the month. Well, I do not know how much money was involved and I do not want to be uncharitable, but in my view the money should have been banked or invested on a daily basis so it would earn some interest and not be left lying around for days, if not weeks, earning absolutely nothing. I am sure the credit unions, banks and building societies would be only too pleased to assist, so if you are ever involved in raising money for a charity do not assume good management. Ask the organisers if the money is being handled along the lines I have suggested. These days every dollar counts.

**Do not be Bulldozed**

Reports alleging that people are being frightened into thinking that they cannot complain about a certain product or the way a product is being marketed is a cause of great concern. New investors should take careful note of what is happening and the quality of advice they are receiving. There are some good advisors, there are some average advisors and there are some appalling advisors. And while on the subject, make sure you are dealing with people, institutions or companies that have a proven track record going back a number of years.

What I am saying is that you cannot be taught to be an investment advisor by taking a two week crash course. It takes years and years of experience. So if you do not like the advisor's tactics, then don't hesitate to complain to the Department of Corporate Affairs in your state.

## Illegal Advice

I never cease to be amazed at the tactics some people adopt to get business and this includes people in high places who should know better. By way of example, a young couple recently went to a certain financial institution seeking advice on investing $100,000.

The first piece of advice received was to open accounts in fictitious names in order to evade tax. Now I am sure there are not too many people who like paying tax, least of all at 48 cents in the dollar, but to be advised to open accounts in fictitious names is more than extreme — it is highly dangerous.

It is also dangerous for the organisation the advisor represents, and if not stopped quickly it could cause the loss of one's name and reputation. Let me again repeat, there are legal ways and means of reducing the tax burden, so please do not use the illegal ones. For what it is worth, the couple have gone elsewhere.

## Poor Advice

At a recent seminar I was appalled to hear that one lady had been induced to sell all her shares and reinvest the proceeds of the sales in just one property trust. Now I have never been against taking profits on shares, indeed I have constantly advised people to do that very thing, but to be advised to sell out, so to speak, at the time the stockmarket was beginning to move up is poor advice.

The shares this lady owned included companies like ANZ Bank, BHP, James Hardie, just to name a few. So, in your own interests, please seek a second opinion before making a final decision.

## Admit Problems

A lot of small business people go to the wall simply because they are not good managers and a lot go to the wall because they have been badly advised by so-called professionals. To make matters worse, many of them end

135

up bankrupt. According to recent comments, the vast majority of bankruptcies could be avoided with the right sort of caring counselling, and this counselling is still available through a number of sources like Small Business Associations etc.

The most important thing of all is to recognise and admit that you have a problem and try to do something about it. If you lay your cards on the table, most people will try to help you out of your difficulties. Remember, there is no embarrassment in getting out of your depth.

Some years ago a group of retired businessmen formed themselves into an advisory group to help bankruptcies be avoided. Their members were prepared to go into a business and help iron out the problems.

Would it not be nice to see an organisation such as this established nationwide. It could be staffed by retired professional and business people, many of whom would be only too pleased to do the job for a nominal payment and in some cases for expenses only.

## Hidden Commissions

An acquaintance of mine received quite a large legacy and she sought the advice of her accountant regarding the investment of this money. Much to her surprise, the accountant suggested she should invest the entire amount in one of the better known property trusts.

As far as doing this with *some* of the money, I would not disagree. What concerned me, however, was the advice to invest the lot in just one trust and not spread it around. At my suggestion, the lady again contacted her accountant and asked if he received any commission on the business introduced. After a slight pause he reluctantly admitted he did.

In the normal course of events, there is nothing wrong with accountants receiving commission, providing they disclose their position at the time. So next time your accountant, solicitor or financial advisor suggests putting all your eggs in one financial basket, ask what *he* is getting out of it and, more important, why he did not volunteer the information.

## Spotting Fees

Competition for the investor's dollar is now so intense that *spotting fees* are now part and parcel of the investment scene.

It is a practice that carries *grave risks* not only for the well-dressed persuasive *spotters* but, more important, for the potential victims who could well find their entire life savings including lump sum superannuation payments tied up in the wrong type of investment.

Although some investments might enjoy certain tax privileges at the moment, the tax advantages in some cases — as we have seen by recent events — could well be *short lived*.

While it is indeed a sad thing to contemplate, there is more than enough evidence to suggest that *the spotters* exist in so-called 'hallowed halls', which might include any financial institution as well as trade union offices. If past experience is any guide, some government departments would not be immune either, nor would some professionals.

There are of course a number of investment advisors who have been officially appointed by certain institutions to act in a professional capacity and the majority — if not all — would not come under the category of spotters.

## First Home Owners

The changes to the First Home Owners Assistance Scheme have, sad to say, virtually eliminated single home buyers, for in most cases their incomes well and truly exceed the new threshold which has (literally) been halved. The changes have been too severe and already the impact is being felt in the all important building industry. I hope the government will rethink the matter and ease the rules for single home buyers in the not too distant future. While I am critical of the changes, I am far from critical of the way the money is paid. In fact, I am quite impressed. Normally it takes weeks and weeks if not months to receive payment from a government department, but in the case of the First Home Owners Assistance Scheme we are talking about days. So let us give credit where credit is due.

## Buying Land

Land is not always a good investment. Some time ago I met a man who seemed terribly depressed. I asked what the problem was and he told me he had lost his block of land. As it turned out, he had bought a block of land during an earlier land boom. He had not lost his block of land . . . he could not find it.

If you are tempted to buy land as an investment, make sure you inspect the property first, otherwise you might find when the tide comes in your land has disappeared under water.

## Guarantees

You know it is quite on the cards that one day you will be asked to guarantee a loan. It might be for your son, daughter or a close friend. But, before you sign that piece of paper, make sure you know what you are letting yourself in for. It is not a token signature as many people think, it is a reality.

If the borrower defaults, you are the one that will have to cough up the money. No, I am not suggesting that you do not help out where you can, what I am saying is make sure you know what your legal obligations are before you put your name to that piece of paper. Depending upon the amount of money involved, it could mean you might be forced to sell the family home. For this reason, I must strongly criticise some lending bodies for not explaining your legal obligations when they ask you to act as guarantor.

**Home Unit — Anticipating Expenses**

If you own a home unit or an apartment, naturally you will have your regular maintenance costs to meet. If there is an unexpected expense, however, each owner will be asked to pay an extra levy to meet this, and on many occasions this can strain the purse strings, particularly if you are living on a fixed income.

One way of overcoming this problem is for every home unit owner to contribute extra money each week or month, as a form of compulsory saving.

This extra money can then be invested in a bank, building society, credit union or savings bonds, so that when there is a major repair to be met, the money will be available in this special reserve.

Next time there is a meeting of owners, why not put forward this suggestion. Better still, why not suggest it immediately. It could be to your advantage.

**Redundancy and a New Start**

If you are ever made redundant, buying or starting a business of your own could be your salvation. The loss of one's job frequently means loss of dignity as well as loss of income. This being so, I was delighted to run into a taxi driver who had followed some advice I had given years before. He was a professional person who had been made redundant following a company takeover. In this particular case, the golden handshake was worth a considerable sum of money. Realising it would be difficult, if not impossible, to find a similar position, he bought a taxi. Although he is working long hours, he is occupied and he is earning a respectable living. On top of that, the market value of his taxi licence has also increased appreciably.

**Work Insurance**

If you are an employee, make sure you are covered by workers compensation insurance and let me explain why.

An associate of mine was recently involved in an industrial accident at work. Fortunately he was not badly injured, but he did require hospital treatment and that of course required time off from work. On asking his employer about workers compensation, he was shocked to find that workers compensation insurance had not been renewed for some years because the employer 'could not afford to pay the premiums'. While appreciating and sympathising with the employer about the very high cost of workers compensation, the costs of not being insured could be even more horrendous. With small business employing the bulk of Australia's workers, it is essential to know if you are insured, so go and ask your employer right now if you are covered.

**Leasing is Practical**

Recently we decided to lease a bike for use on our farm. The purchase price of the bike by the way was around $2,000. We wanted a four year lease and accordingly started looking around for the best deal. First, let me say that there was more than a nominal difference in the base price offered from various dealers. Second, there was more than a nominal difference in the leasing quotes received. Not differences of a few dollars over the life of the lease, but differences of hundreds of dollars.

And on an item with a value of around $2,000, these are differences that cannot be ignored. There are two schools of thought about whether one should lease or one should buy the item outright, but as far as we are concerned we normally lease.

Not only does it help our cash flow, but it also means that we can invest the cash we might have paid for the bike, and after allowing for tax deductions for its 'business' use the extra interest earned on our money, leasing will cost us next to nothing.

**Read the Fine Print**

Recently I was asked to comment on the extra charges incurred when a housing loan was refinanced. The extra charges were in excess of $1,000 and that is a lot of money by any standard. The person concerned quite obviously had not read the fine print. Refinancing a loan or paying off a loan before the due date usually incurs a penalty. If you do not understand the fine print, then do not hesitate to ask some questions. And do not feel embarrassed when you ask them. I say that even allowing for the penalty incurred in refinancing the loan, the person concerned was still thousands of dollars in front, but it again illustrates the importance of knowing just what you are signing up for.

**Keep Copies**    Over the years, I have frequently suggested that people should copy, duplicate or photograph items of importance — be they letters, documents or taxation records. So, in practising what we preach, we make copies of everything — the company accounts, stock records for the farm investment, copies of taxation returns and annual reports. Whenever we go overseas, we always take with us not only our passports but copies of our passports in case of theft. Those important passport details, even using the photocopy, could save a lot of hassles while you are overseas. As a colleague recently suggested, take a list of important home telephone numbers with you, particularly if you are heading overseas.

**Rights on Deposits**    On a recent talk back programme, a lady informed me that the solicitor involved in a real estate transaction would not invest the deposit money paid with regard to the purchase of a sizeable piece of real estate. The purchase price, incidentally, was $200,000 so the 10 per cent deposit was not an inconsiderable sum of money. When I asked if the opposite party — in this case the vendor — was agreeable to the arrangement, she said yes. That being so, the solicitor does not have any say in the matter whatsoever nor, for that matter, does the real estate agent. Whether they like it or not, you can insist that the instructions to invest be carried out and, if they are not, then there is a simple solution. Change the solicitor and, if you feel it is appropriate, report the matter to the Law Society or a similar body, depending upon the state or territory in which you live. There can be variations to this right in some states, but in principle it is your money and you have the final say.

**Land — Selling too Cheaply**    Another reason for delays in selling land is because it often appears to be too cheap and people think there is a catch to it.

One person I know bought a few acres of land some years ago and later subdivided it. He worked out what appeared to be a reasonable profit and offered the land for sale. Some months later he was still waiting to sell the first block. Puzzled by the lack of buyer interest, he went to a major real estate group and sought their advice.

After inspecting the property, they advised him to withdraw the land for a few months and then place it on the market again, but this time at a higher price. He did just that and he sold the lot in a very short time.

**Rural Acres**

When you are thinking about retirement, and it might be 5 or 10 years away, some thought could be given to buying a farm. Those same comments could also apply to others who might be sick and tired of the rat race.

Just on 5 years ago we bought a farm and already it is one of our greatest investments, not only in the financial sense but also as a way of life. Later on, I had one hell of a fright medically, but even before that I had decided I was not going to sit around and wait to die after I retired.

And that is the major point I am making when I suggest the purchase of a farming property. When we bought the property, a lot of people commented 'But there is a drought on. Why buy now? The drought could last for years'.

Well, they could have been right, but, like the share-market, you buy property when the market is down and you sell when the market is up. Incidentally, in a recent issue of a national farm magazine, it was predicted that there would be an acute shortage of small holdings of rural acres in the future because of their popularity. And I am inclined to agree.

**Mortgage — Final Settlement**

What is a day or two worth? When it comes to paying off your mortgage, it could be worth quite a lot of interest and let me quote just one example. Some three years ago a property was purchased on vendor finance which means the vendor (the owner) carried the mortgage which was due to be repaid on 29 March 1986.

Well, 29 March 1986 was Easter Saturday, so as far as the purchaser was concerned he either had to bring the settlement date forward two days or put it back two days. Either way he was up for two days extra interest and on a substantial sum of money, that interest is more than petty cash. It is a point worth noting and it is a point that solicitors should note as well.

**Rent before Deciding**

I have suggested it could be unwise to rush in and sell the family home upon one's retirement or in the case of job transfer until such time as you see how things work out. The same situation would apply in reverse when it comes to buying real estate.

Although with any luck the move will be a happy one, there can be no guarantee and that is why it would be wise to try out the new surroundings for six months or so before you buy another home. And if you can afford to hold on to the old home as well, say by renting it out, then you can look upon this as an investment.

Of course in some cases, people would not have the necessary cash to keep both properties, but even if it means waiting to sell, I would still be inclined to do so even if it should cost you a few extra dollars. It will be money wisely spent.

**Do not Defer on Property**

For most people, their greatest investment is their own home, a house, a home unit, town house or even a block of land, if that is all you can afford. I bought my first block of land when I was 17 and I am pleased to see that a growing number of young people are doing the same thing. One question I am frequently asked relates to deferring the purchase, say for a year or two, to enable the people concerned to save a larger deposit. While in one sense that is not unreasonable, it must be realised that building costs will probably be higher two years from now and so too will be the value of real estate in many areas. On top of that there can be no guarantee that the First Home Owners Assistance Scheme will not be changed again. Apart from these features, rent is money wasted, so even if it means sleeping on the floor, I would be buying now rather than waiting.

**Interstate Planning**

If you are thinking of moving interstate and buying a home at some time in the future you should start planning. If you have a bank account with a national bank (not a state bank) then there should not be any problems, providing of course the bank is prepared to lend the money and you can meet their requirements. Building society finance is a different matter, for, in normal circumstances, building societies can lend only in their own state. You should open a building society account in the state to which you plan to move as soon as possible. By doing this, you will eliminate, or partly eliminate, any possible waiting period in order to qualify for a home loan.

**Early Planning**

From time to time, I do counselling sessions for a number of institutions, and the advice ranges from planning for retirement to starting an investment plan. The people I speak to range in age from 14 upwards and sometimes even younger and they come from all walks of life. Like the 17 year old young lady who is about to receive a compensation settlement of some $20,000. Still in school uniform, she came in to see me and asked for some general guidance on what to do with the money and how she should plan for the future. Quite obviously she was not overwhelmed in any way but she had the common sense to realise that the right decisions made now could have an important bearing on her future. So the first priority was to establish links with banks, building societies and credit unions, particularly from the point of view of buying some real estate as soon as possible.

**Hidden Costs**

Whether buying or selling real estate, watch out and allow for hidden costs — in other words do not throw money away!

For example, a couple were buying a home; finance had been approved yet they were informed by a solicitor that a separate valuation costing hundreds of dollars had to be obtained.

By chance they queried the need for the valuation with the solicitor, who was none too pleased with the question. Yet within half an hour the solicitor confirmed the valuation was not necessary. On the first advice they would have thrown away hundreds of dollars.

Another recent case involved a family also buying their first home. At first, finance had been approved by a bank under very favourable terms but, on calling in to sign the documents, the customer was informed the interest rate had been increased.

Another bank granted a loan under more favourable terms, they declined the first offer, only then were they told of extra costs — loan application fees etc.

Two points must be made. At no stage were they told of extra costs in advance and the bank changed the conditions of the loan, not the customer.

Not unnaturally, a letter of complaint is already on its way to the general manager of the bank, but no payment has been or is likely to be made.

**Know your Entitlements**

With all the talk about changes to superannuation schemes, the introduction of new schemes and changes in the tax rules, one thing stands out — not many people really understand just what their rights, privileges and entitlements are. The time is long overdue for a more enlightened approach from both employer and employee. By way of example, let us look at the problems of redundancy and how people can throw away benefits through ignorance or for the sake of pride.

To illustrate further, a friend of mine in a very senior

position was given the option of retiring gracefully or being sacked. Before talking to me he was on the verge of retiring gracefully. When I pointed out to him that retiring could mean loss of superannuation benefits as well as other benefits, he decided to swallow his pride and wait to be sacked. In being sacked, the benefits were his: if he had retired he would have lost quite a lot. So find out about your superannuation benefits.

**Business Partnership**

Recently I met a couple who were in business together. The business had been going for some five years and all in all they were doing pretty well. The day they saw me they were wanting some advice on superannuation which they believed was an important priority, and on that point they were certainly right.

In fact, they should have considered superannuation long before now. They should also have considered the right sort of life assurance, particularly death cover or term assurance, as it is frequently called.

In this particular situation, the wife should have a policy on her husband's life and the husband should take out a policy on his wife's life. They should also be looking at other forms of protection like personal accident and sickness insurance as well as cover for loss of profits, public risk etc. As I have said in relation to workers compensation insurance, it is penny wise and pound foolish not to have the right insurance.

**ADFs and Super**

Recently an investment advisor approached a 60-year-old about the man's $100,000 lump sum superannuation.

Apart from wondering how the investment advisor found out about his retirement and the money involved — and that is a question all pending retirees should ask — he was intrigued by the advice given.

It looked like a shopping list — and was top heavy with trusts of one kind or another. But it was not what was *on* the list that was important, it was what had been left off. There was not one mention of Approved Deposit Funds.

Wisely, the man is seeking other options. And when he retires next month, he will indeed be parking his money in an Approved Deposit Fund. And he can leave the money in one or more funds until the age of 65.

**Too Many Stocks in a Portfolio**

Recently, I reviewed a share portfolio which consisted of 63 different companies. That is right, 63 different companies. Some of the shareholdings ran into hundreds of shares and others into thousands. Many of these investments, however, involved just a handful of shares.

If you are ever lucky or unlucky enough to be in this situation, progressively sell your smaller holdings, for in my experience no one can successfully manage a share portfolio with more than, say, 20 stocks unless it is a full time job, and even then there might be difficulties unless you are an expert.

## Selling Shares

If you bought some shares for 50 cents, would you be happy to sell them for a dollar? Some people would but others would want more.

You must always remember that many people can think only in round figures. This means that when they decide to sell some or all of their shares, they will place a limit on them of, say, a dollar, two dollars, three dollars and so on and they might get their price.

But I approach the sharemarket in a slightly different way, knowing most of the sellers will be wanting at least a dollar for their shares. I ask my broker to sell my shares for 99 cents.

Of course, much will depend on whether the market is strong or weak. If it is strong you will probably get a dollar for your shares, but if it is weak, giving your broker a one cent discretion could mean the difference between selling the lot, a hundred or two or missing out entirely.

## Take a Loss

If you own shares in a number of companies and suddenly find you need money, you may have to sell some of your shares.

If you are like most people, you will probably sell the shares that are showing a profit and keep the shares that are showing a loss. This can be a costly mistake, for no matter how good the advice you receive from your stockbroker or investment advisor, you will normally own one or two disappointing stocks.

In this situation, take my advice. Cut your losses and sell out the bad stocks. Yes, I know it is easier said than done, but by keeping your good shares you will make up your losses with higher dividends, new issues, bonus issues and takeovers.

Do not forget, keep the good shares and get rid of the bad ones, for in the long run it will save you money.

**Delays can be Costly**

A few days ago a friend of mine wrote to his stockbroker and instructed him to buy some shares in three leading Australian companies.

The day he wrote the letter (and incidentally he lives in Sydney) the market started to move up again. This letter took three days to reach its destination, which of course is absurd, and so by the time the order was received the shares in question had gone up in price quite dramatically. As the orders to buy were without limits, the stockbroker carried out his instructions and purchased the shares.

Why my friend did not telephone the orders to his broker is beyond me, for had he done so instead of writing he would have saved himself a lot of money!

Even if you live in the country, a telephone call can save you money, so next time you want to buy or sell some shares, do not delay placing the order and do not depend on the mail.

**Debenture — Note Applications — Lodge Promptly**

A few years ago CSR made an unsecured note issue which opened and closed — fully subscribed — within a matter of seconds. With interest rates of 16 and 16.25 per cent and a company of this calibre it is no surprise to me that the issue was rushed. What is surprising is the number of investors who missed out on the issue simply because they did not know the correct procedures. While 'technically' this issue was to remain open for around 30 days, it was a foregone conclusion it would be rushed and would close immediately — oversubscribed. In all fairness to CSR, they made it quite clear they would accept applications before the opening date. Well, if you missed out on this issue because your application was not lodged in time, it has been a very valuable lesson and one you will remember next time there is a quality debenture or note issue.

**Unsecured Notes — Be Careful**

The other day a listener was on the verge of investing $80,000 in the unsecured notes of a well known finance company. The finance company, let me add, is one of the leaders, but even so $80,000 is a lot of money to tie up in just one company, and it is a lot of money to invest in unsecured notes. In the unlikely event of the company going out backwards, unsecured note holders would be close to last on the list for repayment. On the other hand, if you owned debentures you would be one of the first in line for repayment. Whether you buy unsecured notes or debentures is up to you, but quite frankly I do not think the extra interest earned is worth the risk.

**Tax Evasion — 49 Separate Accounts**

Some time ago I told you of a lady who kept 20 separate savings bank accounts, the purpose being to keep her interest below $100 on each account and evade the taxman.

At the time, I thought this took the cake, but experience can prove just how wrong you can be. A few days ago I met a man with 49 separate bank, building society and credit union accounts, and he'd had them going for 15 years. During this time his interest had grown progressively to more than $20,000 and he had not declared one cent of this income in his income tax returns during this time. For some strange reason he is a little worried. A little worried! I would be petrified every time I heard a knock at the door.

Despite my suggestion that he make a voluntary disclosure to the taxation department and suffer only a nominal penalty, believe it or not, he is still toying with the idea of continuing to run the risk. Quite frankly, I have no sympathy for him and think he deserves all he gets.

Tax evasion is, of course, illegal but tens of thousands are evading tax every year. In many cases it is deliberate but in other cases it is through ignorance. If by chance you find you have failed to include some bank, building society or credit union interest in your income tax returns, do not despair.

Sit down immediately and write to the Taxation Department in your state or territory explaining the oversight. You will be obliged to pay the tax owing and you might even be penalised. But the penalties you will suffer by making voluntary disclosure will be nominal compared to the penalties you will suffer if the taxation department is the first to find out you have omitted income from your return, and do not think they will not find out. The choice is yours, but I know what I would do.

**The Honest Way**

A few days ago I was asked what ought to be done if a late payment which should have been included in total earnings for the year is received after your tax return has been sent in. Do you hold the amount over until next year or do you send in an amended return.

Well, to be strictly correct, you send in an amended

return, noting, of course, your file number etc. and the amount of taxable income involved. Incidentally, you do not have to complete a second return, just fill in the appropriate section, sign it and send it to the department, making sure you keep a duplicate copy.

**Fight Tax Disallowance**

Tens of thousands of taxpayers this financial year — as in previous years — will have some of their deductions disallowed. If you are like most taxpayers you will probably say 'Well I tried' and leave it at that. But, do not leave it at that.

If you are convinced that your claim is justified, appeal against the decision and appeal on as many grounds as possible. Most important of all, make sure your appeal is lodged within 60 days of notice of assessment, otherwise, and unfairly, you will be too late. If the amounts involved are large then it could pay you to employ a professional who specialises in such matters. Lodging an appeal will not always be successful but it is quite remarkable how frequently taxpayers' appeals are allowed.

**Settlement Delays**

Some time ago a lady contacted me regarding the settlement of a workers compensation claim. The matter had been finalised some eight weeks previously, but despite repeated requests to her solicitor, she had not received settlement of the claim.

To make matters worse, the solicitor was urging her to invest this money in a mortgage. As there was $40,000 involved, naturally she was very worried.

Acting on advice, this lady sent the solicitor a telegram demanding immediate settlement, together with interest. She told him that if the money was not forthcoming, she would contact the Law Society. The effect of her telegram on the solicitor was electrifying and within 24 hours she got her money. There can be valid reasons for settlements of this kind being delayed but the question is, why did it take so long, in this case?

**Laziness can be Costly**

A few days ago, an acquaintance of mine asked me if I would help him rearrange his financial affairs. Although he was earning a substantial income, he admitted he was very casual about money.

After discussing his situation for about 10 minutes, I was horrified. By the time I had finished with him so was he. First, he had not lodged income tax returns for five years. When I asked why, he said he had not got around to it.

But that is not the end of the story. He is also buying a block of land with a finance company loan. This loan still has three years to run. I suggested he should refinance this loan through his credit union and then he would be able to reduce his interest by more than half. And to make matters worse, he was already a member of a credit union.

If you want to be casual about money, that is up to you. But, do not complain, if, because of this, you have very little to show for your labours.

**Pay Bills on Time**

I have just received notice that the final call on some partly paid shares we own will be due for payment in a couple of weeks from now. The amount involved is not large and we could pay the final call now without any hassles, but that is not the point.

The point is that paying for the shares before we have to will not give us any extra dividends and in fact it could cost money if one is using, say, a bank overdraft. These comments do not apply only to the sharemarket. They also apply to one's personal dealings in more than a dozen ways. We make a list of each bill as it is received, noting in particular the final date for payment.

It certainly helps to remind us and to make sure we have the money available.

**Do not put off the Trip**

Recently, I was asked if, in view of the fall in the value of the Australian dollar, a couple should put off an overseas trip for a couple of years. They had worked all their lives and the overseas trip was a lifetime dream. I advised them to go now. First, I do not know what the value of the Australian dollar will be in a couple of years from now, and I really do not think anyone does. Of even greater importance is the need to enjoy your money.

If the couple concerned delayed their trip, one or both could be dead two years from now and they would have missed out on their dream trip. Somehow I think they are packing their bags right now and if you have been wondering the same thing, then you too should start packing.

**Left over Currency**

After an overseas trip, like most travellers, we came back with an assortment of overseas currency and a few travellers' cheques. All told, we are probably talking about the

149

equivalent of a thousand US dollars. While the Australian dollar continues to decline, one might be tempted to hold on to the overseas currency, but unless you are going overseas again in the immediate future, there seems little point in holding on to small sums of money.

First, your money is not earning any interest, and, second, you might well find in a month or two the Australian dollar has regained part of its former value in relation to the other currencies. Australian banks and currency exchanges do not take small change, so spend it or convert it to notes before you leave for home.

**Buy Before Retirement**

The replacement of obsolete items of furniture and household appliances and the renovation of one's home should be seen to before retirement begins. You should also make any other major capital outlays, particularly the purchase of a new car. Expenditure on high quality clothing is a good idea as it will reduce the need after retirement for expensive outlays on clothing, shoes etc.

**Don't Keep Cash at Home**

A few days ago we heard about the sad plight of an elderly pensioner who had his savings stolen by a scoundrel. While in one sense I can understand why some people keep cash at home, these days it really is a dangerous exercise. But it is not only pensioners who do this. I know of dozens of people if not hundreds who do the same thing with cash and other assets. One lady, and I do not know her address, bought a few bars of gold some years ago and rather than pay someone to look after the gold on her behalf, she decided to keep them at home. Rather than try to hide them in the accepted sense, she kept the gold under the kitchen sink. I hope the gold is still there but, as I said, leaving cash or kind around the home is foolhardy.

# Appendix 1

**The CSR
Share
Purchase
Plan**

## 1. What is the CSR Share Purchase Plan?

The plan provides two optional and convenient investment services:

- The *dividend reinvestment service* which allows shareholders to purchase CSR shares by automatically reinvesting all or part of their dividends in new shares
- The *cash contribution service* which allows shareholders and holders of CSR loan securities (debentures, notes and convertible notes) to purchase CSR shares by contributing cash, which can include all or part of their interest on CSR loan securities, up to a limit of $1,200 each year. Dividends reinvested automatically under the dividend reinvestment service are not included in the cash contribution limit of $1,200.

All shares issued under the plan are allotted at a 5% discount from market price and you pay no brokerage or other costs.

The closing date for dividend reinvestment is the close of books for each dividend. The closing date for cash contributions is the last business day in Sydney each month.

## 2. Who can participate in the plan?

All shareholders and holders of CSR loan securities (except those with registered addresses in the United States of America) may participate in the plan subject to any regulations governing specific countries.

## 3. How do I join the plan?

Complete a plan *application form* and return it to CSR, together with your cheque or money order or completed *bank transfer forms* if applicable. The application form explains the choices open to you.

## 4. Can I make cash contributions without reinvesting dividends?

Yes. If you are a shareholder, you can take advantage of either service or both. If you hold only loan securities (or shares being purchased under the CSR Employee Share Plan) you may initially only take advantage of the cash contribution service. But once shares are allotted to you under the plan you may then also take advantage of the dividend reinvestment service.

## 5. Need I reinvest all my dividends?

No. When reinvesting dividends you have a choice between full participation and limited participation:

FULL PARTICIPATION

This choice maximises the benefits of reinvesting dividends because dividends on all shares you hold now, or may hold in the future, are automatically reinvested in new shares.

This includes dividends on:
- Shares held now
- Shares you acquire in the future
- Shares allotted under the plan (whether for reinvested dividends or cash contributions)
- Shares allotted through future rights or bonus issues

LIMITED PARTICIPATION

This choice provides for reinvestment of dividends on only the number of shares you nominate. Dividend payments will be made in the normal way for shares not subject to the plan.

## 6. How much cash can I contribute and how often can I make payments?

You can make cash contributions up to a limit of $1,200 each financial year, 1 July to 30 June. Contributions can be made at any time and shares are priced and allotted during the following month. The minimum deposit for cash contributions is $20. There is no minimum for interest automatically applied as cash contributions. A completed *cash contribution form* (or an *application form* with the cash contribution section completed) must be sent with cheques and money orders. A cash contribution form is attached to each plan *statement*. Additional copies are available on request.

## 7. Can interest on my CSR loan securities be used to make cash contributions?

Yes. Interest on loan securities may be used as contributions, but only up to the overall cash limit of $1,200 each year. CSR can arrange for all or a nominated amount of the interest on any of your CSR debentures, notes or convertible notes to be automatically applied as cash contributions.

## 8. When must I notify CSR if I wish to use interest on loan securities as cash contributions?

Notifications to use interest as cash contributions need to be received by CSR at least 10 business days (in Sydney) before the payment of interest.

## 9. Can I make regular cash contributions direct from my bank account?

Yes. You can have cash contributions deducted automatically each month from a bank account within Australia. See the plan *application form* and *bank transfer forms*.

## 10. How can I vary the amount of dividends being reinvested?

Send a completed *variation notice* to CSR to arrive on or before the next closing date for dividends (the close of CSR's share register).

**11. How can I vary cash contributions being made by monthly bank transfers or by automatic investment of interest on CSR loan securities?**

Send a completed *variation notice* to CSR to arrive at least 10 business days prior to the closing date for cash contributions (the last business day in Sydney each month).

**12. Can I withdraw cash contributions?**

Yes. You may withdraw all or part of your cash contributions including interest on loan securities. Requests for withdrawal need to be signed and must reach CSR on or before the closing date for the month in which the contributions are made.

**13. If I purchase shares with a cash contribution, will the dividends on these shares be reinvested automatically?**

This will happen if you are a full participant for dividend reinvestment. If you are not a participant for dividend reinvestment you will receive dividend payments in the normal way.

**14. What are the costs to me if I participate in the plan?**

CSR meets all administration costs of the plan and you pay no brokerage or other costs when purchasing shares under the plan.

**15. How is the price of shares allotted under the plan determined?**

Shares are allotted at a 5% discount from the weighted average market price of all CSR shares sold on the Sydney and Melbourne stock exchanges during the three trading days immediately following the closing date for dividends and the monthly closing date for cash contributions. The Sydney Stock Exchange calculates the relevant market price.

**16. How are shares purchased under the plan?**

Dividends and cash contributions are used to purchase as many new shares as possible at the allotment price. There will usually be a small cash balance left over (always less than the allotment price of one share). This balance is added to the next dividend or cash contribution (whichever comes first) for investment.

**17. How can I keep a record of my participation in the plan?**

You are sent a detailed statement after every allotment of shares in which you participate.

**18. What is my taxation position?**

Dividends and interest used to purchase shares under the plan are assessable for income tax as if received in the normal way. Investors resident outside Australia, unless exempted by the Australian Taxation Office, have withholding tax deducted from dividends and interest invested under the plan. Your plan *statements* and interest advices provide details.

**19.  Is there any difference between shares allotted under the plan and other CSR shares?**

No. Shares allotted under the plan rank equally with existing fully-paid ordinary shares, and carry the same voting rights and the same entitlements to dividends and bonus and rights issues.

**20.  Can I round up my holding to a nominated number of shares?**

No. As the price at which shares are allotted under the plan is not known until after the closing date for each allotment, and in view of the administration costs involved, it is not practicable to do this.

**21.  Do I receive certificates for shares allotted under the plan?**

Certificates are not issued except on request or upon withdrawal from the plan. You may request a certificate at any time. Your plan *statements* show the number of shares for which no certificate has been issued.

**22.  How do I obtain a certificate?**

Send CSR a signed *variation notice* indicating the number of shares for which you require a certificate.

**23.  Is there a problem in selling shares allotted under the plan?**

No. You own the shares even if you do not hold a certificate for them. However, you will need a certificate for these shares if you sell them as CSR does not register transfers of shares without the corresponding share certificate(s). If you wish to sell the shares and want the certificate to be given to your stockbroker, please complete the 'authority to deliver' section on the *variation notice*. CSR will then forward the certificate to your stockbroker.

**24.  If I intend to sell shares for which a certificate has not been issued, should I obtain a certificate first?**

Yes. This will help to ensure that all the CSR shares you own are included in the sale. It will also assist your broker.

**25.  If I wish to sell all my shares should I first withdraw from the plan?**

Yes, especially if you intend to sell just before a dividend payment date. This will ensure that no further shares are allotted to you under the plan.

**26.  How do I withdraw from the plan?**

Send a completed *variation notice* to CSR.

# Appendix 2

## TABLE 1 — APPROVED DEPOSIT FUNDS

### Group 1: Capital Stable Investments

| | Size of Fund at 31/7/89 $ M | 3 months % | 1 year %(p.a.) | 2 years %(p.a.) | Entry Fee | Exit Fee | Annual Fee | Unit Linked/ Capital Gteed | Minimum Invest $ | Pres. Fac. |
|---|---|---|---|---|---|---|---|---|---|---|
| Advance — Capital (Note 1) | 8 | 3.1 | 11.8 | 12.6 | Nil | Note 1 | 1.0% | U/Y | 1,000 | Yes |
| AFT — Security | 4 | 3.8 | 12.8 | n/a | Nil | Nil | Nil | U/N | 1,000 | No |
| AMP — Capital Stable (Note 4) | 189 | 3.4 | 12.6 | 12.4 | Nil | Nil | Nil | N/Y | 1,000 | No |
| ANA — Capital Stable (Short Term) | <1 | 4.7 | 14.5 | n/a | Nil | Nil | 1.0% | N/N | 2,000 | Yes |
| — (Medium/Long Term) | <1 | 4.6 | n/a | n/a | 3.5% | Nil | 1.0% | N/N | 2,000 | Yes |
| ANZ Bank — Income Accumulation | 510 | 3.5 | 12.9 | 11.9 | Nil | Note 5 | 1.0% | U/N | 1,000 | Yes |
| — Maxi Safe (Note 6) | 32 | n/a | n/a | n/a | Nil | Nil | Nil | N/Y | 5,000 | Yes |
| Aust. Funds — Cap. Secure | 36 | 3.5 | 12.5 | n/a | Nil | Nil | Nil | N/N | 1,000 | Yes |
| — Cap. Maint. (Note 9) | 22 | 3.5 | 12.1 | 12.1 | Closed | Nil | 0.75% | N/N | Closed | Yes |
| Aust-Wide — Deposit (Note 10) | 1 | 3.2 | 13.0 | 13.7 | Nil | Nil | 1.0% | N/N | 1,000 | Yes |
| Barclays — High Income (Note 11) | <1 | 2.3 | n/a | n/a | 0.5% | Nil | 1.75% | N/N | 1,000 | Yes |
| Brick Securities — Capital Maint. | 62 | 2.5 | 12.2 | 19.3 | 2.0% | Note 13 | 1.06% | U/N | $1,000 | Yes |
| BT — Deposit | 120 | 3.7 | 13.3 | 12.1 | 1.25% | Nil | 1.5% | U/N | 1,000 | Yes |
| — Property | 15 | 3.3 | 10.5 | n/a | 4.0% | Nil | 0.5% | U/N | Note 14 | Yes |
| — Capital Stable | 33 | 3.4 | 11.5 | n/a | 4.0% | Nil | 1.25% | U/N | Note 14 | Yes |
| Capita — Capital Secure | 5 | 3.5 | 12.8 | n/a | Nil | Nil | 1.25% | U/N | Note 14 | Yes |
| Capital Building Society | 2 | 3.6 | 12.5 | 12.3 | Nil | Nil | 1.5% | N/N | 2,000 | Yes |
| Colonial Mutual — Capital Stable | 5 | 2.7 | 9.9 | 10.3 | Closed | Nil | 1.0% | N/Y | None | Yes |
| Commonwealth Bank — Cap. Stable | 1,320 | 3.1 | 12.0 | 12.2 | Nil | Nil | Excess | N/N | Closed | Yes |
| County NatWest — Capital Stable | 1 | 6.6 | 8.8 | n/a | 4.0% | Nil | 1.0% | N/Y | None | Yes |
| EquitiLink — Capital Stable | 12 | 5.1 | 10.3 | 12.2 | 5.0% | Nil | Note 19 | U/N | 1,000 | Yes |
| Farmers Trustee (SA) | 2 | 3.4 | 12.6 | 13.8 | Nil | Nil | 1.1% | N/N | 1,000 | Yes |
| Fidelity — Capital Stable | <1 | 3.3 | 13.5 | n/a | 0.5% | Nil | 1.0% | N/N | 2,000 | Yes |
| Friends Provident — Capital Safe | <1 | 4.1 | 14.6 | n/a | Nil | Nil | 1.5% | U/N | 100 | Yes |
| — Capital Secure | <1 | 4.1 | 14.3 | n/a | 5.0% | Nil | 1.5% | U/N | 100 | Yes |
| GIO (NSW) — Cash | 16 | 3.6 | 12.8 | 11.9 | Nil | Nil | 1.0% | N/Y | Note 21 | Yes |
| Global — Preservation | <1 | 0.2 | 7.6 | n/a | 0.5% | Nil | 1.25% | U/Y | 1,000 | Yes |
| Grosvenor Pirie — Income | <1 | 3.3 | 16.6 | 18.5 | Nil | Nil | Note 22 | U/N | None | No |
| Growth Equities — Income | 8 | 4.1 | 13.9 | 13.6 | 0.5% | Nil | Note 23 | U/N | 1,000 | Yes |
| Hambros — Capital Security | 3 | 3.5 | 12.2 | n/a | 0.5% | $25 | 0.75% | U/N | Note 25 | Yes |
| IMB | 6 | 3.0 | 10.6 | 10.9 | Nil | Nil | Nil | N/N | 500 | Yes |
| IOOF — Short Term | 19 | 2.7 | 10.8 | 12.5 | Nil | Nil | 1.0% | N/Y | 500 | Yes |
| — Long Term | 170 | 3.0 | 11.8 | 13.5 | 3.5% | Nil | Nil | N/Y | 500 | Yes |
| Macquarie Bank — Deposit | 223 | 3.1 | 12.2 | 11.9 | Nil | Nil | 1.0% | N/N | Note 29 | Yes |
| — Balanced | <1 | 8.7 | n/a | n/a | 4.0% | Nil | 1.5% | U/N | Note 29 | Yes |
| — Property | <1 | 2.4 | n/a | n/a | 4.5% | Nil | 1.25% | U/N | Note 29 | Yes |
| McIntosh — Transit | n/p | n/p | n/p | n/p | Nil | Nil | 1.0% | U/Y | 1,000 | Yes |
| Metway Bank — MetwayFund | 1 | 5.0 | 14.5 | 9.0 | Nil | Nil | 1.0% | U/N | 1,000 | Yes |
| National Australia — Income (Series I) | 16 | 3.5 | 8.1 | 11.7 | Closed | Note 32 | n/p | U/N | Closed | Yes |
| National Credit Union — Cap. Maint. | 178 | 3.3 | 12.3 | 11.8 | Nil | Nil | 1.0% | N/N | None | Yes |
| National Mutual — Bankguard | 13 | 3.0 | 11.5 | 11.5 | Nil | Nil | Excess | N/N | 1,000 | Yes |
| Norwich — Deposit | 21 | 3.3 | 6.2 | 10.3 | Nil | Nil | 1.2% | U/N | 2,000 | Yes |
| Oceanic — Capital Preservation | <1 | 2.5 | 12.4 | 16.0 | Nil | Nil | 1.25% | U/Y | 1,000 | Yes |
| Over 50's Friendly Society (The) | 4 | n/p | 12.0 | 16.0 | Note 39 | Nil | 0.5% | N/Y | 1,000 | Yes |
| Perpetual Trustees — High Income | 14 | 3.5 | 12.3 | 12.7 | Nil | Note 40 | 1.0% | N/N | 5,000 | Yes |
| Potter Warburg — Capital Secure | 9 | 4.2 | 11.8 | 10.6 | Nil | Nil | 0.75% | U/N | 1,000 | Yes |
| (ex KB) — Capital Secure No. 2 | 1 | 2.4 | 9.2 | n/a | Nil | Nil | 1.6% | U/N | 2,000 | Yes |
| R&I — Supersure | 40 | 3.0 | 11.2 | 12.3 | Nil | Nil | 1.0% | N/N | 500 | Yes |
| REI Building Society | 1 | 3.5 | 13.1 | 13.3 | Nil | Nil | 0.5% | N/Y | 1,000 | No |
| Resi Statewide Building Soc. — Flexi | n/p | n/p | n/p | n/p | Nil | Nil | 1.0% | U/Y | 1,000 | Yes |
| Rothschild — Deposit | 15 | 3.2 | 11.2 | 10.3 | Nil | Nil | 1.1% | U/N | 5,000 | Yes |
| Sandhurst Trustees | 4 | 3.1 | 12.8 | 12.9 | Nil | Nil | 1.0% | U/N | None | No |
| State Bank (NSW) — Minder Cap. Sec. | 194 | 3.4 | 12.5 | 12.6 | Nil | Nil | 1.0% | N/N | None | Yes |
| State Bank (SA) — Superflex | 72 | 3.0 | 11.6 | 13.2 | Nil | Nil | 1.0% | N/N | None | Yes |
| State Bank (VIC) — SuperSafe | 794 | 3.2 | 11.8 | 12.1 | Nil | Nil | 1.0% | N/Y | None | Yes |
| St George — Super Future | 50 | 3.3 | 11.2 | 12.7 | Nil | Nil | Nil | N/Y | None | Yes |
| Suncorp | 7 | 2.9 | 10.4 | 11.7 | Nil | Nil | 1.0% | N/Y | None | Yes |
| Trust | 2 | 3.5 | 12.2 | 12.2 | Nil | Nil | 1.0% | U/N | 5,000 | Yes |
| Union (Municipal Officers) Fund No. 2 | 2 | 4.5 | 8.5 | n/a | Nil | Nil | 1.1% | U/N | 1,000 | Yes |
| V S & L — Capital Guaranteed | 5 | 3.3 | 12.0 | 12.8 | Nil | Nil | Nil | N/Y | 500 | Yes |
| Wardley — Trustee Investment | 17 | 3.9 | 9.3 | 9.2 | 0.5% | Nil | 1.0% | U/N | 5,000 | Yes |
| Were, J B — Income (Note 49) | 1 | 3.6 | 12.7 | n/a | Nil | Nil | 0.575% | U/N | 10,000 | Yes |
| Westpac Bank — Capital Stable | 400 | 3.3 | 12.2 | 11.3 | Nil | Note 50 | 1.5% | U/N | 1,000 | Yes |
| Total | 4,696 | | | | | | | | | |

## TABLE 1 — APPROVED DEPOSIT FUNDS

### Group 2: Equity Type Investments

| | Size of Fund at 31/7/89 $ M | 3 months % | 1 year %(p.a.) | 2 years %(p.a.) | Entry Fee | Exit Fee | Annual Fee | Unit Linked/ Capital Gteed | Minimum Invest $ | Pres. Fac. |
|---|---|---|---|---|---|---|---|---|---|---|
| Advance — Growth (Note 1) | 24 | 3.3 | 14.2 | 7.1 | 5.0% | Nil | 1.5% | U/N | 1,000 | Yes |
| AFT — Performance | 3 | 8.4 | 17.2 | n/a | 4.0% | Nil | 1.5% | U/N | 1,000 | No |
| ANA — Managed | n/a | n/a | n/a | n/a | 4.0% | Nil | 1.0% | U/N | 2,000 | Yes |
| ANZ Bank — Growth | 125 | 7.4 | 9.0 | - 6.2 | 3.0% | Note 5 | 1.5% | U/N | 1,000 | Yes |
| Armstrong Jones — Property | 38 | 4.0 | 18.0 | n/a | 4.5% | Nil | 1.0% | U/N | 2,000 | Yes |
| Australian Funds — Performance | 2 | 5.2 | - 0.8 | n/a | 4.0% | Nil | 2.0% | U/N | 1,000 | Yes |
| — Index | 4 | 11.3 | 4.1 | n/a | 4.0% | Nil | 1.5% | U/N | 1,000 | Yes |
| — Share | <1 | 11.0 | 6.6 | n/a | 4.0% | Nil | 2.0% | U/N | 1,000 | Yes |
| — International | <1 | 8.7 | 22.7 | n/a | 4.0% | Nil | 2.0% | U/N | 1,000 | Yes |
| — Managed | 8 | 6.2 | 9.1 | n/a | 4.0% | Nil | 0.75% | U/N | 1,000 | Yes |
| — Fixed Interest | 1 | 2.6 | 7.4 | n/a | 2.5% | Nil | 1.0% | U/N | 1,000 | Yes |
| — Growth (Note 9) | 7 | 5.3 | 11.0 | -16.2 | Closed | Nil | 1.0% | U/N | Closed | Yes |
| Aust-Wide — Investment (Note 10) | 46 | 8.7 | 16.8 | 4.7 | 4.0% | Nil | 2.0% | U/N | 1,000 | Yes |
| Barclays — Growth (Note 11) | n/a | 3.0 | n/a | n/a | 4.0% | Nil | 1.06% | U/N | 1,000 | No |
| Brick Securities — Growth | 16 | 4.0 | 13.9 | 14.5 | 3.0% | Note 13 | 1.5% | U/N | 1,000 | No |
| BT — Investment | 476 | 7.4 | 12.8 | 7.0 | 4.0% | Nil | 1.25% | U/N | Note 14 | Yes |
| Capita — Managed Growth | <1 | 7.1 | 17.4 | n/a | 4.0% | Nil | 1.5% | U/N | 2,000 | Yes |
| Clayton Robard (Note 17) | 24 | 3.0 | 0.0 | -28.5 | 4.0% | Nil | 1.5% | U/N | 1,000 | Yes |
| County NatWest — Growth | 4 | 7.8 | 10.3 | - 3.9 | 4.0% | Nil | Note 19 | U/N | 1,000 | Yes |
| EquitiLink — Growth | 13 | 8.0 | 8.3 | 1.8 | 5.0% | Nil | 1.5% | U/N | 1,000 | Yes |
| Fidelity — Managed | <1 | 5.9 | 14.1 | n/a | 5.0% | Nil | 1.5% | U/N | 2,000 | Yes |
| Friends Provident — Managed Growth | <1 | 4.1 | 14.0 | n/a | 5.0% | Nil | 1.5% | U/N | 100 | Yes |
| Global — Growth | 3 | 2.2 | 4.5 | n/a | 4.0% | Nil | 1.25% | U/N | 1,000 | Yes |
| Grosvenor Pirie — Equity | <1 | 1.8 | 9.9 | n/a | Nil | Nil | Note 22 | U/N | None | No |
| Growth Equities — Managed | 13 | 7.5 | 2.1 | -14.6 | 4.0% | Nil | Note 23 | U/N | 1,000 | Yes |
| — Property (Note 23) | 69 | 3.2 | 13.4 | n/a | 4.0% | Nil | Note 23 | U/N | 1,000 | Yes |
| Hambros — Managed | 13 | 5.8 | 4.9 | - 6.7 | 4.0% | Nil | 1.5% | U/N | Note 25 | Yes |
| — Property Securities | 7 | 5.9 | - 4.0 | - 9.4 | 4.0% | Nil | 1.5% | U/N | Note 25 | Yes |
| — International | 10 | 8.5 | 17.4 | - 6.5 | 4.0% | Nil | 1.5% | U/N | Note 25 | Yes |
| IOOF — Managed | n/a | 4.9 | n/a | n/a | 4.0% | Nil | Nil | U/N | 500 | Yes |
| JF — International | 9 | 8.7 | 23.5 | - 6.5 | 5.0% | Nil | 1.5% | U/N | 1,000 | Yes |
| Macquarie Bank — Personal | 51 | Note 29 | Note 29 | Note 29 | 1.75% | Nil | 1.5% | Note 29 | 100,000 | Yes |
| McIntosh — Investment | n/p | n/p | n/p | n/p | 4.0% | Nil | 1.5% | U/N | 1,000 | Yes |
| Metway Bank — MetwayGrowth | n/p | n/p | n/p | n/p | 3.0% | Nil | 1.5% | U/N | 1,000 | Yes |
| National Australia — Investment | 17 | 2.4 | 4.9 | 8.4 | Closed | n/p | n/p | U/N | Closed | Yes |
| National Credit Union — Growth | 38 | 6.2 | 10.9 | 6.2 | 4.0% | Nil | 1.0% | U/N | None | Yes |
| — Property | 5 | 4.8 | 17.1 | n/a | 4.0% | Nil | 1.0% | U/N | None | Yes |
| National Mutual — Super Manager | n/a | 2.7 | 11.8 | n/a | 4.5% | Nil | 1.5% | U/N | 5,000 | Yes |
| Norwich — Investment | 18 | 8.8 | 9.3 | 3.4 | 5.0% | Nil | 1.7% | U/N | 2,000 | Yes |
| Oceanic — Growth | <1 | 0.5 | 7.4 | 1.0 | 4.0% | Nil | 1.25% | U/N | 1,000 | Yes |
| Perpetual Trustees — Personal | 14 | Note 40 | Note 40 | Note 40 | 2.0% | Note 40 | 1.5% | Note 40 | 100,000 | Yes |
| Potter Warburg — Capital Growth | 17 | 8.9 | 7.3 | 3.0 | 4.0% | Nil | 1.5% | U/N | 1,000 | Yes |
| (ex KB) — Growth No. 2 | n/a | 10.0 | 11.2 | n/a | 5.0% | Nil | 1.6% | U/N | 2,000 | Yes |
| (ex KB) — Australian | n/a | 9.4 | 5.8 | n/a | 5.0% | Nil | 1.6% | U/N | 2,000 | Yes |
| (ex KB) — International | n/a | 1.5 | 9.0 | n/a | 5.0% | Nil | 1.9% | U/N | 2,000 | Yes |
| Resi Statewide Building Soc. — Growth | n/p | n/p | n/p | n/p | 3.0% | Nil | 1.5% | U/N | 1,000 | Yes |
| Rothschild — Investment | 64 | 7.5 | 12.3 | 6.2 | 4.0% | Nil | 1.1% | U/N | 5,000 | Yes |
| State Bank (NSW) — Minder Growth | 6 | 8.0 | 9.5 | n/a | 1.0% | Nil | 1.5% | U/N | 5,000 | Yes |
| State Bank (SA) — Supergrowth | 4 | 10.6 | 10.9 | 7.5 | 1.5% | Nil | 1.0% | U/N | None | Yes |
| State Bank (VIC) SuperSafe — Growth | 23 | 7.7 | 7.2 | - 8.8 | 4.0% | Note 45 | 1.35% | U/N | 5,000 | Yes |
| Union (Municipal Officers) Fund No. 1 | <1 | - 2.2 | 4.5 | n/a | Nil | Nil | 1.1% | U/N | 1,000 | Yes |
| Wardley — Capital Growth | 70 | 8.5 | 7.7 | - 1.8 | 4.0% | Nil | 1.25% | U/N | 5,000 | Yes |
| — International | 4 | 9.1 | 10.6 | - 4.3 | 4.0% | Nil | 1.5% | U/N | 5,000 | Yes |
| Were, J B — Growth (Note 49) | 1 | 7.8 | 6.5 | n/a | 2.0% | Nil | 0.575% | U/N | 10,000 | Yes |
| Westpac Bank — Equity/Growth | 134 | 8.1 | 15.8 | 6.4 | Nil | Note 50 | 1.5% | U/N | 1,000 | Yes |
| Total | 1,389 | | | | | | | | | |
| Total ADFs | 6,085 | | | | | | | | | |

## TABLE 2 — DEFERRED ANNUITIES

### Group 1: Capital Stable Investments

| | Size of Fund at 31/7/89 $ M | 1 year %(p.a.) | 2 years %(p.a.) | 3 years %(p.a.) | Entry Fee | Exit Fee | Annual Fee | Unit Linked/ Capital Gteed | Minimum Invest $ | Pres. Fac. |
|---|---|---|---|---|---|---|---|---|---|---|
| Adriatic — Capital Guaranteed | n/p | 13.5 | 14.5 | 15.4 | 5.0% | Nil | 1.6% | N/Y | 2,500 | No |
| AETNA — Preservation | 29 | 7.5 | 7.9 | 9.5 | 5.0% | Nil | Nil | N/Y | 2,500 | No |
| — Capital | 1 | 12.0 | 11.6 | n/a | Note 2 | Note 2 | 1.26% | U/N | 2,000 | No |
| AMEV Life — Cash Plus | <1 | 10.6 | n/a | n/a | 6.0% | Note 3 | 1.2% | U/N | Note 3 | Yes |

| | Size ($M) | 1 year | 2 years | 3 years | Entry Fee | Exit Fee | Annual Fee | Unit Linked/Capital Greed | Minimum Invest $ | Pres. Fac. |
|---|---|---|---|---|---|---|---|---|---|---|
| AMP (Note 4) — Invest. Account | 451 | 15.8 | n/a | n/a | 5.0% | Nil | $17.52 | N/Y | 5,000 | Yes |
| — Invest. Linked — Sec. | 53 | 10.3 | 12.1 | 13.6 | 5.0% | Nil | $17.52 | U/Y | 5,000 | Yes |
| — Capital Secure | 167 | n/p | n/a | n/a | Nil | Note 4 | $17.52 | N/Y | 5,000 | Yes |
| ANZ Life — Capital Stable | 12 | 11.5 | 12.4 | 13.2 | 5.0% | Nil | 1.2% | U/Y | 1,000 | Yes |
| APFS (Telecom/Lumley) | 6 | 9.0 | n/a | n/a | Nil | Note 7 | Note 7 | N/Y | 3,000 | Yes |
| Australian Eagle — Capital Guaranteed | n/p | 14.5 | 16.3 | 16.8 | $60+5.0% | Note 8 | 1.3% | N/Y | 2,500 | No |
| BMA — Capital Guaranteed | 5 | 11.1 | 13.8 | 14.8 | 5.0% | Nil | Note 12 | N/Y | Note 12 | Yes |
| Capita — Capital Guaranteed | n/p | 14.6 | 15.6 | 16.6 | Note 15 | Note 15 | Nil | N/Y | 2,000 | Yes |
| Citicorp (Note 16) | 159 | 12.8 | 15.0 | n/a | Nil | Nil | Nil | N/Y | 5,000 | Yes |
| Colonial Mutual — Superbridge Cap. Gtd. | 215 | 16.4 | 16.9 | 17.0 | 5.0% | Nil | 0.9% | N/Y | 5,000 | Yes |
| — Superspan II | 31 | n/a | n/a | n/a | Nil | Note 18 | 2.0% | N/Y | 5,000 | Yes |
| Equity Life — Capital Guaranteed | 32 | 12.2 | 12.1 | 13.5 | Nil | Nil | 1.3% | U/Y | 1,000 | Yes |
| FAI — Capital Stable (Note 20) | 7 | 7.1 | 0.0 | 7.2 | Note 20 | Nil | 1.2% | U/Y | 1,000 | No |
| Friends Provident — Capital Ins. | 27 | 13.0 | 12.5 | 13.7 | 5.0% | Nil | Nil | N/N | 1,000 | Yes |
| GIO (NSW) — S Unit | 245 | 12.4 | 12.5 | 13.5 | Note 21 | 1.0% | $32+0.6% | U/Y | Note 21 | Yes |
| Guardian — Fixed Interest | 9 | 11.9 | 13.1 | 20.7 | Note 24 | Nil | 1.3% | U/N | 2,500 | No |
| — Cash | <1 | 12.8 | 11.2 | 13.0 | Note 24 | Nil | 1.3% | U/N | 2,500 | No |
| IFMA (Lumley) — Capital Secure | <1 | 8.3 | n/a | n/a | 5.0% | Nil | 1.2% | U/N | 2,000 | Yes |
| Inlife — Capital Guaranteed | 16 | 13.6 | 14.3 | 15.5 | Note 26 | Nil | 1.5% | N/Y | 2,000 | No |
| IOOF — Capital Guaranteed | <1 | n/a | n/a | n/a | Nil | Note 27 | 0.75% | N/Y | 500 | No |
| Investment Action Friendly Society | 2 | 13.5 | 17.1 | n/a | 4.0% | Nil | Nil | N/Y | None | No |
| Legal & General — Capital Gtd. No. 1 | 252 | 12.3 | 14.6 | 15.7 | 5.0% | Nil | 1.5% | U/Y | 1,000 | Yes |
| — Capital Gtd. Cash | 60 | 12.0 | 14.7 | 15.4 | 5.0% | Nil | 1.5% | U/Y | 1,000 | Yes |
| Lumley Life — Capital Gtd. (Note 27) | 34 | 11.1 | 13.3 | 17.2 | 5.0% | Note 28 | Nil | N/Y | 2,000 | Yes |
| — Capital Secure | 1 | 9.6 | n/a | n/a | 5.0% | Nil | 1.2% | U/N | 2,000 | Yes |
| Macquarie Bank — Capital Guaranteed | <1 | n/a | n/a | n/a | 5.0% | Nil | 1.5% | N/Y | 5,000 | Yes |
| Mercantile Mutual — Cap. Gtd. | 520 | 13.5 | 14.3 | 15.7 | Note 30 | Nil | Nil | N/Y | 1,000 | Yes |
| — Cap. Stable | 7 | n/a | n/a | n/a | Note 30 | Nil | 1.5% | Y/N | 1,000 | Yes |
| MLC Life — Capital Guaranteed | 28 | 12.6 | 12.0 | n/a | Note 31 | Note 31 | 1.32% | U/Y | 3,000 | No |
| — Cap. Gtd. Roll-Over | n/p | 16.5 | n/a | n/a | Nil | Note 31 | Nil | N/Y | 10,000 | Yes |
| Five Star Investment | | | | | | | | | | |
| — Rollover Cash Option | 15 | n/a | n/a | n/a | Nil | Note 31 | 1.8% | U/Y | 3,000 | Yes |
| National Australia — Cash (Old) | 1 | 11.3 | n/a | n/a | Closed | n/p | n/p | N/Y | Closed | No |
| — Group Deposits | 8 | 11.1 | n/a | n/a | Closed | n/p | n/p | U/Y | Closed | Yes |
| — Cash (New) | 4 | 12.0 | n/a | n/a | Closed | n/p | n/p | U/N | Closed | Yes |
| — Income | 16 | 10.0 | n/a | n/a | Nil | n/p | n/p | U/N | 500 | Yes |
| — Fixed Interest | 7 | 5.9 | n/a | n/a | Closed | n/p | n/p | U/N | Closed | Yes |
| National Credit Union — Cap. Gtd. | 25 | n/a | n/a | n/a | Nil | Note 33 | Nil | N/Y | 5,000 | Yes |
| Nat. Mutual — Supgd. Cap. Gtd. | 1,386 | 13.2 | 14.1 | 14.5 | Nil | Nil | Excess | U/Y | 2,000 | Yes |
| — Supgd. + Cap. Gtd. | 224 | 14.6 | 15.5 | 15.9 | 5.0% | Nil | 1.35% | U/Y | 3,000 | Yes |
| — Supgd. + Cap. Stable | n/a | 15.7 | 12.1 | 18.0 | 5.0% | Nil | 1.35% | U/N | 3,000 | Yes |
| Norwich — Cash | 52 | 12.9 | 12.2 | 13.7 | 5.0% | Nil | 1.6% | U/Y | 1,000 | Yes |
| — Capital Guaranteed | 138 | 13.5 | 16.5 | 17.5 | 5.0% | Nil | 0.6% | N/Y | 1,000 | Yes |
| NRMA — Capital Secure | 4 | 10.5 | n/a | n/a | Note 35 | Note 35 | 1.2% | U/N | $1,000 | Yes |
| NZI Life — Capital Guaranteed | 43 | 14.8 | 17.0 | 17.0 | Note 36 | Nil | Nil | N/Y | Note 36 | Yes |
| — Invest. Linked — Cash | <1 | 10.3 | 24.1 | n/a | Closed | 1.0% | 1.4% | U/N | Closed | Yes |
| Occidental — Capital Guaranteed | 12 | n/a | n/a | n/a | 5.0% | Nil | 1.9% | U/Y | Note 37 | Yes |
| OST Friendly Society | 80 | 17.2 | 18.1 | 19.0 | 4.0% | Nil | Note 38 | N/Y | None | Yes |
| Over 50's Friendly Society (The) | 27 | 14.0 | 16.7 | 20.0 | Note 39 | Nil | 0.5% | N/Y | 1,000 | Yes |
| Prudential — Cash | 32 | 12.7 | 11.9 | 13.1 | Nil | Nil | 1.25% | U/Y | 100 | Yes |
| — Capital | 121 | 15.4 | 15.8 | 15.9 | Note 41 | Nil | Nil | N/Y | 2,000 | Yes |
| Scottish Amicable Life | n/p | 12.1 | 11.7 | 12.7 | Note 43 | 3.0% | 1.2% | U/Y | Note 43 | Yes |
| SGIC (SA) (Note 44) | 96 | 15.2 | 16.5 | 17.2 | Note 44 | Note 44 | Nil | N/Y | 500 | Yes |
| State Bank (Vic) SuperSafe (Note 45) | | | | | | | | | | |
| — Capital Stable | 10 | 11.6 | 11.9 | n/a | 4.0% | Note 45 | 1.2% | U/N | 5,000 | Yes |
| Sun Alliance — Cash Guaranteed | 24 | 12.4 | 11.8 | 12.7 | 5.0% | Nil | 1.2% | U/Y | Note 46 | Yes |
| — Fixed Interest | 4 | 10.6 | n/a | n/a | 5.0% | Nil | 1.2% | U/N | Note 46 | Yes |
| Suncorp — Capital Guaranteed | 119 | 13.8 | 14.3 | 14.8 | Note 47 | $22 | Nil | N/Y | 2,000 | Yes |
| Tyndall Life — SERIES I — Capital Gtd. | 35 | 11.2 | 11.9 | 13.8 | 5.0% | Nil | 1.2% | U/Y | 1,000 | Yes |
| (Note 48) — SERIES II — Capital Gtd. | <1 | n/a | n/a | n/a | 5.0% | Nil | 1.2% | U/Y | 1,000 | Yes |
| Westpac — Cap. Gtd. Rollover | 3 | n/a | n/a | n/a | Nil | Note 50 | 1.5% | U/Y | 10,000 | Yes |
| Zurich — Capital Guaranteed | n/p | 12.1 | 13.8 | 14.8 | 5.0% | Nil | 1.2% | N/Y | 2,000 | Yes |
| **Total** | **4,862** | | | | | | | | | |

### TABLE 2 — DEFERRED ANNUITIES

#### Group 2: Equity Type Investments

| | Size of Fund at 31/7/89 $M | Yields for periods ended 31 July 1989 (net of all ongoing fees) | | | Entry Fee | Exit Fee | Annual Fee | Unit Linked/ Capital Gteed | Minimum Invest $ | Pres. Fac. |
|---|---|---|---|---|---|---|---|---|---|---|
| | | 1 year %(p.a.) | 2 years %(p.a.) | 3 years %(p.a.) | | | | | | |
| Adriatic — Managed Invest. — Linked "Series B" | n/p | 11.3 | n/a | n/a | 5.0% | Nil | 1.6% | U/N | 2,500 | No |
| AETNA — Squirrel | 2 | 7.4 | 9.7 | n/a | Note 2 | Note 2 | 1.26% | U/N | 2,000 | No |
| — Bear | 2 | 8.4 | 8.9 | n/a | Note 2 | Note 2 | 1.44% | U/N | 2,000 | No |
| — Beaver | 2 | 5.2 | - 1.2 | n/a | Note 2 | Note 2 | 1.62% | U/N | 2,000 | No |
| — Bull | <1 | 2.1 | - 6.7 | n/a | Note 2 | Note 2 | 1.74% | U/N | 2,000 | No |
| — Stag | n/a | - 6.6 | -32.1 | n/a | Note 2 | Note 2 | 1.92% | U/N | 2,000 | No |
| AFT — BOAB | 2 | 9.6 | - 9.0 | n/a | 5.8% | Nil | 1.5% | U/N | 1,000 | No |

| | | | | | | | | | | |
|---|---|---|---|---|---|---|---|---|---|---|
| AMEV Life — Managed | 1 | 6.3 | n/a | n/a | 6.0% | Note 3 | 1.2% | U/N | Note 3 | Yes |
| — Share Market | <1 | 11.0 | n/a | n/a | 6.0% | Note 3 | 1.2% | U/N | Note 3 | Yes |
| — Property | <1 | 3.0 | n/a | n/a | 6.0% | Note 3 | 1.2% | U/N | Note 3 | Yes |
| AMP (Note 4) — Inv. Linked | | | | | | | | | | |
| — Balanced | 328 | 16.1 | 7.3 | 13.8 | 5.0% | Nil | $17.52+1.32% | U/N | 5,000 | Yes |
| — Broadly Based | 13 | 15.4 | 3.9 | 13.0 | 5.0% | Nil | $17.52+1.32% | U/N | 5,000 | Yes |
| — Equity Based | 57 | 17.2 | -0.3 | 11.2 | 5.0% | Nil | $17.52+1.32% | U/N | 5,000 | Yes |
| — Property | 132 | 21.5 | 22.9 | 22.1 | 5.0% | Nil | $17.52+1.32% | U/N | 5,000 | Yes |
| — Australian Equity | 3 | 13.3 | -1.2 | 20.0 | 5.0% | Nil | $17.52+1.32% | U/N | 5,000 | Yes |
| — International | <1 | 21.7 | -1.9 | 1.4 | 5.0% | Nil | $17.52+1.5% | U/N | 5,000 | Yes |
| — Cash Based | <1 | 12.8 | n/a | n/a | 5.0% | Nil | $17.52+1.32% | U/N | 5,000 | Yes |
| ANZ Life — Managed | 30 | 8.1 | 0.4 | 11.6 | 5.0% | Nil | 1.5% | U/N | 1,000 | Yes |
| Australian Eagle — Linked | n/p | 8.6 | -1.2 | 9.7 | $60+5.0% | Note 8 | 1.3% | U/N | 2,500 | No |
| Capita | n/p | 9.0 | -5.5 | 10.2 | Note 11 | Note 15 | 0.72% | U/N | 2,000 | Yes |
| Colonial Mutual — Superbridge | 11 | 4.6 | -8.3 | 5.0 | 5.0% | Nil | 1.2% | U/N | 5,000 | Yes |
| Equity Life — Managed | 38 | 8.0 | -3.7 | 12.7 | 5.0% | Nil | 1.3% | U/Y | 1,000 | Yes |
| FAI — Performance (Note 20) | 12 | 7.5 | 2.4 | 15.6 | Note 20 | Nil | 1.2% | U/N | 1,000 | No |
| Friends Provident — Cash | 11 | 12.5 | 11.6 | 13.0 | 5.0% | Nil | 1.2% | U/N | 1,000 | Yes |
| — Ethical | 5 | 6.3 | -7.8 | n/a | 5.0% | Nil | 1.2% | U/N | 1,000 | Yes |
| — Cap. Accumulation | 25 | 8.7 | 10.9 | n/a | 5.0% | Nil | 1.2% | U/N | 1,000 | Yes |
| — Property Plus | 4 | 2.5 | -8.0 | n/a | 5.0% | Nil | 1.2% | U/N | 1,000 | Yes |
| — Mixed | 50 | 8.6 | -8.2 | 8.0 | 5.0% | Nil | 1.2% | U/N | 1,000 | Yes |
| — International | 34 | 24.2 | 2.1 | 5.3 | 5.0% | Nil | 1.2% | U/N | 1,000 | Yes |
| — Multibond Capital | 6 | 10.3 | n/a | n/a | 6.0% | Nil | 1.5% | U/N | 1,000 | Yes |
| — Multibond Managed | 2 | 9.2 | n/a | n/a | 6.0% | Nil | 1.5% | U/N | 1,000 | Yes |
| GIO (NSW) — O Unit | 127 | 8.8 | 0.1 | 20.4 | Note 21 | 2.0% | $32+0.6% | U/N | Note 21 | Yes |
| — L Unit | 297 | 10.7 | 17.0 | 17.9 | Note 21 | 2.0% | $32+0.6% | U/N | Note 21 | Yes |
| — G Unit | 109 | 10.8 | 11.8 | 15.2 | Note 21 | 1.0% | $32+0.6% | U/N | Note 21 | Yes |
| — I Unit | 58 | 7.9 | 11.2 | 13.4 | Note 21 | 1.0% | $32+0.6% | U/N | Note 21 | Yes |
| — F Unit | 1 | 26.3 | n/a | n/a | Note 21 | 2.0% | $32+0.1% | U/N | Note 21 | Yes |
| Guardian — Managed | 32 | 5.1 | -17.2 | 12.3 | Note 24 | Nil | 1.3% | U/N | 2,500 | No |
| — Equity | 2 | -2.8 | -25.2 | 2.6 | Note 24 | Nil | 1.3% | U/N | 2,500 | No |
| IFMA (Lumley) — Managed | <1 | 3.9 | n/a | n/a | 5.0% | Nil | 1.2% | U/N | 2,000 | Yes |
| Inlife — Linked | 14 | 16.1 | -5.1 | 8.7 | Note 26 | Nil | 1.5% | U/N | 2,000 | No |
| IOOF — Managed | n/a | n/a | n/a | n/a | Nil | Note 27 | 1.25% | U/N | 500 | Yes |
| Legal & General — Managed | 202 | 8.0 | -7.0 | 10.4 | 5.0% | Nil | 1.5% | U/N | 1,000 | Yes |
| — International | 13 | 26.4 | 3.5 | 6.1 | 5.0% | Nil | 1.5% | U/N | 1,000 | Yes |
| Lumley Life — Growth | 2 | -1.6 | 34.0 | n/a | 5.0% | Nil | 1.2% | U/N | 2,000 | Yes |
| — Managed Flexibond | <1 | 1.0 | n/a | n/a | 5.0% | Nil | 1.2% | U/N | 3,000 | Yes |
| Mercantile Mutual — Man. Growth | 2 | n/a | n/a | n/a | Note 30 | Nil | 1.5% | U/N | 1,000 | Yes |
| MLC Life — Balanced | 18 | 10.6 | 0.5 | n/a | Note 31 | Note 31 | 1.32% | U/N | 3,000 | No |
| — Growth | 1 | 18.0 | -4.7 | n/a | Note 31 | Note 31 | 1.32% | U/N | 3,000 | No |
| — Equity | <1 | 10.7 | -7.3 | n/a | Note 31 | Note 31 | 1.32% | U/N | 3,000 | No |
| — International Equity | <1 | 29.3 | -0.2 | n/a | Note 31 | Note 31 | 1.32% | U/N | 3,000 | No |
| — Share Index | 1 | 6.0 | -6.7 | n/a | Note 31 | Note 31 | 1.32% | U/N | 3,000 | No |
| — Property | 1 | 2.0 | -4.4 | n/a | Note 31 | Note 31 | 1.32% | U/N | 3,000 | No |
| — Interest Bearing Securities | 1 | 6.2 | 9.4 | n/a | Note 31 | Note 31 | 1.32% | U/N | 3,000 | No |
| Five Star Investment | | | | | | | | | | |
| — Balanced | 9 | n/a | n/a | n/a | Nil | Note 31 | 1.8% | U/N | 3,000 | Yes |
| — Growth | <1 | n/a | n/a | n/a | Nil | Note 31 | 1.8% | U/N | 3,000 | Yes |
| — Equity | <1 | n/a | n/a | n/a | Nil | Note 31 | 1.8% | U/N | 3,000 | Yes |
| — International Equity | <1 | n/a | n/a | n/a | Nil | Note 31 | 1.8% | U/N | 3,000 | Yes |
| — Share Index | 2 | n/a | n/a | n/a | Nil | Note 31 | 1.8% | U/N | 3,000 | Yes |
| — Property | <1 | n/a | n/a | n/a | Nil | Note 31 | 1.8% | U/N | 3,000 | Yes |
| — Interest Bearing Securities | 1 | n/a | n/a | n/a | Nil | Note 31 | 1.8% | U/N | 3,000 | Yes |
| National Australia — Growth | <1 | 7.3 | n/a | n/a | Closed | n/p | n/p | U/N | Closed | No |
| — Equity | 1 | 5.9 | n/a | n/a | Nil | n/p | n/p | U/N | 500 | Yes |
| — International | <1 | 31.8 | n/a | n/a | Nil | n/p | n/p | U/N | 500 | Yes |
| — Managed | 8 | 9.1 | n/a | n/a | Nil | n/p | n/p | U/N | 500 | Yes |
| — Property | 6 | -2.2 | n/a | n/a | Nil | n/p | n/p | U/N | 500 | Yes |
| National Mutual | | | | | | | | | | |
| — Superguard Plus Managed | 146 | 12.4 | 5.8 | 16.7 | 5.0% | Nil | 1.35% | U/N | 3,000 | Yes |
| Norwich — Managed (Note 34) | 91 | 9.3 | -1.0 | 10.9 | 5.0% | Nil | 1.6% | U/N | 2,000 | Yes |
| — Growth (Note 34) | 26 | 10.3 | 0.5 | 12.6 | 5.0% | Nil | 1.6% | U/N | 2,000 | Yes |
| NRMA — Managed | 27 | 19.8 | n/a | n/a | Note 35 | Note 35 | 1.2% | U/N | 1,000 | Yes |
| NZI Life — Inv. Linked — Australian | 5 | 9.1 | 55.2 | n/a | 5.0% | 1.0% | 1.4% | U/N | 2,000 | Yes |
| — International | <1 | 19.6 | 27.9 | n/a | Closed | 1.0% | 1.4% | U/N | Closed | Yes |
| Occidental — Managed | 39 | 14.2 | n/a | n/a | 5.0% | Nil | 1.9% | U/N | Note 37 | Yes |
| Prudential — Linked | 44 | 13.8 | 0.6 | n/a | Note 41 | Nil | 1.2% | U/N | 2,000 | No |
| Scottish Amicable Life | n/p | 10.2 | -6.1 | 8.0 | Note 43 | 3.0% | 1.2% | U/N | Note 43 | Yes |
| State Bank (Vic) — SuperSafe (Note 43) | | | | | | | | | | |
| — Growth | 4 | 8.1 | -10.9 | n/a | 4.0% | Note 45 | 1.2% | U/N | 5,000 | Yes |
| Sun Alliance — Growth | 72 | 9.3 | -3.4 | 10.4 | 5.0% | Nil | 1.2% | U/N | Note 46 | Yes |
| — Managed | 59 | 9.3 | 1.0 | 11.4 | 5.0% | Nil | 1.2% | U/N | Note 46 | Yes |
| Suncorp — Linked | 6 | 7.3 | 2.9 | 11.8 | Note 47 | $22 | 0.65% | U/N | 2,000 | Yes |
| Tyndall Life — SERIES I — Equity | 13 | -16.6 | -43.2 | -17.1 | 5.0% | Nil | 1.2% | U/N | 1,000 | Yes |
| (Note 48) — Managed | 27 | -2.8 | -28.1 | -6.3 | 5.0% | Nil | 1.2% | U/N | 1,000 | Yes |
| — International | 16 | 0.5 | -19.7 | -6.2 | 5.0% | Nil | 1.2% | U/N | 1,000 | Yes |
| SERIES II — Equity | 8 | -29.6 | -40.6 | n/a | 5.0% | Nil | 1.2% | U/N | 1,000 | Yes |
| — Managed | 23 | -5.9 | -18.8 | n/a | 5.0% | Nil | 1.2% | U/N | 1,000 | Yes |
| — International | 10 | 6.5 | -10.9 | n/a | 5.0% | Nil | 1.2% | U/N | 1,000 | Yes |
| — Optimum | 22 | 7.3 | 2.1 | n/a | 5.0% | Nil | 1.2% | U/N | 1,000 | Yes |
| — Gold | <1 | n/a | n/a | n/a | 5.0% | Nil | 1.2% | U/N | 1,000 | Yes |
| — Property | <1 | n/a | n/a | n/a | 5.0% | Nil | 1.2% | U/N | 1,000 | Yes |
| Westpac — Balance Growth Rollover | 1 | n/a | n/a | n/a | Nil | Note 50 | 1.5% | U/Y | 10,000 | Yes |
| Zurich — Managed | 101 | 14.9 | -0.5 | 11.3 | 3.0% | 3.0% | 1.3% | U/N | 2,000 | Yes |
| — Equity | 11 | 18.5 | -6.5 | 10.1 | 3.0% | 3.0% | 1.3% | U/N | 2,000 | Yes |
| — Fixed Interest | 3 | 9.6 | 2.5 | 8.5 | 3.0% | 3.0% | 1.3% | U/N | 2,000 | Yes |

| | | | | | | | | | | |
|---|---|---|---|---|---|---|---|---|---|---|
| — Public Securities | 4 | 10.2 | 17.5 | 17.6 | 3.0% | 3.0% | 1.3% | U/N | 2,000 | Yes |
| — Property | 1 | 8.1 | 5.5 | 10.0 | 3.0% | 3.0% | 1.3% | U/N | 2,000 | Yes |
| Total | 2,455 | | | | | | | | | |
| Total DAFs | 7,317 | | | | | | | | | |

## EXPLANATION OF HEADINGS IN TABLES 1 AND 2

**Investment Medium:** The ADFs and DAFs have been divided into two Groups:-
- Group 1 "Capital Stable Investments" consist of those products which give a high priority to the maintenance of capital values. Some products in this group consist only in fixed interest securities e.g., Government securities, debentures, mortgages, etc., whereas others including some of the life offices products, invest in a wider range of assets but smooth the investment return and give a capital guarantee.
- Group 2 "Equity Type Investments" can invest in equity type assets such as shares, property, etc., as well as fixed interest securities. The division into two groups does not indicate how actively an investment policy is being pursued by managers.

**Size of Fund:** This column shows the size to the nearest million dollars. Where several products are invested in one fund, as with most life offices, the size shown relates only to the product described.

**Net Investment Return:**
- The columns for ADFs (Table 1) indicate the percentage yields of $10,000 invested for 3 months, 1 year and 2 years to 31 July 1989.
- The columns for DAFs (Table 2) indicate the percentage yields of $10,000 invested for 1 year, 2 years and 3 years to 31 July 1989.

The returns for ADFs and DAFs are calculated "net of all ongoing fees" — ie they represent the return to the fund manager after annual fees are deducted, but without any deduction for entry or exit fees.
Returns are also net of the 15% Investment tax as from 1 July 1988.
Returns for 2 and 3 years periods are expressed as equivalent annual rates of return.

THE PERCENTAGE YIELDS SET OUT IN TABLES 1 (ADFs) AND 2 (DAFs) MAY NOT PROVIDE A RELIABLE GUIDE TO FUTURE YIELDS THAT WILL BE ACHIEVED.

**Fees:**
- Three columns set out the amount charged:
  1. to enter the Fund
  2. to leave the Fund
  3. the annual charge whilst in the Fund.

Fees quoted as a percentage are calculated on the assets invested in the Fund. Further,
- Some Funds (e.g. AMP, CML, Capital Building Society, NMLA) declare an investment return and the Manager is entitled to any return in excess of the declared rate. This is shown as "Excess" in the Table.
- Certain ADF Trust Deeds allow the Manager to charge higher fees than is currently charged. In such cases the fees shown in the table are what the Manager is currently charging.
- Some ADFs use an associated investment product run by their Manager. There may also be expenses applying to the associated investment product.
- Some Funds impose additional fees for brokerage and stamp duty.

**Capital Guaranteed:** This column indicates if the investment is guaranteed or not. Different managers use a variety of definitions of the amount they guarantee including:
- the amount invested in the Fund,
- the amount invested less fees,
- the amount invested plus declared investment return, and
- the amount invested plus part of the declared investment return.

Some ADFs (National Credit Union, Farmers Trustee and Sandhurst Trustee) are not capital guaranteed but only invest in authorised Trustee Investments.

**Preservation Facilities:** This column indicates if the Manager can provide preservation facilities, not necessarily in the fund indicated. Those interested should contact the respective Managers for further details.

### TOTAL FUNDS OF $200m AND OVER

| Manager | ADFs Stable $m | ADFs Equity $m | ADFs Total $m | DAFs Stable $m | DAFs Equity $m | DAFs Total $m | Total ADFs & DAFs $m | % of Grand Total of $13.402m |
|---|---|---|---|---|---|---|---|---|
| National Mutual | 13 | — | 13 | 1,610 | 146 | 1,751 | 1,769 | 13.2 |
| AMP | 189 | — | 189 | 671 | 535 | 1,206 | 1,395 | 10.4 |
| Commonwealth Bank | 1,320 | — | 1,320 | — | — | — | 1,320 | 9.9 |
| GIO — NSW | 16 | — | 16 | 245 | 592 | 837 | 853 | 6.4 |
| State Bank — Vic. | 794 | 23 | 817 | 10 | 4 | 14 | 831 | 6.2 |
| ANZ Bank | 542 | 125 | 667 | — | — | — | 667 | 5.0 |
| BT | 168 | 476 | 644 | — | — | — | 644 | 4.8 |
| Westpac Bank | 400 | 134 | 534 | 3 | 1 | 4 | 538 | 4.0 |
| Mercantile Mutual | — | — | — | 527 | 2 | 529 | 529 | 4.0 |
| Legal & General | — | — | — | 312 | 215 | 527 | 527 | 3.9 |
| Norwich | 20 | 18 | 38 | 190 | 117 | 307 | 345 | 2.6 |
| Macquarie Bank | 225 | 51 | 276 | 1 | — | 1 | 277 | 2.1 |
| Colonial Mutual | 5 | — | 5 | 246 | 11 | 257 | 262 | 2.0 |
| National Credit Union | 178 | 43 | 221 | · 25 | — | 25 | 246 | 1.8 |
| State Bank — NSW | 194 | 6 | 200 | — | — | — | 200 | 1.5 |

## NOTES TO TABLES 1 AND 2

THE YIELDS INDICATED IN THE TABLES ARE INTENDED TO PROVIDE A GUIDE TO THE RELATIVE INVESTMENT PERFORMANCE OF THE VARIOUS MANAGERS. THE FIGURES ARE BASED ON AN INVESTMENT OF $10,000 AFTER PAYMENT OF ANY INITIAL FEES AND ARE NET OF ALL ONGOING FEES.

| | | | |
|---|---|---|---|
| n/a: Not Applicable | n/p: Not Provided | U: Unit Linked | N: Not Unit Linked |
| Y : Fund is "capital guaranteed" | N : Fund is not "capital guaranteed" | | |

Note 1: ADVANCE — Funds may be switched at any time. Switching during the first twelve months from "Capital" to "Growth" a fee of 5.0% is payable. No fee is payable if switching after twelve months.
"Capital" — The exit fee is 2.0% within the first 12 months and Nil after twelve months.

Note 2: AETNA — Managed "Capital" "Squirrel" "Bear" "Beaver" "Bull" "Stag" — The entry fee is 5.0% plus $75 up to $50,000 for initial investments but only the 5.0% fee is applicable to additional deposits or fund switches on the same contract. A fee of 1.0% with a minimum charge of $50 is applicable when more than one switch in a year is involved.
The minimum investment, initial or balance, is $2,000. The minimum per fund is $1,000. The minimum additional investment is $1,000.

Note 3: AMEV Life — Funds may be switched at any time. The first switch is free, subsequent switches are subject to a fee of $20 or 1.0% of the value switched, whichever is greater.
The minimum investment, initial or balance, is $2,000 and the minimum additional investment is $1,000.
The first withdrawal in any one year is free and subsequent withdrawals are subject to a $25 exit fee.

Note 4: AMP — The entry fee is for amounts up to $100,000. For larger amounts the rate is reduced.
DAF "Capital Secure" — The exit fee for the first year is 3.0%, for the second year is 1.5% and Nil after two years.

Note 5: ANZ BANK — Although the exit fee is Nil, $30 may be charged upon the second and any subsequent redemption made within a 12 month period.
The minimum investment of $1,000 may be in one fund or spread between "Income"and "Growth".
"Maxi Safe" — The fund guarantees the return of investors' capital and a predetermined rate of interest for the full term of the investment from one to five years.

Note 6: ANZ LIFE — A fee of 0.5% is charged when switching between funds.
"Capital Stable" — The unit price is guaranteed never to fall.

Note 7: APFS (Telecom) — The exit fee is $75 in the first twelve months and Nil after the first twelve months.
The annual fee is 1.7% reducing progressively to 0.5% in year six and thereafter.

Note 8: AUSTRALIAN EAGLE — The exit fee for total withdrawal or one partial withdrawal per calendar year is Nil and $60 for each additional withdrawal. The minimum investment balance is $500.

Note 9: AUSTRALIAN FUNDS — "Capital Maintenance" and "Growth" — are now closed to new applications and have been superceded by the new ADF, an umbrella trust offering seven individual investment options

Note 10: AUST-WIDE — The investment may be switched from one fund to the other at minimal or no cost.

Note 11: BARCLAYS — The initial minimum investment is $1,000 and $500 thereafter. Investors may convert their investment from one fund to the other at a charge of 3.5% from the "High Income" Fund to the "Growth" Fund.

Note 12: BMA — The annual fee is $42.60, subject to annual CPI increase. The minimum initial investment is $1,000 and the minimum additional investment is $500.

Note 13: BRICK SECURITIES — No exit fee is charged after two months from creation of the Unit. An exit fee of 2.0% is charged within the first two months. Investment may be split between the two funds. Switching from "Capital Maintenance" to "Growth" a fee of 1.0% is charged but no fee is charged for switching in reverse.

Note 14: BT — The minimum initial investment is $5,000 and the minimum additional investment is $1,000.

Note 15: CAPITA — DAF — The entry fee is 5.0% with reduced rates for amounts over $100,000, plus up to $100 for amounts less than $10,000. The exit fee is Nil for the first withdrawal in any calendar year and $25 for each subsequent withdrawal.

Note 16: CITICORP — Capital and return are guaranteed for up to 5 years. Current rate, guaranteed in advance, for 3, 4 or 5 years is 13.3%.

Note 17: CLAYTON ROBARD — Funds may be switched to any of the Tyndall Life Series II Funds at a fee of 1.0%. Tyndall Life is a wholly owned subsidiary of the Clayton Robard Group.

Note 18: COLONIAL MUTUAL — "Superspan II" — The exit fee ranges from 5.0% of the amount withdrawn during the first year to Nil in the fifth year and thereafter.

Note 19: COUNTY NATWEST — The management fee is one twelfth of 1.25% of the value of the fund on the last day of each month and is payable monthly.

Note 20: FAI — "Stable" and "Performance" — The entry fee is 5.0% up to $40,000 and 4.0% for $40,000 or more. Incentive Performance fee — when during a financial year the percentage growth in the unit exceeds one and a half times the "Ten Year Commonwealth Bond" rate a fee of 25.0% of the excess is charged.

Note 21: GIO (NSW) — The entry fee on initial and additional deposits, during any twelve months, is 4.0% of the first $10,000 with reduced rates for larger amounts.
The minimum initial investment is $500 and $100 for additional investments, with the exception of Cash ADF which is $1,000.
The minimum withdrawal is $500 with at least $1,000 worth of units remaining in the account.

Note 22: GROSVENOR PIRIE — "Income" — The management fee is 0.075% of the average value of the fund for each month. The Trustee Fee is 0.008333% of the value of the fund at the end of each month.
"Equity" — The manager's fee is 0.125% of the average value of the fund for each month. The Trustee Fee is 0.01333% of the value at the end of each month plus 1.25% of the Cash Produce of the fund at the end of each financial year.
Units may be switched from "Income" to "Equity" or vice versa. No fees are charged for the switching.

Note 23: GROWTH EQUITIES — Switching from "Income" to "Managed" or "Property" can be effected, at the current value of a unit at each fund, as at the end of each weekly "accrual period". A once only service fee of 3.5% of the amount switched from the "Income" to "Managed" or "Property" is payable but there is no fee when switching from "Managed" or "Property" to "Income".
The annual fee for all Funds is 0.5% plus 7.5% of the net return.
The "Property" Fund is aimed at an investment in bricks and mortar (50.0%-60.0%), listed properties (10.0%-20.0%) and liquids (balance). Investment returns do not include capital growth in physical property. (Additional units are issued to investors.) Unit prices do not include issue of additional units for property revaluation.

Note 24: GUARDIAN — "Managed" "Equity" "Fixed Interest" "Cash". The entry fee is $100 plus up to 5.0%.

Note 25: HAMBROS — Investments can be made in any combination of funds subject to a total minimum investment of $2,000 and $1,000 in any chosen fund. Presently there is no fee charged on switching unless from the Capital Security fund in which case a fee of 3.5% will apply.

Note 26: INLIFE — "Unit Linked" and "Capital Guaranteed" — No initial fee is charged but a 1.5% p.a. establishment fee is charged for the first four years.

Note 27: IOOF — DAF "Capital Guaranteed" and "Managed" — The exit fee before one year is 4.0% and reduces by 0.5% every 6 months to Nil after 54 months.

Note 28: LUMLEY LIFE — "Capital Guaranteed" — On withdrawal, a depositor will receive no less than the initial amount invested, less fees plus credited interest. No fee is charged on the first four withdrawals in each of the first two years. Thereafter the first two withdrawals in the year are free of charge. Withdrawals in excess of these limits are subject to $25 each.

Note 29: MACQUARIE BANK — "Personal" — A separate ADF is set up for each individual with investments being chosen by the individual. Each ADF achieves a different return.
"Deposit" "Balanced" "Property" — The minimum deposit for all 3 funds together is $5,000 and $2,000 in each fund.

Note 30: MERCANTILE MUTUAL — The entry fee is 4.5% plus $30 if ETP is less than $5,000 with reduced fees for larger amounts. Minimum withdrawal is $1,000 or account balance (whichever is the lesser).

Note 31: MLC LIFE — The entry fee is 5.0% for investments less than $50,000, for larger amounts the rate is reduced. An additional fee of $36 is payable for deposits less than $10,000. The exit fee is Nil for total withdrawal and for the first withdrawal each twelve months, otherwise $25. The annual management fee is 1.32% p.a./0.11% p.m. A single switching fee of $30 is payable regardless of the number of investment options switched at any one time.
"Capital Guaranteed Roll-Over" — The exit fee after three years is Nil. For fees up to three years refer Manager's brochure. The minimum additional investment is $2,500.
"Five Star Investment Roll-over" — The exit fee after five years is Nil. For fees up to five years refer Manager's brochure. The minimum additional investment is $1,000.

Note 32: NATIONAL AUSTRALIA — ADF "Income" and "Investment" NOW CLOSED TO NEW INVESTORS.
DAF "Cash (Old & New)", "Group Deposits", "Fixed Interest" and "Growth" NOW CLOSED TO NEW INVESTORS.

Note 33: NATIONAL CREDIT UNION — DAF — "Capital Guaranteed" — The exit fee is 5.0% for the first year, 4.0% for the second year, 3.0% for the third year and Nil after three years.

Note 34: NORWICH — DAF — Figures quoted are based on full entry fee option, a Nil entry fee option is also available.
"Managed" "Growth" — These funds become capital guaranteed after deferral period.

Note 35: NRMA — The entry fee for the "Capital Secure" is 2.5% of the first $10,000 with reduced rates for larger amounts and for the "Managed" 3.0% of the first $50,000 with reduced rates for larger amounts.
The exit fee, for both funds, is 1.0% in the first twelve months and Nil thereafter.

Note 36: NZI Life — "Capital Guaranteed" — The entry fee for initial investments up to $100,000 is 6.0% plus $40 with reduced rates for larger amounts and for subsequent investments 6.0%. The minimum initial investment is $2,000 and for subsequent investments $1,000.
On transfers or withdrawals within the first five years the income credited will be reduced to reflect a rate of 1.5% lower than the actual rate declared for each year. However, this does not apply to partial withdrawals which in any twelve month period, does not exceed 20.0% of the amounts deposited.

Note 37: OCCIDENTAL — The minimum initial investment is $3,000 with minimum subsequent deposits of $1,000.

Note 38: OST — The annual fee is 0.3 of 1.0% of the balance of the fund.

Note 39: OVER 50's FRIENDLY SOCIETY (The) — The entry fee for the ADF is 3.5% for the first $100,000 and 3.0% on any excess over $100,000.

Note 40: PERPETUAL TRUSTEES — "High Income" — The exit fee is Nil except when there are more than four withdrawals in any one year, a fee of $50 for each additional withdrawal may be charged.
"Personal" — The exit fee is Nil except when there are more than four withdrawals or investment transactions exceeding twenty in any one year. A separate ADF is set up for each individual with investments being chosen by the individual. Each ADF achieves a different return.

Note 41: PRUDENTIAL — "Capital" "Linked" — The entry fee is 5.0% of $50,000 plus 4.75% of the balance.
Gold Seal Linked contracts up to 31 October 1986 were invested in the No. 3 Fund. As from 1 November 1986 Gold Seal Linked contracts have been invested in the No. 5 Fund. Performance information for No. 3 Fund is available from the Prudential.

Note 42: R & I — The details, excluding the yields, recorded apply also to the Fixed Interest-Fixed Term Option which guarantees a predetermined rate of interest for periods from 3 to 96 months.

Note 43: SCOTTISH AMICABLE LIFE — The entry fee is 2.9% for amounts up to $100,000 with reduced rates for larger amounts. The minimum initial investment is $2,000 and $1,000 for subsequent additional investments.

Note 44: SGIC (SA) — The entry fee is 1.5% of the first $50,000 and 0.5% of any balance.
The exit fee is Nil except when there is more than one withdrawal in any six month period, a fee of $50 for each additional withdrawal may be charged.
The current yields are based on an interim interest rate. Actual interest rates are declared annually at 30 June when the investment results are known.

Note 45: STATE BANK (VIC) — "Growth" — The exit fee for the ADF and DAF is 1.5% in the first twelve months or $25 whichever is the greater, 1.0% in the twelve to twenty-four months following or $25 whichever is the greater and after twenty-four months $25.
"Capital Stable" — The exit fee for the DAF is $25 in the first three months of lodgement and Nil after three months. The DAF is operated in conjunction with the Australian American Assurance Co. Ltd.

Note 46: SUN ALLIANCE — The minimum investment is $2,000 with a minimum of $1,000 in any one fund.

Note 47: SUNCORP — The entry fee is 5.0% of the first $10,000, 2.0% of the next $40,000 and 1.0% of the balance in excess of $50,000.

Note 48: TYNDALL LIFE — Funds may be switched at any time with a fee of 1.0% of the value of the units being switched.

Note 49: WERE, J B — Units may be switched from "Growth" to "Income" or vice versa at any time. Switching from "Income" to "Growth" will attract a 2.0% Service Fee. The minimum amount that may be switched is $10,000.

Note 50: WESTPAC BANK — ADFs — The exit fee is Nil except where more than one request is received within any three month period when the fee of 3.0% applies.
DAFs — The exit fee is 3.0% in the first two years and Nil thereafter.

## ADDITIONAL FEATURES OF ADFs AND DAFs

**Minimum Withdrawals:** The minimum withdrawals are equivalent to the minimum investments in Tables 1 and 2, except for:-
- AETNA DAF $1,000
- AMEV Life DAF $1,000
- AMP ADF $500
- AUSTRALIAN EAGLE DAF $500
- CAPITA ADF and DAF $500
- COMMONWEALTH BANK ADF $1,000
- GIO (NSW) ADF and DAF $500
- MLC LIFE DAF $500. Capital Guaranteed Roll-Over $1,000. Five Star Investment Roll-over DAFs $1,000.
- NATIONAL AUSTRALIA ADF Nil
- NATIONAL MUTUAL ADF Bankguard $500, ADF Supermanager $1,000, DAFs $500
- REI BUILDING SOCIETY ADF $500
- STATE BANK (SA) SuperFlex ADF $1,000, SuperGrowth ADF $2000
- SUN ALLIANCE DAF $1,000
- SUNCORP DAF Nil
- TRUST ADF Nil
- WARDLEY ADF $1,000
- ZURICH DAF $500

## ANNUITIES PAYABLE IMMEDIATELY

The following Tables show the immediate annuities payable per annum for a purchase price of $50,000. The figures quoted are net of all fees (including commission), levied by Life Offices. However, in some States an additional amount for Stamp Duty may be payable when the annuity is purchased. Annuities are payable at the end of each month. Figures are quoted as at 1 August 1989.

(SEE NOTES AFTER TABLE 6 FOR EXPLANATION OF EACH TYPE OF ANNUITY)

### TABLE 3 — IMMEDIATE ANNUITIES WITH NO GUARANTEE AND TEN YEAR GUARANTEE

| | Single Life | | | | Last Survivor (2/3 annuity payable to survivor)[3] | | | |
| | No Guarantee[1] | | 10 year Guarantee[2] | | No Guarantee[1] | | 10 year Guarantee[2] | |
| Company | Male 65 | Female 60 | Male 65 | Female 60 | Male 65 | Female 62 | Male 65 | Female 62 |
|---|---|---|---|---|---|---|---|---|
| | $p.a. | $p.a. | $p.a. | $p.a. | $p.a. | | $p.a. | |
| AETNA | 8,291 | 7,206 | 7,567 | 7,019 | 7,483 | | 7,181 | |
| AMP | 8,415 | 7,222 | 7,710 | 7,050 | 7,440 | | 7,179 | |
| ANZ Life | 7,872 | 6,804 | 7,212 | 6,648 | 7,080 | | 6,816 | |
| Capita | 8,112 | 7,056 | 7,512 | 6,912 | 7,320 | | 7,080 | |
| Colonial Mutual | 8,413 | 7,386 | 7,786 | 7,223 | 7,508 | | 7,311 | |
| Friends Provident | 8,143 | 7,086 | 7,479 | 6,925 | 7,358 | | 7,089 | |
| GIO (NSW) | 7,692 | 6,492 | 7,020 | 6,336 | 6,804 | | 6,540 | |
| Legal & General | 8,201 | 7,134 | 7,537 | 6,974 | 7,411 | | 7,139 | |
| Mercantile Mutual | 8,602 | 7,482 | 7,889 | 7,304 | 7,771 | | 7,476 | |
| MLC Life | 8,112 | 7,009 | 7,443 | 6,848 | 7,295 | | 7,025 | |
| National Mutual | 8,465 | 7,313 | 7,769 | 7,133 | 7,577 | | 7,289 | |
| Norwich | 8,177 | 7,102 | 7,496 | 6,932 | 7,340 | | 7,059 | |
| Prudential | 8,259 | 7,017 | 7,515 | 6,856 | 7,347 | | 7,057 | |
| Suncorp | 8,586 | 7,422 | 7,868 | 7,188 | 7,698 | | 7,380 | |

### TABLE 4 — IMMEDIATE ANNUITIES WITH BALANCE OF PURCHASE PRICE RETURNED ON DEATH[4]

| | Single Life | | | | Last Survivor (2/3 annuity payable to survivor)[3] | | | |
| Company | Male 65 | Female 60 | Male 60 | Female 55 | Male 65 | Female 62 | Male 60 | Female 57 |
|---|---|---|---|---|---|---|---|---|
| | $p.a. | $p.a. | $p.a. | $p.a. | $p.a. | | $p.a. | |
| AMP | 7,959 | 7,096 | 7,519 | 6,843 | 7,502 | | 7,135 | |
| Friends Provident | 7,701 | 6,963 | 7,320 | 6,773 | 7,331 | | 7,031 | |
| Legal & General | 7,842 | 7,037 | 7,435 | 6,839 | 7,256 | | 6,994 | |
| MLC Life | 7,660 | 6,881 | 7,259 | 6,677 | 7,263 | | 6,946 | |
| National Mutual | 8,009 | 7,181 | 7,589 | 6,941 | n/a | | n/a | |
| Norwich | 7,686 | 6,965 | 7,315 | 6,777 | n/a | | n/a | |

### TABLE 5 — IMMEDIATE ANNUITIES INDEXED AT 5% PER ANNUM[5]

| | Single Life | | | | Last Survivor (2/3 annuity payable to survivor)[3] | | | |
| | No Guarantee[1] | | 10 year Guarantee[2] | | No Guarantee[1] | | 10 year Guarantee[2] | |
| Company | Male 65 | Female 60 | Male 65 | Female 60 | Male 65 | Female 62 | Male 65 | Female 62 |
|---|---|---|---|---|---|---|---|---|
| | $p.a. | $p.a. | $p.a. | $p.a. | $p.a. | | $p.a. | |
| AETNA | 6,351 | 5,196 | 5,788 | 5,066 | 5,501 | | 5,283 | |
| AMP | 6,438 | 5,125 | 5,892 | 5,008 | 5,480 | | 5,281 | |
| ANZ Life | 6,060 | 4,908 | 5,436 | 4,716 | 5,208 | | 4,932 | |
| Capita | 6,336 | 5,088 | 5,760 | 4,932 | 5,412 | | 5,172 | |

| | | | | | | |
|---|---|---|---|---|---|---|
| Colonial Mutual | 6,478 | 5,365 | 5,983 | 5,249 | 5,523 | 5,380 |
| Friends Provident | 6,110 | 5,003 | 5,594 | 4,888 | 5,297 | 5,101 |
| GIO (NSW) | 5,724 | 4,476 | 5,232 | 4,368 | 4,812 | 4,632 |
| Legal & General | 6,155 | 5,034 | 5,641 | 4,918 | 5,330 | 5,136 |
| Mercantile Mutual | 6,430 | 5,229 | 5,889 | 5,109 | 5,550 | 5,345 |
| MLC Life | 6,059 | 4,914 | 5,546 | 4,801 | 5,220 | 5,026 |
| National Mutual | 6,545 | 5,249 | 5,987 | 5,129 | 5,549 | 5,339 |
| Norwich | 6,219 | 5,044 | 5,702 | 4,934 | 5,318 | 5,126 |
| Prudential | 6,175 | 4,880 | 5,600 | 4,768 | 5,232 | 5,024 |
| Suncorp | 6,402 | 5,142 | 5,868 | 4,992 | 5,460 | 5,250 |

### TABLE 6 — IMMEDIATE ANNUITIES INDEXED WITH THE CPI[6]

| | Single Life | | | | Last Survivor (2/3 annuity payable to survivor)[3] | |
|---|---|---|---|---|---|---|
| | No Guarantee[1] | | 10 year Guarantee[2] | | No Guarantee[1] | 10 year Guarantee[2] |
| Company | Male 65 | Female 60 | Male 65 | Female 60 | Male 65   Female 62 | Male 65   Female 62 |
| | $p.a. | $p.a. | $p.a. | $p.a. | $p.a. | $p.a. |
| AETNA | 4,709 | 3,537 | 4,304 | 3,457 | 3,856 | 3,715 |
| AMP | 4,651 | 3,457 | 4,262 | 3,384 | 3,780 | 3,649 |
| Friends Provident | 4,448 | 3,335 | 4,077 | 3,264 | 3,639 | 3,512 |
| National Mutual | 5,021 | 3,677 | 4,601 | 3,599 | 3,995 | 3,851 |
| Norwich | 4,351 | 3,193 | 3,990 | 3,126 | 3,460 | 3,339 |

### NOTES TO TABLES 3 TO 6

n/a: Not available

1. No guarantee — Once the annuitant dies (or both lives die for a last survivor annuity) the annuity ceases to be paid.

2. Ten year guarantee — The initial amount of the annuity is paid for at least ten years and subject to this ceases to be paid on the death of the annuitant (or the death of both lives for the last survivor annuity).

3. In the case of the last survivor annuity two thirds of the amount of the annuity is paid to the surviving life on the death of the first life. However, for an annuity with a ten year guarantee the full amount will be payable until the expiration of the ten year period even if the first life dies during that period.

4. A lump sum payment is made on death of the life (or in the case of a last survivor annuity, on the death of both lives). The lump sum equals the difference between the purchase price and the total of the annuity payments made to the date of death provided the amount is positive.

5. The amount of the annuity increases at the end of each year by 5%. Table 5 shows the initial amount of the annuity payable in the first year.

6. The amount of the annuity increases at the end of each year in line with the Consumer Price Index (National Mutual limits any increase to a maximum of 10.0% a year). Table 6 shows the initial amount of the annuity payable in the first year.

Annuity rates can change frequently and the rates in the Tables 3 to 6 may not be those applicable at the time of purchase.

# Appendix 3

**CASH APPLICATION FORM**

| Stockbroker's Stamp | 🔵 **Telecom Australia** | Date Stamp of Commonwealth Bank/Telecom |
|---|---|---|
| | **BOND ISSUE No. 40–1989** | Date Lodged: / / |

In accordance with the terms of the Prospectus of the above Bond Issue I/we apply for Inscribed Stock as shown hereunder, and I/we undertake to pay in full for the amount of Inscribed Stock applied for or any less amount that may be allotted to me/us in conformity with the terms of the said Prospectus.

| | |
|---|---|
| FULL CHRISTIAN OR GIVEN NAME(S) | SURNAME(S) |
| Mr/Mrs/Miss/Ms | |
| Mr/Mrs/Miss/Ms | |
| Mr/Mrs/Miss/Ms | |
| Mr/Mrs/Miss/Ms | |
| Trustees and unincorporated bodies: Please note Prospectus Terms and Conditions | OCCUPATION |
| ADDRESS | |
| Postcode | TELEPHONE No. (Priv.) / (Bus.) |

*PLEASE USE BLOCK LETTERS*

**OPTIONAL** AGE ☐ under 30 ☐ 31-40 ☐ 41-50 51-60 ☐ 61 +

| TERM | MATURITY | QUARTERLY INTEREST P.A. | HALF YEARLY INTEREST P.A. | COMPOUND ANNUALLY TO MATURITY |
|---|---|---|---|---|
| 2 Years | August 1st, 1991 | 15.00% $ Q1 | 15.50% $ H1 | 16.00% $ C1 |
| 3 Years | August 1st, 1992 | 14.00% $ Q2 | 14.50% $ H2 | 15.00% $ C2 |
| 5 Years | August 1st, 1994 | 13.50% $ Q3 | 14.00% $ H3 | 14.00% $ C3 |

*AMOUNT MUST BE IN MULTIPLES OF $100 (MINIMUM $1,000)*

The sum $_____ being payment ☐ in full OR ☐ of is tendered herewith

A DEPOSIT OF NOT LESS THAN 10% OF TOTAL AMOUNT APPLIED FOR (Balance to be paid on or before August 11th, 1989).

**PLEASE PAY INTEREST AND PRINCIPAL ON REDEMPTION TO THE FOLLOWING ACCOUNT:**

| | |
|---|---|
| Bank/Building Society/Credit Union | |
| Branch Address | Postcode |
| Bank/State/Branch (BSB) No. — | savings ☐ or trading ☐ |
| Account Number | Account Name |

*PLEASE COMPLETE DETAILS FOR PAYMENT OF INTEREST*

Signature of Applicant(s) (Usual signature)

Should this document be signed under Power of Attorney, the grantee of such Power declares that no notice of revocation thereof, by death or otherwise, has been received and that the Power has been/will be forwarded to the Registrar for noting ☐

*PLEASE SIGN*

Date: ...... / ...... /1989

| REGISTRY USE ONLY | |
|---|---|
| DOC. NO. | |
| LODGE DATE | |
| TRANS. CODE | C1 |
| INV. | |
| NAME 1 | |
| 2 | |
| 3 | |
| 4 | |
| I.I. | |
| BR/IHSE | |
| MKT CODE | MSI |
| ENT. | EXAM. |
| CORRES. | MRKG. |
| NEW INV./SIG CARD | |

**LODGEMENT OF APPLICATION** Cheques should be made payable to TELECOM AUSTRALIA and crossed "Not Negotiable".

The application may be lodged at any:
► Commonwealth Bank,
► Member of a recognised Stock Exchange in Australia;

Or complete and mail today to:
**Freepost 18
Telecom Australia Stock Registry,
GPO Box 2867DD Melbourne, Vic 3001**
(No postage stamp required.)

✂ ☐ ✂

Sample application Telecom Bond issue (see page 27)

# Money and Bond Markets

## Authorised Dealers in the short-term money market
Secondary market transactions in Commonwealth Government securities

| | Purchases | | Sales | |
|---|---|---|---|---|
| | Amount $m | Range of yields (%pa) | Amount $m | Range of yields (%pa) |
| **TREASURY BONDS:** | | | | |
| No transactions | – | – | – | – |
| **TREASURY NOTES:** | | | | |
| 36 to 70 days to maturity ...... | 50.0 | 16.90 | 50.0 | 16.88 |
| Total | 50.0 | | 50.0 | |

*Transactions are those arranged for Wednesday; settlement date may vary from this. Buy-back transactions are excluded, as are subscriptions to new issues and redemptions/rediscounts. Yields reflecting non-market influences are excluded from the range shown.

## THE WHOLESALE MARKET

Most trades in government securities are now done off stock exchanges. The most active traders in bonds hold reporting bond dealer status with the Reserve Bank of Australia and must report trades daily to the bank. Here is a summary of yesterday's reporting bond dealer trades:

### Securities of more than one year to maturity

| Stock | pct | Amount $m | Yield range | Weighted av yield |
|---|---|---|---|---|
| Apr 1991 ............. | 12.0% | 22.0 | 15.33-15.58 | 15.41 |
| Mar 1992 ............. | 12.0% | 135.0 | 14.43-14.58 | 14.52 |
| May 1993 ............. | 13.0% | 107.0 | 14.22-14.37 | 14.28 |
| Sep 1994 ............. | 12.5% | 1.0 | 14.03 | 14.03 |
| Apr 1995 ............. | 12.5% | 10.0 | 14.01 | 14.01 |
| Jul 1995 ............. | 13.0% | 25.0 | 14.04-14.08 | 14.06 |
| Nov 1995 ............. | 13.0% | 15.0 | 14.04-14.10 | 14.08 |
| Jul 1996 ............. | 13.0% | 30.0 | 14.00 | 14.00 |
| Oct 1996 ............. | 9.1% | 7.0 | 13.91 | 13.91 |
| Nov 1996 ............. | 12.0% | 20.0 | 14.01 | 14.01 |
| Mar 1997 ............. | 12.5% | 55.0 | 13.81-13.95 | 13.83 |
| Sep 1997 ............. | 12.5% | 41.0 | 13.60-13.70 | 13.64 |
| Jan 1998 ............. | 12.5% | 166.0 | 13.47-13.62 | 13.57 |
| Jul 1999 ............. | 12.0% | 154.0 | 13.38-13.51 | 13.45 |
| May 2000 ............. | 13.0% | 10.0 | 13.50-13.51 | 13.51 |
| Jul 2000 ............. | 13.0% | 59.0 | 13.35-13.46 | 13.41 |
| Dec 2000 ............. | 13.0% | 5.0 | 13.52 | 13.52 |

Transactions are those arranged on 5 July 1989; settlement date may vary from this. Transactions with the Reserve Bank are included. Transactions between reporting dealers are adjusted to avoid double counting. Buy-back transactions, subscriptions to new issues, redemptions and transactions conducted at non-market yields are excluded. (Source: Reserve Bank).

## CASH MANAGEMENT TRUSTS

| | Jul 4 | Jul 5 |
|---|---|---|
| AFT Cash Management Trust ............... | 16.34pc | 16.28pc |
| AFT Govt. Securities Trust. ................... | 16.09pc | 16.04pc |
| Australian Liquid Assets Trust ................ | 16.38pc | 16.39pc |
| Australian Prime Fund ......................... | 16.50pc | 16.50pc |
| Australia Wide Fund .......................... | 16.70pc | 16.70pc |
| BT Hi—Yield Trust ........................... | 17.00pc | NA |
| Capita Cash M'ment Trust .................... | 16.52pc | 16.54pc |
| Hambros Cash Management Trust ............. | 16.69pc | 16.61pc |
| Macquarie Cash Management Trust ........... | 16.64pc | 16.68pc |
| McIntosh Asset Management CMT ........... | 17.01pc | 17.01pc |
| Ordmin Cash Management Trust .............. | 16.43pc | 16.35pc |
| PP Cash Management Trust ................... | 16.64pc | 16.59pc |
| Rothschild's Five Arrows CMT ............... | 17.19pc | 17.17pc |
| Tricontinental Multitrust CMT ................ | 15.94pc | 15.94pc |
| Were Securities Cash Trust ................... | 16.67pc | 16.63pc |
| **CASH COMMON FUNDS:** | | |
| ANZ Trustees Cash Trustee C.Fund V2 .......... | 16.72pc | 16.72pc |
| Burns Philp Trustee Melb Cash Common Fund ... | 17.18pc | 17.15pc |
| Burns Philp Trustee Syd Call Common Fund ..... | 16.57pc | 16.46pc |
| Elders Trustee Cash Common Fund No 16 ...... | 16.41pc | 16.41pc |
| Executor Trustee SA Commn Fund 20V ......... | 17.15pc | 17.15pc |
| National Mutual Trustees Common Fund ....... | 17.05pc | 17.05pc |
| Perpetual Trustees Common Fund ............. | 16.93pc | 16.94pc |
| Sandhurst 11am Call Common Fund ........... | 16.65pc | 16.65pc |
| Trust Company of Australia Common Fund ...... | 16.06pc | 16.06pc |
| Winchcombe Carson Tr Cash C. Fund No.10 ..... | 16.36pc | 16.09pc |

All rates for cash management trusts and common funds are average percentages which are updated each day.

Sample Melbourne stock exchange bond report   (see pages 23 & 32)

Sample Premier State bonds prospectus cover   (see page 27)

## YOUR INVESTMENT APPLICATION FORM

I hereby apply for debenture stock and/or unsecured notes of Australian Guarantee Corporation Limited as set out below:

Bank /Broker's Stamp

### A  SELECT YOUR INVESTMENT OPTION(S)

#### INCOME BONDS

BSB No.

**DEBENTURE STOCK**

| TERM | 1 YEAR | 2 YEARS | 3 YEARS | 4 YEARS |
|---|---|---|---|---|

**MONTHLY**

| RATE | | 15.0 % P.A. | 14.6 % P.A. | 14.1 % P.A. |
|---|---|---|---|---|
| AMOUNT (MIN $15,000) | | $ | $ | $ |

**QUARTERLY**

| RATE | 16.0 % P.A. | 15.1 % P.A. | 14.7 % P.A. | 14.2 % P.A. |
|---|---|---|---|---|
| AMOUNT (MIN $2,000) | $ | $ | $ | $ |

**ANNUALLY**

| RATE | 17.0 % P.A. | 16.0 % P.A. | 15.5 % P.A. | 15.0 % P.A. |
|---|---|---|---|---|
| AMOUNT (MIN $2,000) | $ | $ | $ | $ |

#### GROWTH BONDS

**DEBENTURE STOCK**

| TERM | 2 YEARS | 3 YEARS | 4 YEARS |
|---|---|---|---|
| RATE | 16.2 % P.A. | 15.7 % P.A. | 15.2 % P.A. |
| AMOUNT (MIN $500) | $ | $ | $ |

077

#### READY ACCESS ACCOUNT

**UNSECURED NOTES**

| | AT - CALL |
|---|---|
| AMOUNT (MIN $2,000) $ | (RATE REVIEWED EACH WEEK) |

**PLEASE ENSURE BANK/BLDG. SOC. DETAIL IN SECTION C IS COMPLETED**

To meet the requirements of the Companies (NSW) Code this application form must not be issued, circulated or distributed unless accompanied by this prospectus. No securities will be issued under the short form prospectus 77 dated 25 September, 1989 after 24 September, 1990.

### E  ATTACH A CHEQUE OR MONEY ORDER marked
"Not Negotiable" to Australian Guarantee Corporation Limited.

### B  YOUR DETAILS
(PLEASE PRINT IN CAPITAL LETTERS)

MR / MRS
MS / MISS
_____ FULL FIRST NAMES

MR / MRS _____ SURNAME
MS / MISS
_____ FULL FIRST NAMES

_____ SURNAME

POSTAL ADDRESS: _____

_____ STATE _____

POSTCODE _____ PHONE _____
(DAYTIME)

### C  YOUR INTEREST INSTRUCTIONS

[ ] I AM ALREADY AN AGC INVESTOR. Please credit my payments to the same account as nominated for
OR my other AGC investment payments.

[ ] I WISH TO ESTABLISH A DIRECT CREDIT FACILITY. My nominated bank/building society account is:

ACCOUNT NAME: _____

ACCOUNT NO: _____

ACCOUNT TYPE: SAVINGS [ ] CHEQUE [ ]

BANK/BLDG SOC: _____

BRANCH : _____

BANK/STATE/BRANCH NO: [ ][ ][ ][ ][ ][ ]
OR

[ ] AGC READY ACCESS ACCOUNT
REFERENCE NO: [0][ ][ ][ ][ ][ ][ ]

### D  YOUR SIGNATURE(S)

Date / / 19

**IMPORTANT:** Before signing this application you should read the prospectus to which this application relates. The donee of Power of Attorney states that no notice of revocation has been received.

Australian Guarantee Corporation Limited

_____ 19 _____

Received from _____

The sum of $ _____ being application moneys for INCOME BONDS / GROWTH BONDS

( _____ months. @ _____ % p.a ) / READY ACCESS ACCOUNT at call.

Thank you for your subscription. Your certificate will be forwarded shortly.

Bank /Company Stamp

INVESTMENTS MAY BE MAILED TO YOUR AGC INVESTOR CENTRE, FREEPOST 9908, IN STATE OF POSTING, OR LODGED AT ANY AGC OFFICE, WESTPAC BRANCH OR INVESTMENT ADVISER

3

**APPLICATION FORM**

Sample application for AGC debenture stock   (see page 30)

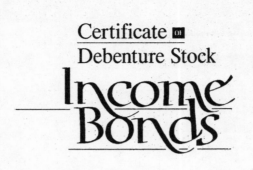

# Certificate of
# Debenture Stock
## Income Bonds

**AGC**
**Australian Guarantee**
Corporation Limited
(Incorporated in NSW)
A member of the Westpac Group

Issued in accordance with the trust deed 20th December, 1954 made between the Company of the first part certain Subsidiaries of the Company of the second part and Permanent Trustee Company Limited (as trustee for the stockholders) of the third part and issued with the benefits of and subject to the provisions of such trust deed. Interest is payable as set out in the schedule below.

**This is to certify that**
The person whose name and address are set out in the schedule appearing below is the registered holder of the stock specified therein.

| Holder Number | Register | Certificate Number |
|---|---|---|
| 0900240001 | SYDNEY | 17 917543 |

Name and Address of Registered Holder

MR JOHN D CITIZEN
100 SMITH STREET
SYDNEY   NSW     2000

| Amount | Interest Commences | Interest Rate % P.A. | Redeemable Date |
|---|---|---|---|
| **$9,000.00** | 1/10/89 | 15.400 | 1/10/1991 |

Interest Payments

INTEREST IS PAYABLE DURING THE CURRENCY ON THE LAST DAYS OF MARCH, JUNE, SEPTEMBER AND DECEMBER AND ON MATURITY.

Dated this   TWELFTH   day of   OCTOBER   1989

Executed by
**AUSTRALIAN GUARANTEE CORPORATION LIMITED**
by its duly appointed attorneys

| New South Wales | Victoria | Queensland | South Australia | Western Australia | Tasmania | A.C.T. |
|---|---|---|---|---|---|---|
| 12-22 Langston Place | 277 William Street | 18 Tank Street | 10 Pulteney Street | 165 Adelaide Terrace | 161 Collins Street | 11 London Circuit |
| Epping 2121 | Melbourne 3000 | Brisbane 4000 | Adelaide 5000 | Perth 6000 | Hobart 7000 | Canberra 2600 |
| Tel : 868 0765 | Tel : 608 6666 | Tel : 226 4100 | Tel : 223 4455 | Tel : 425 6222 | Tel : 34 8500 | Tel : 48 7644 |

**PLEASE KEEP THIS CERTIFICATE IN A SAFE PLACE AS IT WILL BE REQUIRED FOR REINVESTMENT OR REDEMPTION**

№ 005320

Sample AGC certificate of debenture stock   (see page 30)

APPLICATION FOR

*Money Market*

ACCESS ACCOUNT

UNSECURED NOTES

To meet the requirements of the Companies (NSW) Code this application form must not be issued, circulated or distributed unless accompanied by this prospectus. No securities will be issued under this short form prospectus dated 25th September, 1989 after 24th September, 1990.

Bank/Broker's Stamp

I HEREBY APPLY FOR UNSECURED NOTES of Australian Guarantee Corporation Limited as set out below.

■ **TO INVEST IN MONEY MARKET ACCESS ACCOUNT PLEASE FOLLOW THESE 5 STEPS**

**1** **Complete name and address details**
(Trustees must record their own names)

Mr, Miss
Mrs, Ms _____
(Full First Names)          (Surname)

Address _____

State _____ Postcode _____ Telephone _____

If already an AGC investor please indicate with ✓ ☐

**2** **Enter the amount of your investment**

Initial Deposit (min. $15,000)          $_____

Additional Deposits (min. $2000)          $_____

Reference No.          |0| | | | | | | | | | |

**3** **Supply bank or building society account details.**
Repayment by direct credit will be made to this account only

On my instructions please redeem my investment into my bank or building society account as detailed below

Account Name _____

Account No. _____

Bank _____ Branch _____

**4** **Sign your name**
● Individuals or their attorney
● Joint applications — by all parties
● Organisations — person signing for or on behalf of, must show their title

Signature(s) _____ Date _____

_____

The donee of Power of Attorney states that no notice of revocation has been received

**IMPORTANT:** Before signing the application form applicants should read the prospectus to which this application relates.

SER No.          | | | | | | | |

**5** Attach a 'Not Negotiable' cheque payable to Australian Guarantee Corporation Limited and mail to AGC in the capital city in your State, or lodge with any AGC office or Westpac branch

Received from _____          _____ / _____ / 19          Bank/Company Stamp

The sum of $ _____ being application moneys for Unsecured Notes

**AGC**
Australian Guarantee

Thank you for your subscription. Your Certificate will be forwarded as soon as possible.

For Australia Guarantee Corporation Limited

3

Sample application for AGC unsecured notes   (see pages 33-4)

### READY ACCESS ACCOUNT

31st October 1989                    Our Ref:  09 0024001

Mr John D Citizen
100 Smith Street
SYDNEY   NSW   2000

Dear Investor

Thank you for your investment in the AGC Ready Access Account. This certificate confirms our acceptance of your investment as at 01/11/89. Please note the following details:

ACCOUNT NO:      70193024
AMOUNT:          $4,000.00
TERM:            48 HOUR CALL (Subject to cheque clearance).
INTEREST RATE:   16.800 (Subject to weekly change, as published every
                 Friday in the Australian Financial Review).

Your interest will be calculated on a daily basis on and from the date of acceptance. At the end of each quarter interest will be reinvested automatically and paid when you withdraw the full balance. You will receive a statement detailing transactions and your account balance each quarter. Your June statement will record total interest credited to your account for the full year to 30th June.

Your Ready Access Account can be added to at any time in amounts of at least $500, up to an account balance of $250,000 without referral, by completing our application form and attaching your cheque. Additional investments may then be made by any one of the following methods:

1. Mailed to AGC at P O Box 419, Epping   NSW   2121.
2. Lodged at any AGC or Westpac Branch.
3. Lodged with your stockbroker, accountant or investment adviser.

Should you have any enquiries regarding your account please contact the Ready Access Account Investment Centre on 868 0765 or (008) 01 1844, toll free for callers outside the Metropolitan area. Please quote the above reference and account numbers in any correspondence.

Yours faithfully

INVESTOR SERVICES MANAGER

**AGC**
Australian Guarantee

**Sample AGC Ready Access account certificate**   (see pages 33-4)

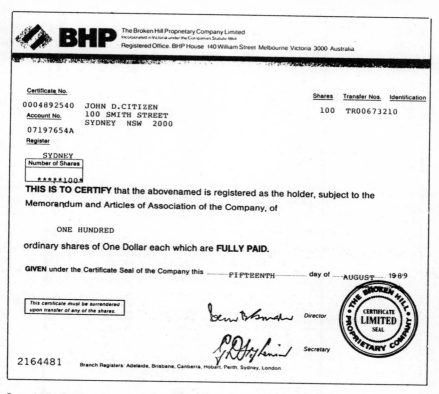

Sample BHP share certificate   (see page 47)

# RISES — CN Gold 30 c

## INDUSTRIAL

AJ Prime $1 110 4
AAM 20c 58 3
AAM opt89 30 4
ACI $1 372 1
AFL $1 170 5
AMI Tyota 175 5
ANI 91 nts 3.10 420 b 5
ANZ $1 558 6
AWA 610 10
Acmex 1450 150
Adel Stm 1370 70
Adel Stm opt86 1500 b 40
Allwood 20c 63 b 3
Alpha opt87 40 10
Amcor $1 390 10
Ampol 230 2
Ariadne 335 5
Ariadne rts 128 13
Ariadne bndsl 315 3
Ausmintec $1 550 b 20
Auspharm 65 3
Aust Agr 480 20
Aust N Fd 20c 30 2
Aust Ovrs opt87 45 3
A.P.R. 67 5
Aust Vent opt87 225 10
Austen B 20c 180 b 15
BCS Cemt 435 5
BTR Nylex 850 10
BWD Ind 1150 50
BWD Ind opt88 1050 30
Bank Sing $1 125 5
Barlow 30c 112 2
Barrack $1 280 5
Barwon 20c 70 5
Barwon opt86 55 b 3
Battery 205 5
Battery opt89 170 b 5
Bell G $1 1040 20
Beltech 25c 22 1
Bisley 40c 1200 20
Boral 400 5
Brambles 730 10
Bram 90 nts 2.05 700 10
Burns P $1 780 10
CA Prop 52 b 1

Melcorp 10c 11 3
Metal Man 185 3
Miniskips 235 b 5
Miniskips opt87 190 5
Monier 208 3
Mono Aust 170 10
NZ For 40c 212 b 2
Nat Aust $1 560 4
Nat Prop opt91 120 b 15
Ncorp Inv dd 20c 195 b 5
News Corp 3250 80
Oakbridge 90 3
Oceanic 280 b 5
P.A.L. 20c 60 6
P.A.L. opt87 42 4
Pac Dunlp 365 15
P P Trust $1 88 3
Perm Tst $1 1050 b 100
Peters Si 219 4
Pioneer C 280 4
P Metal 55 3
Powerplay 25c 38 2
QMH 20c 18 1
Qld Press nts $9 1000 b 44
Rothwells new 360 b 10
Sarich $1 2300 190
Siddons 240 6
Sthn Farm 550 10
Sunshine 330 5
Sunshine opt88 190 10
TNT 350 5
Taubmans 192 2
Taylor 720 b 20
Taylor opt86 490 10
Teltronic 84 1
Transcon 5c 8 1
Undrwater 25c 300 10
Unity Crp 490 15
Vestcorp 78 b 2
Viking 20c 87 2
WAM opt89 27 1
Wardley opt88 40 5
Watkins P 25c 48 1
Wes Cap opt91 107 2
West Brke 610 b 20
Westpac $1 480 5
Woolworth 355 5

Elders Rs opt86 65 10
Electrum 20c 22 2
Electrum opt88 11 1
Elf Trlak 25c 44 1
Emperor 10c 630 20
Emu Hill 20c 16 1
Endeavour 20c 33 1
E'prise 25c 73 1
Euralba 20c 16 1
Falcona 20c 30 2
Fst Inv opt91 30 3
Forsayth 25c 170 10
GM Kalg 25c 1560 10
Genoa Res 200 5
G'Shamrock 20c 80 5
Gold Copp 15c 18 1
Golden Gr 25c 85 b 3
Grants 20c 63 5
Gt Cent 20c 26 1
Gt Cent opt90 16 2
Gt Fngall 20c 27 1
HMC Aust 20c 8 1
Haoma 25c 24 4
Hartogen $1 235 5
Hawk Inv 20c 310 10
Hill 50 10c 74 2
Hunter R 25c 134 4
Ivanhoe 20c 120 10
J'lana 36 1
J'lana opt87 12 1
Julia Min 25c 85 3
Kalg Res 25c 15 1
Keela Wee 25c 74 9
Kitchener 25c 80 5
Kukim 25c 115 b 3
Lachlan 25c 78 3
Lennard 14 b 1
MIM 245 5
Magellan 200 10
Metana 25c 586 6
Mincoa 25c 54 2
Minoil 25c 82 4
Moonie 25c 250 5
Mt Burges opt87 21 b 1
Mt Carrin 170 1?
Mt Carrin opt87 12?

# FALLS — IEL 18 c

## INDUSTRIAL

ACI opt86 190 2
Aus Stock 105 5
A Wide opt89 450 s 10
BBJ Comp 87 s 3
BHP $1 860 2
Bond Corp 282 3
Brunckhst opt89 36 2
Burswood opt89 16 1
Campbell 20c 100 10
Century 25c 230 5
Cherry Ln 420 s 30
Circadian 20c 100 5
Comalco $1 253 2
Dawebanke 20c 72 3
Dylup dd 42c 135 5
EA Coffee 70c 480 20
Equity F 20c 12 s 2
First Inv 25c 102 3
Fletcher del 260 s 5
GPT $1 280 2
GPT Incme $1 160 5
Goodman 355 5
Hanimex 25c 93 4
Herbert 20c 10 s 1
Houseware 20c 85 5
Humes 322 3
Ind Equit 730 18
I.M.T. 120 1
Jupiters $1 130 10
Kemtron optdl 6 1
Koitaki 650 10
Kostech 24 1
Kurts 177 3
L Lease 930 10
Loscam 80 5
Moore B $1 370 10
NZI Corp 40c 163 2
Nat Mutl $1 112 5
OPSM 300 10
Panfida 25c 105 5
Radtek 70 5

Rover 125 5
SA Brwing 288 5
Scalzo 145 1
TNT opt91 150 10
Unity Crp new 450 10
Wes Cap 165 3
West Bio 25c 100 10

## MINING

A.U.R. 25c 42 3
ARI 20c 26 1
Aberfoyle 1030 20
Aus Emrld opt89 19 1
A Hydro 25c 15 1
Aztec 37 2
BH Metals 25c 120 10
Bamboo opt89 10 1
Bendigo M 25c 130 s 5
Bridge 80 4
Bridge ctgcp 35c 23 2
C Coast 82 s 3
Callina 20c 127 5
Centenary opt87 32 3
Cent Kalg 25c 87 s 5
Cent Min 20c 39 1
Chrchll R dd $1 75 s 5
Cool Gold 30c 38 1
Coronet 20c 120 5
Croesus 19 1
Croesus opt91 10 1
Crusader 20c 190 5
Delta G 25c 44 1
East Pet del 25c 35 b 1
Energy O 19 s 1
Ero Hydro ctg 10c 8 2
Gippsland 200 20
Golden V 20c 22 s 3
Gt Fngall opt89 12 1
Greenbush 10c 65 5
Hannans 20c 95 5
Helix Res 25c 125 5
Home E 32 1
Horizon 20c 50 2

Ind Ocean 25c 72 1
Intermin 20c 120 s 10
Invincble 30c 77 b 3
Jason Min 20c 100 2
Kidston 20c 780 6
Laurel B 25c 12 1
MC Mining 25c 48 2
Maitland 25c 68 s 2
Meridian ctg 40c 9 1
Metals Ex 105 10
Metramar 20c 140 s 2
Mistral 20c 6 1
Mt Gipps 25c 38 4
Newmex opt87 45 s 5
Nicron 20c 48 2
North BH 260 8
Nth Kalg opt87 95 s 5
Nullarbor 10c 100 5
Oilmet 25c 122 b 3
Pact Res 25c 18 1
Pancont M 25c 315 5
Peko Oil 105 1
Planet 25c 15 s 1
Ramsgate 20c 32 1
Santos 25c 445 5
Stellar opt 12 s 2
Sthn Gold 20c 28 1
Strategic 260 35
Sundowner 10c 34 1
Sundowner opt86 23 1
Swan Res 20c 28 s 2
Technomin 45 3
Thames Mn 25c 43 2
Thames Mn opt87 19 s 1
Vultan 20c 28 2
West Gold 20c 29 1
Whim Crk 20c 510 10
Windsor 25c 100 2
Woodside 98 5
Yinnex 20c 30 5
Yinnex opt88 18 b 1
Zanex opt87 21 1

Sample Sydney stock exchange report on market trends  (see page 49)

## INDUSTRIAL

| 1989 High | Low | | Buy | Sell | Move | Last | Sales 100 | Div Yld | P/E |
|---|---|---|---|---|---|---|---|---|---|
| 380 | 235 | A.D.T. 1c | 380 | 410 | | 360 | | | |
| | | A.D.T. bnadl 1c | | | | | | | |
| 22 | 1 | A.Invest dd 20c | 3 | 6 | | 4 | | | |
| 41 | 30 | A.Invest nts | 10 | | | 30 | | 30 43 | |
| 2 | 1 | A.Invest opt92 | | 1 | | 1 | | | |
| 106 | 75 | AJ Prime $1 | 80 | 83 | 3 | 83 | 10 | 13.78 | 7 3 |
| 70 | 60 | AP Group | 58 | 65 | | 60 | | 8 33 | 7 3 |
| 70 | 64 | AP Group pref 65c | | 64 | | 64 | | 8 63 | |
| 3 | 1 | AP Group opt90 | 1 | | | 1 | | | |
| 155 | 100 | AFP Grp 10c | 145 | 150 | | 148 | 7000 | | 30 9 |
| 75 | 41 | AFP Grp opt | 70 | | | 70 | | | |
| 80 | 70 | ANG 1.55 | 70 | | | 70 | | | 4 5 |
| 180 | 106 | ANI 30c | 133 | 134 | −1 | 134 | 55 | 7.90 | 6 6 |
| 566 | 446 | ANZ $1 | 506 | 508 | 2 | 508 | 185 | 8.66 | 7 2 |
| 340 | 250 | ANZ clg | 300 | 305 | | 305 | | | |
| 11 | 2 | APA | 2 | 3 | | 3 | | | |
| 115 | 40 | APA nts 2.55 | | | | | | | |
| 18 | 6 | APR | 6 | 8 | | 8 | | | |
| 4 | 1 | APR opt90 | | 1 | | 2 | | | |
| 52 | 38 | ASC | 40 | 41 | | 40 | | | |
| 170 | 152 | AUI $1 | 155 | 164 | | 155 | | 3 87 | 22 5 |
| 130 | 90 | AWA dd 5c | 118 | 120 | | 118 | | 8.90 | 17 1 |
| 215 | 180 | AWP | 195 | 203 | | 195 | | | |
| 65 | 55 | Abaldyn | 65 | | | 65 | | 13.85 | 6 5 |
| 21 | 10 | Abigroup dd 20c | 11 | 12 | | 12 | | 8 33 | 2 6 |
| 2 | 1 | Abigroup opkod | | 1 | | 1 | | | |
| 4 | 1 | Access 20c | | 2 | | 1 | | | |
| 200 | 145 | Acmex | 165 | | | 162 | | 6 06 | 26 6 |
| 232 | 180 | Acton $1 | 212 | 215 | −2 | 212 | 14 | 4 72 | 12 6 |
| 248 | 200 | Adel Cem | 237 | 240 | −2 | 238 | 1 | 3 78 | 14 4 |
| 140 | 98 | Adel Cem opt89 | 135 | 138 | | 135 | 6 | | |
| 730 | 550 | Adel Stm | 700 | 710 | | 710 | 4 | 13 24 | 7 0 |
| 83 | 60 | Adel Stm opt92 | 62 | 75 | | 75 | 1 | | |
| 110 | 68 | Adroyal | 78 | 84 | | 84 | | 10.12 | 4 9 |
| | | Adroyal del | | | | | | | |
| 62 | 44 | Adtrans | 50 | 55 | | 55 | | 8 18 | 8 4 |
| 560 | 440 | Advnce Bk $1 | 485 | 490 | | 485 | | 4 43 | 11 9 |
| 70 | 35 | Aerodata | 35 | 45 | | 45 | | | |
| 86 | 38 | Agen 20c | 42 | 43 | −1 | 43 | 40 | | |
| 66 | 50 | Air Inl | 53 | 54 | −1 | 54 | 350 | 5.56 | 16 9 |
| 55 | 55 | Air Inl délxx | 50 | | | 55 | | | |
| 14 | 4 | Airship 26c | 8 | 9 | | 8 | | | |
| 280 | 200 | Alcan $1 | 200 | | | 200 | | 10.00 | 3 3 |
| 990 | 800 | Aldus $1 | 800 | 850 | | 800 | | 4 38 | 8 1 |
| 710 | 600 | Allgas $1 | 670 | 700 | | 680 | | 2 94 | 8 2 |
| 10 | 1 | Allwood 20c | 1 | 2 | | 2 | | | 1 4 |

## MINING

| 1989 High | Low | | Buy | Sell | Move | Last | Sales 100 | Div Yld | P/E |
|---|---|---|---|---|---|---|---|---|---|
| 12 | 5 | A Gold Rs $1 | 7 | 8 | | 7 | | | |
| 2 | 1 | A Gold Rs opt92 | 1 | | | 1 | | | |
| 6 | 2 | A-Cap 5c | 2 | 3 | | 3 | | | |
| | | A-Cap delxo 5c | | | | | | | |
| 2 | 1 | A-Cap opt89 | | 1 | | 1 | | | |
| 65 | 13 | A.O.V Min 20c | 25 | 27 | | 25 | 180 | | |
| 32 | 14 | A.U.R. 25c | 18 | 19 | | 18 | 1070 | 11.11 | 3 0 |
| 3 | 1 | A.U.R. opt90 | 1 | 2 | | 1 | | | |
| 184 | 112 | AC Mins | 182 | 185 | | 182 | | 3.85 | 11 2 |
| 225 | 165 | 'CM Gold 20c | 215 | 223 | | 224 | | | |
| 200 | 185 | ACM Gold new 20c | 175 | | | 200 | | | |
| 10 | 2 | ADEX clg 25c | 3 | | | 3 | | | |
| 20 | 6 | ADEX clg 35c | 10 | | | 12 | | | |
| 89 | 53 | AOG | | 62 | | 62 | | | 17 9 |
| 37 | 18 | APM 20c | 18 | 20 | | 18 | | | |
| 18 | 5 | APMO opt90 | | 9 | | 12 | | | |
| 560 | 450 | Aberfoyle | 510 | 530 | | 520 | | 2.69 | 34 7 |
| 26 | 12 | Acorn 20c | 17 | 25 | | 17 | | | |
| 12 | 5 | Adel Pet 20c | 5 | 6 | | 6 | 500 | | |
| 8 | 3 | Afro-West 20c | 4 | 5 | | 3 | | | |
| 10 | 3 | Alcaston 25c | 3 | 5 | | 3 | | | |
| 2 | 1 | Alcaston opt90 | | 1 | | 1 | | | |
| 5 | 2 | Alkane 25c | 2 | 3 | | 2 | | | |
| 75 | 45 | Alld Gld | 75 | 80 | | 75 | | | |
| 25 | 13 | Allstate 20c | 17 | 20 | −1 | 17 | 20 | | |
| 8 | 3 | Am Bouldr | 3 | 4 | | 3 | | | |
| 1 | 1 | Am Bouldr clg 20c | | 1 | | 1 | | | |
| 1 | 1 | Am Bouldr opt90 | | 1 | | 1 | | | |
| | | Am Bouldr opt89 | | | | | | | |
| 41 | 23 | Amadeus 30c | 25 | 28 | | 28 | | | |
| | | Amadeus clgdl 20c | 15 | 19 | | | | | |
| 11 | 8 | Amadeus optdl | 10 | 11 | | 11 | | | |
| 195 | 145 | Ampol Exp | 180 | 197 | | 180 | 1 | | 10 8 |
| 50 | 24 | Ampol Exp opt93 | 44 | | | 44 | | | |
| 10 | 2 | Ando 25c | 3 | 4 | | 3 | | | |
| 8 | 1 | Ando opt90 | 1 | 2 | | 1 | | | |
| 20 | 5 | Anglo 25c | 4 | 6 | | 5 | 200 | | |
| 3 | 1 | Anglo opt89 | | 1 | | 1 | | | |
| 20 | 8 | Aquarius 25c | 9 | 10 | 1 | 10 | 640 | | |
| 4 | 1 | Aquarius opt89 | | 1 | | 1 | | | |
| 105 | 30 | Arabex 25c | 90 | 92 | | 90 | | | |
| 40 | 22 | Arboyne | 26 | 28 | | 28 | | 10.71 | |
| 8 | 3 | Arboyne opt90 | 6 | 7 | | 7 | | | |
| 5 | 3 | Arcadia 10c | 3 | 4 | | 3 | | | |
| 65 | 46 | Arimco 30c | 54 | 55 | | 55 | | 7.27 | 39 6 |
| 98 | 70 | Asarco 25c | 83 | 85 | | 85 | | 3.53 | 9 3 |
| 145 | 103 | Ashton | 135 | 136 | | 135 | 325 | 4.44 | 11 0 |
| 87 | 65 | Ashton clg 25c | 79 | 90 | | 79 | 8 | | |
| 9 | 1 | Astrik 20c | 2 | 3 | | 3 | | | |
| 2 | 2 | Astrik opt90 | | 1 | | 1 | | | |
| 50 | 5 | Astro Min 25c | 28 | 29 | | 30 | | | |
| 100 | 10 | Astron | 23 | 51 | | 26 | | | |
| 33 | 8 | Audax 25c | 10 | 11 | | 10 | 550 | | |
| 8 | 1 | Audimco 25c | 6 | 7 | | 6 | 700 | | |
| 16 | 4 | Auralia 25c | 5 | 6 | | 6 | 100 | | |
| 10 | 3 | Auridium 25c | 5 | 7 | | 7 | | | |
| 3 | 1 | Auridium opt90 | | 1 | | 1 | | | |
| 4 | 2 | Aurotech 20c | 2 | 3 | | 2 | | | |
| 1 | 1 | Aurotech opt89 | | 1 | | 1 | | | |
| 7 | 3 | Aust Coal 20c | 3 | 4 | | 3 | | | |
| 215 | 130 | Aust Devl 10c | 150 | 170 | | 150 | 60 | 2.00 | 21 4 |
| 6 | 3 | Aust Emrld 20c | 5 | 6 | | 5 | | | |
| | | Aust Emrld opt89 | | 2 | | 2 | | | |
| 10 | 3 | Aust Gold 20c | 5 | 6 | | 5 | | | |

Sample industrial and mining share list showing yield (see page 49)

**The CSR Share
Purchase
Plan**

## Share Purchase Plan Statement

If your address is shown incorrectly please complete the reverse side of this form.

1234567   JOHN DAVID CITIZEN
          182 GEORGE STREET
          SYDNEY   NSW          2000

Name of holding
JOHN DAVID CITIZEN

Statement date   14TH JUNE 1989     Financial year  1 JULY 1988 TO 30 JUNE 1989

### Information about your current allotment

| | Plan transactions | | Details of current dividend reinvestment |
| --- | --- | --- | --- |

| Date | Description | Amount $ |
| --- | --- | --- |
| | BALANCE B/F | 2.88 |
| 22/05/89 | AUTO BANK TRANSFER | 100.00 |
| | TOTAL INVESTED | 102.88 |
| | PURCHASE OF SHARES | 100.97– |
| | BALANCE C/F | 1.91 |

Type of dividend
Dividend per share $
Type of participation
Number of shares participating
– held by you
– held at CSR

| | Dividends reinvested $ | Imputed credit $ |
| --- | --- | --- |
| Franked | | |
| Unfranked | | |
| Total | | |
| Less: Withholding tax | | |
| Total for reinvestment | | |

TOTAL SHAREHOLDING DOES NOT INCLUDE ANY
PARTLY PAID SHARES YOU MAY HOLD

Notes on current allotment:

| Allotment closing date | 31/05/89 | Allotment type | CASH | Date of allotment | 14/06/89 |
| --- | --- | --- | --- | --- | --- |
| Total invested $ | 102.88 | Price per share $ | 4.39 | Shares purchased | 23 |

### Your total transactions for this tax year

| Cash contributions $: | Money | 2300.00 | Interest | 0.00 * | Total | 2300.00 |
| --- | --- | --- | --- | --- | --- | --- |
| Dividends reinvested $: | Franked | 1819.86 * | Unfranked | 0.00 * | Total | 1819.86* |
| | Imputed credit | 1748.49 * | Withholding tax | 0.00 | Total reinvested | 1819.86 |

Amounts marked * are assessable for income tax, however tax payable can be reduced by the imputed credit.

### Your total CSR shareholding — including shares not in the plan

| Shares held by you | 5000 | Shares held at CSR | 2500 | Your current shareholding | 7500 |
| --- | --- | --- | --- | --- | --- |

**CSR Limited**   Level 5 182 George Street Sydney  GPO Box 483 Sydney 2001 Australia  Telephone (02) 235 8382  Facsimile (02) 235 8555

Incorporated in New South Wales

### Form for making optional cash contributions

Make cheque or money order payable to
**CSR Limited** (minimum $20 per deposit,
maximum $2400 per year)

Amount enclosed    $

Telephone number where you can be contacted (    )

Sample CSR share purchase plan statement   (see page 52)

**CSR Limited**
INCORPORATED IN NEW SOUTH WALES

REGISTERED OFFICE:
1-7 O'CONNELL STREET
SYDNEY NSW AUSTRALIA

## CONVERTIBLE UNSECURED NOTE CERTIFICATE

X000001

### NOTES OF $4.00 EACH – 1987 ISSUE MATURING 31 MARCH 1997

This is to certify that the noteholder(s) named below is (are) registered as a holder(s), of the amount as specified in The Schedule below, of 8% per annum Convertible Unsecured Notes of $4.00 each, issued subject to the provisions of a Trust Deed dated 8 May 1987 made between the company and Perpetual Trustee Company Limited as Trustee for the Convertible Unsecured Noteholders and to the conditions appearing on the back of this certificate.

1234567

THE SCHEDULE

NUMBER OF NOTES     DATE

JOHN DAVID CITIZEN     ONE THOUSAND ONLY     *****1000*     30/06/89

MAIN NOTES

REGISTER

SYDNEY

### NOTICE OF EXERCISE OF RIGHT TO CONVERT

To effect conversion in accordance with clause 6 of the conditions of issue on the back of this certificate, this notice must be completed and forwarded to the company between 1 February and 14 February in a year of conversion (each year beginning 1988 and ending 1997).

To **CSR Limited:** I (We) hereby give notice of exercise of my (our) right to convert, into fully-paid one dollar ordinary shares of the company the following number of notes:

\*

Signature(s) ..........................................................

.........................................................................

Date ...................................................................

\* If you wish to convert only part of your entitlement insert the appropriate number in multiples of 100 notes. If this space is left blank the Notice will be deemed to relate to the whole of your holding of 8% per annum Convertible Unsecured Notes as shown by this certificate.

This certificate must be surrendered to the company before any transfer will be registered or new certificate or certificates issued in exchange or on conversion.

**FOR CONVERTIBLE UNSECURED NOTE REGISTERS SEE BACK OF CERTIFICATE**

For and on behalf of CSR Limited

CANCELLED CANCELLED CANCELLED

Sample CSR unsecured note certificate

# SECURITY TRANSFER FORM

| PART 1 | PLEASE USE BLOCK LETTERS | Marking Stamp |
|---|---|---|

| | | |
|---|---|---|
| FULL NAME OF COMPANY OR CORPORATION | | Register |
| DESCRIPTION OF SECURITIES | Class · If not fully paid, paid to | |
| QUANTITY | Words · Figures | Transferor's Broker. hereby certifies:— (i) As to the validity of Documents. (ii) That Stamp Duty (if payable) has been or will be paid. |
| TRANSFER IDENTIFICATION NUMBER | | |
| FULL NAME(S) OF TRANSFEROR(S) (SELLER [S] ) | Surname(s) ............................. Christian Name(s) ............................. | |
| | | Transferor's Broker's Stamp |

I/We hereby transfer the above securities to the transferee(s) named in Part 2 hereof or to the several transferees named in Part 2 of the Broker's Transfer Form(s) or Split Transfer Form(s) relating to the above securities. I/We have no notice of the revocation of the Power of Attorney under which this transfer is signed.

AFFIXED AT SYDNEY ON:—

FOR REGISTRAR USE

| TRANSFEROR(S) (SELLER [S] ) SIGN HERE ➡ | ............................. ............................. | Date Signed |
|---|---|---|

| PART 2 | | |
|---|---|---|
| Surname(s) Mr. Mrs. Miss | ............................. | |
| Christian Name(s) | ............................. | |
| FULL NAME(S) & ADDRESS OF TRANSFEREE(S) (BUYER [S] ) | ............................. ............................. ............................. ............................. State ............................. | |

| Transferee's Broker Hereby Certifies | (i) That the securities set out in Part 1 above having been purchased in the ordinary course of business are to be registered in the name(s) of the transferee(s) named in this Part. (ii) That Stamp Duty (if payable) has been paid or will be paid — and hereby requests that such entries be made in the register as are necessary to give effect to this transfer |
|---|---|

Transferee's Broker's Stamp

DATE OF AFFIXING STAMP

Please enter the above securities on the ............................. Register

Sample security transfer form

## TRUST FUND QUOTES

### UNLISTED MANAGED INVESTMENTS

#### EQUITY TRUSTS

| | Buyer | Seller |
|---|---|---|
| ABC Aggressive | 0.7800 | Closed |
| ABC Trading | 1.1500 | Closed |
| ACC Mgd Gth | 0.9160 | 0.9810 |
| ACC Quadriga Gth | 0.5130 | Closed |
| ACC Quadriga Income | 0.4570 | Closed |
| ACC Austn Leaders | 1.7289 | 1.8469 |
| Adv Aust Sharemkt No.1 | 0.7546 | Closed |
| Adv Imput | 0.6269 | 0.6669 |
| Adv High Perf Sharemkt | 0.4107 | 0.4369 |
| AFT Equity Gth No.1 | 0.5900 | Closed |
| AFT Equity Gth No.2 | 0.1875 | Closed |
| AFT Equity Gth No.3 | 0.1875 | Closed |
| AFT Equity Gth No.4 | 0.1750 | Closed |
| AFT Mgd Inv | 0.6950 | 0.7407 |
| AFT Natu Res | 0.1450 | Closed |
| AFT Oil & Minerals | 0.2250 | Closed |
| AFT Savings | 5.4600 | Closed |
| ANZ Austn Leaders Trust | 2.3550 | 2.4775 |
| AMP Equity | 0.9846 | 1.0557 |
| AMP Imput | 1.0027 | 1.0951 |
| AMP Blue Chip | 1.1003 | 1.1798 |
| AMP Gold | 1.0308 | 1.1053 |
| AMP Res | 1.2324 | 1.3206 |
| AMP Small Coys | 0.9076 | 0.9732 |
| ANZ EQUITY No.1 | 1.8592 | 1.8968 |
| ANZ EQUITY No.2 | 1.3460 | 1.3732 |
| ANZ Res | 0.4832 | 0.4929 |
| ANZ Multitrust | 0.8019 | 0.8059 |
| Arm Jones — Tax Effective | 0.9468 | 0.9914 |
| Audant Res | 0.6125 | 0.6675 |
| Audant High Perfom | 0.5825 | 0.6350 |
| Aust Funds — Index | 1.2482 | 1.3272 |
| Aust Funds — Mgd | 1.0819 | 1.1388 |
| Aust Funds — Share | 1.2198 | 1.2696 |
| BSL HI-Yield | 0.7600 | 0.8100 |
| BSL Trading | 0.6800 | 0.7200 |
| The Rural Invest Trust | 0.9315 | 0.9874 |
| BT Split — Gth | 2.3475 | 2.4750 |
| BT Split — Income | 1.0125 | 1.0675 |
| BT Equity Imput | 2.1200 | 2.2700 |
| Capita 3rd UFT | —— | —— |
| Capita 4th and 5th UFT | 0.4950 | Closed |
| Capita UFT Cap Gth No.1 | —— | —— |
| Capita UFT Cap Gth No.2 | —— | —— |
| Capita UFT Earnings No.1 | —— | —— |
| Capita Div Imput | 0.3050 | 0.3260 |
| Capita Indtl Gth | 0.4100 | 0.4390 |
| Capita Oil & Mining | 0.3000 | 0.3240 |
| Capita Inv Trading | 0.6800 | Closed |
| Clay Robd No.1 | 0.7250 | Closed |
| Clay Robd No.2 | 1.1200 | Closed |
| Clay Robd No.3 | 1.3300 | Closed |
| Clay Robd No.4 | 1.1825 | Closed |
| Clay Robd No.5 | 0.6225 | Closed |
| Clay Robd No.6 | 0.6550 | Closed |
| Clay Robd No.7 | 0.6800 | Closed |
| Clay Robd No.8 | 0.3250 | Closed |
| Clay Robd No.9 | 0.5125 | Closed |
| Clay Robd No.10 | 0.3575 | 0.3750 |
| Clay Robd Special Sitns | 0.5000 | 0.4375 |
| Clay Robd Gold | 0.3175 | 0.3375 |
| Col Mut Prof Perfom | 1.0535 | 1.0939 |
| Col Mut Mgd Gth | 1.0407 | 1.1176 |
| Corcarr High Income | 1.0900 | 1.1050 |
| Corcarr Inv | 0.6750 | 0.6850 |
| DBSM Cont Asset Allocation | 1.0553 | 1.1108 |
| DBSM Austn Share Index | 1.1069 | 1.1652 |
| Elders Equity | 1.7200 | 1.8400 |
| Equitilink — Gthlink | 0.9210 | 0.9830 |
| Fidelity Austn Equity | 0.3630 | 0.3900 |
| Fidelity Equity Income | 0.4060 | 0.4400 |
| First State — Balanced | 1.1120 | 1.1650 |
| First State — Mgd | 1.2010 | 1.2830 |

| | Buyer | Seller |
|---|---|---|
| Wardley General Inv | 0.8810 | 0.9140 |
| Westpac Inv Trust | 3.2500 | Closed |
| Westpac Austn Cap | 6.8600 | Closed |
| Westpac Imput Trust | 1.0720 | 1.0910 |
| Westpac Aust Invest Trust | 1.0670 | 1.0840 |

#### INTERNATIONAL TRUSTS

| | Buyer | Seller |
|---|---|---|
| ABC Intern | 0.5100 | Closed |
| Adv Inter Sharemkt | 0.4345 | 0.4622 |
| AFT Intern | 0.8575 | 1.0000 |
| AMP Intern | 0.7526 | 0.8052 |
| ANZ Intern Trust | 0.7514 | 0.7666 |
| Aust Funds — Intern | 1.1678 | 1.2417 |
| Aust's Baring Japan | 1.6200 | 1.7250 |
| BT Intern Gth | 1.5600 | 1.6700 |
| BT Am Gth | 1.2200 | 1.3100 |
| BT European Gth | 1.5200 | 1.6300 |
| bT Pacific Basin | 3.4300 | 3.6600 |
| Clay Robd 1st Equity | 1.0875 | Closed |
| Clay Robd Equity No.2 | 0.4750 | 0.5050 |
| Clay Robd Tiger | 0.5250 | 0.5575 |
| Clay Robd 1st Income | 0.3475 | 0.3700 |
| DBSM Intern Share Index | 1.1184 | 1.1773 |
| Equitilink — Worldlink | 0.6640 | 0.7080 |
| Fidelity Intern | 0.6550 | 0.7000 |
| Fidelity Am Assets | 0.6340 | 0.6800 |
| Fidelity European | 0.6330 | 0.6800 |
| Fidelity Japan | 0.7530 | 0.8100 |
| Friends Intern Gth | 1.0519 | 1.1190 |
| GIO Intern | 0.8678 | 0.8633 |
| GT Intern Gth | 1.8780 | 2.0350 |
| GT Am Gth | 0.4710 | 0.5100 |
| GT Am Special Sitns | 0.4930 | 0.5340 |
| GT Asian Gth | 0.6940 | 0.7520 |
| GT Aust/asian Gth | 0.6800 | 0.7370 |
| GT European Gth | 0.5270 | 0.5710 |
| GT Germany Gth | 0.5500 | 0.5960 |
| GT Japan Gth | 0.7450 | 0.8070 |
| GT UK Gth | 0.4660 | 0.5050 |
| Hambros Inter Gth | 1.2704 | 1.3515 |
| Hambros Europe | 1.2578 | 1.3381 |
| Hambros Japan and Asia | 1.6582 | 1.7640 |
| Hambros Nth Am | 1.0994 | 1.1695 |
| Hambros S-E Asia | 1.0304 | 1.0962 |
| Hambros UK | 1.2579 | 1.3381 |
| Hambros Intern Bond | 0.9411 | 0.9803 |
| Heine Intern | —— | —— |
| Heine Nth Am | —— | —— |
| JB Were Intern | 1.0703 | 1.0885 |
| JF European Gth | 0.5420 | 0.5840 |
| JF Global | 0.3690 | 0.3990 |
| JF Japan Gth | 0.7640 | 0.8240 |
| JF Bond and Currency Trust | 0.3950 | 0.4260 |
| JF Pacific Gth | 3.0500 | 3.3100 |
| JF Pacific Gth No.2 | 1.1220 | 1.1410 |
| JF US Gth | 0.5350 | 0.5770 |
| Lumley Intern | 1.0046 | Closed |
| Nat Aust Intern | 1.2700 | Closed |
| NatM World Gth | 1.0049 | 1.0791 |
| Nomura Goode Japan Gth | 0.9629 | Closed |
| Nomura Japan Gth Opts | —— | —— |
| Nthn Sec Inter Sec | 0.8700 | 0.9200 |
| NZI Global Equity | 1.3800 | 1.4400 |
| Oceanic Japan | 0.8550 | Closed |
| OST Intern | 1.0000 | 1.0530 |
| Pot Warb Int'l | 1.2860 | 1.3870 |
| Rothschild Intern | 2.5900 | 2.6400 |
| Scott Ami Intern | 1.5877 | 1.7093 |
| Bank of Vic Premium Gth | —— | —— |
| Swiss Intern | 1.6353 | 1.7416 |
| Sydney Fund Mgrs Japan Trust | —— | —— |
| Thornton Opport | 0.2905 | 0.3129 |
| Thornton Tiger Opport | 0.3129 | 0.3379 |
| Ultimate Intern Trading | 0.9218 | 1.0018 |
| Wardley World | 0.8700 | 0.9260 |
| Wardley Intern | 1.2890 | 1.3810 |
| Westpac Intern Inv | 1.4190 | 1.4290 |

#### PROPERTY TRUSTS

| | Buyer | Seller |
|---|---|---|
| ACC Prop Sec | 0.4870 | 0.5210 |
| Adv Aust No.1 | 0.5346 | Closed |
| Adv Split Fund — Income | 1.0263 | 1.0472 |

Sample trust and fund market listing   (see page 77)

## Insurance Bonds

(Insurance Bonds Con't)

| Trust/Fund | Size $m | Fees % Entry/Yrly | Min $ Inv | Entry Cost | Exit Price | Performance 1yr | 2yr | 3yr |
|---|---|---|---|---|---|---|---|---|
| AAA Cap Secure | 19.9 | 5/1.2 | 2,000 | np | - | - | - | - |
| AAA M'ged | 1.5 | 5/1.2 | 2,000 | np | - | - | - | - |
| ACC Life Inter | 0.1 | 6/1.5 | 1,000 | 1.05 | 0.97 | 2.9 | - | - |
| ACC Life M'ged Gwth | 3.4 | 6/1.5 | 1,000 | 1.15 | 1.07 | 4.0 | (5.1) | - |
| Adriatic M'ged | S | 2.5/1.6 | 1,000 | 1.24 | 1.18 | np | - | - |
| Aetna Bear | 6.5 | 5/$75 | 2,000 | 1.22 | 1.16 | 2.9 | 2.8 | - |
| Aetna Beaver | 11.7 | 5/$75 | 2,000 | 1.04 | 0.99 | (1.3) | (7.0) | - |
| Aetna Bull | 4.7 | 5/$75 | 2,000 | 0.93 | 0.88 | (3.5) | (13.2) | - |
| Aetna Squirrel | 7.0 | 5+$75/1.3 | 2,000 | 1.22 | 1.16 | 4.2 | 4.8 | - |
| Aetna Stag | 1.3 | 5/$75 | 2,000 | 0.64 | 0.61 | (11.7) | (28.2) | - |
| Aetna Capital | 2.9 | 5+$75/1.3 | 2,000 | 1.15 | 1.09 | 7.6 | 6.5 | - |
| AMP Aust Equity | 2.7 | 5/1.0 | 4,000 | 0.95 | 0.98 | 3.5 | (2.8) | 7.2 |
| AMP M'ged Brd Based | 1383.9 | 5/1.0 | 4,000 | 1.57 | 1.49 | 7.4 | 1.2 | 6.7 |
| AMP M'ged Equity | 342.9 | 5/1.0 | 4,000 | 1.70 | 1.61 | 5.5 | (2.6) | 7.1 |
| AMP Inter | 1.1 | 6/1.3 | 4,000 | 0.88 | 0.84 | 5.4 | (6.1) | (0.3) |
| ANZ Life Cap G'teed | 38.8 | 5.8/1.2 | 1,000 | 2.64 | 2.48 | 8.4 | 8.8 | - |
| ANZ Life M'ged | 170.1 | 5.8/1.5 | 1,000 | 2.20 | 2.07 | 42 | 1.2 | 6.0 |
| Aust Eagle Eclipse | S | 5/1.6 | 1,500 | np | - | - | - | - |
| Aust Eagle M'ged | S | $60/1.3 | 2,500 | np | - | - | - | - |
| Capita Inv Lkd Cash | 7.5 | $100/0.7 | 2,000 | 1.54 | 1.46 | 8.9 | 11.9 | 11.1 |
| Capita Inv Lkd Equity | 1.2 | $100/0.7 | 2,000 | 1.64 | 1.56 | 11.3 | (1.4) | 10.0 |
| Capita Inv Lkd Inter | 2.7 | $100/0.7 | 2,000 | 1.36 | 1.30 | (2.3) | (8.9) | (0.4) |
| Capita Inv Lkd M'ged | 64.6 | $100/0.7 | 2,000 | 1.42 | 1.35 | 5.2 | (4.7) | 5.3 |
| Capita Inv Lkd Prop | 6.8 | $100/0.7 | 2,000 | 1.84 | 1.75 | 8.2 | 8.4 | 13.6 |

## Friendly Societies

| Trust/Fund | Size $m | Date of Launch | Fees % Entry/Yrly | Min $ Inv | Last Decl'n | Decl Bonus Rates 1988 | 1987 | 1986 |
|---|---|---|---|---|---|---|---|---|
| Amicus Invest | 6.2 | - | 4/nil | 1,000 | Jun 88 | 12.6 | 11.0 | 10.9 |
| ANA Capital Stable | 152.6 | - | 3.6/nil | - | Jun '88 | 11.3 | 13.1 | 14.3 |
| ANA Mortgage | - | - | 3.6/1 | 500 | np | - | - | - |
| AOF Perf | S | - | 3.5/nil | - | May '88 | 11.80 | 12.60 | 13.60 |
| Aus Pac M'ged Inv 2 | S | - | nil/1.7 | 2,000 | Jun '88 | 10.7 | 12.55 | - |
| HBF Benefit 1 | 13.8 | - | nil/2 | 100 | Sep '88 | 10.00 | 12.25 | 13.25 |
| HBF Benefit 3 | 5.1 | - | 4/nil | 500 | Sep '88 | 10.00 | 12.25 | 13.25 |
| Hibernian Blue Chip | 7.6 | - | 3.5/0.5 | - | Jun '88 | 10.34 | 14.10 | 15.23 |
| Inv Action Index Plus | 16.9 | - | 4/nil | 2,000 | Jun '88 | 10.1 | 16.30 | - |
| Inv Action Perf | 43.0 | - | 4/nil | 5,000 | Jun '88 | 10.1 | 15.20 | - |
| Inv Act'n Inc Index | 16.0 | - | 4/nil | 2,000 | Jun '88 | 10.1 | 15.20 | - |
| Inv Action Inc Perf | 15.0 | - | 4/nil | 2,000 | Jun '88 | 10.1 | 16.10 | - |
| IOOF SA Super | 82.0 | July 82 | 4/nil | 1,000 | Jun '88 | 12.05 | 13.05 | 13.05 |
| IOOF SA State Inv | 38.5 | - | 4/nil | 1,000 | Jun '88 | 12.56 | 13.60 | - |
| IOOF Vic Super | 1221.0 | Apr 81 | 3.6/0.3 | 500 | Jun '88 | 12.38 | 12.58 | 12.10 |
| IOOF Vic BT Inv | S | - | 4/nil | 500 | Jun '88 | 13.02 | 14.60 | 13.40 |
| Lifeplan Flexi | 15.3 | - | 2/nil | 1,000 | Jun '88 | 12.50 | 13.50 | 13.20 |
| Manch Blue (Vic) Chip 2 | 194.9 | Nov 82 | 3.6/0 | 500 | May '88 | 13.00 | 13.00 | 14.65 |
| Mutual RESI Bond | S | - | nil/0.7 | 500 | Jun '88 | 10.30 | 12.60 | 13.00 |
| Mutual Baby Bond | S | - | nil/0.7 | 250 | Jun '88 | 10.30 | 12.60 | 13.00 |

## Deferred Annuities

| Trust/Fund | Size $m | Fees % Entry/Yrly | Min $ Inv | Entry Cost | Exit Price | Performance 1yr | 2yr | 3yr |
|---|---|---|---|---|---|---|---|---|
| Adriatic Managed | S | 2.5/1.6 | 1,000 | 1.36 | 1.30 | np | - | - |
| Aetna Squirrel Fund | 2.1 | $75/1.3 | 2,000 | 1.34 | 1.27 | 7.5 | 10.7 | - |
| Aetna Bear Fund | 2.1 | $75/1.4 | 2,000 | 1.39 | 1.33 | 10.1 | 11.5 | - |
| Aetna Beaver Fund | 2.8 | $75/1.6 | 2,000 | 1.22 | 1.16 | 7.0 | 2.4 | - |
| Aetna Bull Fund | 0.6 | $75/1.7 | 2,000 | 1.12 | 1.07 | 4.0 | (2.5) | - |
| Aetna Stag Fund | 0.1 | $75/1.9 | 2,000 | 0.60 | 0.57 | (8.0) | (30.2) | - |
| Aetna Capital Fund | 1.2 | $75/1.3 | 2,000 | 1.26 | 1.19 | 11.9 | 11.7 | - |
| AMP Aust Equities | 2.3 | 5/1.0 | 5,000 | 1.03 | 0.98 | 7.1 | 1.4 | 14.0 |
| AMP International | 0.8 | 5/1.0 | 5,000 | 0.90 | 0.85 | 14.4 | (5.4) | 4.8 |
| AMP M'ged Broad Based | M | 5/1.0 | 5,900 | np | - | - | - | - |
| AMP M'ged Equity | 56.6 | 5/1.0 | 5,000 | 2.07 | 1.96 | 10.8 | (0.3) | 11.6 |
| AMP Managed Bal | 978.8 | 5/1.0 | 5,000 | 2.07 | 1.96 | 13.2 | 7.3 | 12.7 |

Sample insurance bonds listing    (see page 82)

# APPLICATION

**Friends Provident**
**Managed Insurance Bond**

## APPLICANT (if other than Life to be Insured)

☐ Mr ☐ Mrs ☐ Miss ☐ Ms ☐ Other _____

Given Names _____ Surname _____

Address _____

_____

_____

Postcode _____

Telephone Number: Home ( _____ ) _____ Work ( _____ ) _____

Relationship to Life to be Insured ("Insurable Interest")

☐ Spouse ☐ Partner ☐ Parent ☐ Other _____

## LIFE TO BE INSURED

☐ Mr ☐ Mrs ☐ Miss ☐ Ms ☐ Other _____

Given Names _____ Surname _____

Address _____

_____

_____

Postcode _____

Telephone Number: Home ( _____ ) _____ Work ( _____ ) _____

Date of Birth _____ Place of Birth _____ Occupation _____

The Applicant requires a Child's Advancement Plan to be issued in accordance with the provisions of the Life Insurance Act 1945 to vest in the Life Insured on the anniversary of the date of the commencement of the Plan preceding his/her _____ birthday. ☐ Yes ☐ No

## INVESTMENT DETAILS

I/We request that Friends' Provident Life Office allocate units in the Cash Fund to be reallocated after 21 days, in proportion, to the following allocations:

Please tick:

☐ Mixed Fund Contribution $_____ ☐ Cash Fund Contribution $_____ ☐ International Fund Contribution $_____

☐ Ethical Fund Contribution $_____ ☐ Capital Accumulation Fund Contribution $_____ ☐ Property Plus Fund Contribution $_____

Total Contribution: $_____

(NB Minimum contribution $1,000, and minimum in each Fund $500.)

The number of units allocated in the Cash Fund will depend upon the selling price of the cash units at the date upon which the contribution is received by Friends' Provident Life Office. On the 21st day from the date on which the contribution is received by the Office, units will be reallocated in proportion to the above Fund allocations. Units allocated in each Fund will be the number obtained by dividing the amount directed to that Fund by the current buying price of the units in that Fund. The buying price of each unit varies in accordance with the market value of the assets of the Fund.

## DECLARATION

I/We agree that this Application will be the basis of the contract subject to the Act of Incorporation and Statutory Rules for time being of Friends' Provident Life Office, to the extent that if the answers are not in my own handwriting, they have been checked by me and I certify that they are correct.

Signed at _____

on this _____ day of _____ 19 _____

X (1) _____ 1st Applicant

X (2) _____ 2nd Applicant

X (1) _____ 1st Life Insured

X (2) _____ 2nd Life Insured

**FOR OFFICE USE ONLY**

Introduced by: _____ Agency No: _____

Bond No: _____ Application No: _____ Date Received: _____ 19 _____

Sample Friends' Provident application for managed insurance bond   (see page 81)

AUSTRALIAN TAXATION OFFICE

# STATEMENT OF TERMINATION PAYMENT

To be completed by:
APPROVED DEPOSIT FUND. SUPERANNUATION FUND. LIFE ASSURANCE COMPANY or OTHER REGISTERED ORGANISATION

**PAYING INSTITUTION:** Before completing this form you MUST read either the relevant instructions printed in the booklet 'Procedures for Group Employers' or those in the tax stamps book.
This form consist of four parts.
Parts A and B are to be completed by the paying institution.  **PART D** is to completed by the paying institution.
**PART C** is to be completed by the payee.

| | ORIGINAL |

**PART A**
Name of Paying Institution: ABC Engineering Superannuation Fund.   Group No. 99.99.99.99.
Name of Recipient of Eligible Termination Payment— Surname: Citizen
Christian or Given Name: John David.   Date of Birth: 31.10.28
Eligible Service Period (show number of days)—Pre 1.7.83: 6205   Post 30.6.83: 1095.
Type of Eligible Termination payment: Lump Sum Payment.

**N.B.** If a commutation payment use Statement of Termination Payment (Commutation).

**PART B—COMPOSITION OF ELIGIBLE TERMINATION PAYMENT**
The Eligible Termination Payment consists of the following amounts.
Concessional Component   : $ .............(1)
Pre 1.7.83   Component   : $ 85,000— .............(2)
Post 30.6.83 Component   : $ 15,000— .............(3)
Undeducted Contributions   : $ .............(4)

Eligible Termination Payment: $ 100,000—

NOTE: Components (1) and (2) are not subject to tax instalment deductions but 5% of these amounts will be included in assessable income. Component (3) is subject to tax instalment deductions at the rate of 31% unless the payee is aged 55 or more in which case the rate is 16% for the first $55000 being retained by the payee, and 31% for the balance. Component (4) is tax free and is not included in assessable income.

**PART C—PAYEE "ROLL-OVER" NOMINATION**

To the PAYEE: Before completing this Part you should read the notes on the last page of this Statement. Complete this part if you wish to have the institution from which you are receiving your Eligible Termination Payment "roll-over" all or part of it on your behalf. Otherwise, write 'NIL' at (5) below and sign the declaration. Where amount(s) are to be paid to "roll-over" institution(s) you must also complete a Roll-Over Payment Notification in respect of each "roll-over" institution nominated.

FILE NUMBER
AS SHOWN ON
LAST INCOME TAX
NOTICE OF
ASSESSMENT

**DECLARATION BY PAYEE**

I (full name) John David Citizen.   hereby request
and authorise the above paying institution to pay the amount(s) below to the nominated "roll-over" institution(s).

| NAME OF "ROLL-OVER" INSTITUTION | CONCESSIONAL COMPONENT $ | PRE 1.7.83 COMPONENT $ | POST 30.6.83 COMPONENT $ | UNDEDUCTED CONTRIBUTIONS $ | TOTAL TO BE "ROLLED-OVER" $ |
|---|---|---|---|---|---|
| State Bank Minder A.D.F. | | 85,000 | 15,000 | | 100,000—0 |
| | | | | | |
| TOTAL TO BE "ROLLED-OVER" | (1) 85,000—00 | 85,000—00 | 15000— (3) | (4) | 100,000— (5) |

JD Citizen
Payee's Signature

19.9.89.
Date

**PART D—DECLARATION BY PAYING INSTITUTION**

I (full name) Herman Brown   being an authorised person of the paying institution named above, declare to the best of my knowledge that the information at PARTS A and B is correct. I have have not*. paid the amount(s), if any, set out in PART C to the "roll-over" institution(s) nominated.

H. Brown.
Signature of Authorised Person

Date of payment of Eligible Termination Payment 19.9.89.

*Delete whichever is not applicable
NAT 945-9.85   ORIGINAL—This copy to be retained by the Payee for inclusion in his or her income tax return.

**Sample Australian Taxation Office statement of termination payment** (see page 107)

# Deposit Application

**The Trustee,
State Bank Minder Fund.**

Mr/~~Mrs/Miss/Ms~~ ___John David___ ___Citizen___
<sub>Given Names</sub> <sub>Surname</sub>

Date of Birth ___31 | 10 | 28.___ Telephone Number _____

Residential Address ___100 Smith Street, Sydney. NSW___ Postcode ___2000___

Address for correspondence (if not as above) ___"As Above"___

_____ Postcode _____

    I hereby apply to Deposit the amount of ($100,000 ) to the State Bank Minder Fund – an Approved Deposit Fund upon and subject to the provisions of the Trust Deed, constituting the Trust Fund known as the State Bank Minder Approved Deposit Fund.

    If this application is granted, I agree to be bound by the provisions of the Trust Deed and any rules made thereunder.

    I enclose herewith a cheque for the sum of ($100,000.) and also enclose Australian Taxation Office Statement of Termination Payment and Rollover Payment Notification relating to my Deposit.

    In signing this Application I hereby agree to be bound by all of the terms and conditions and provisions contained in the Trust Deed.

_____ ___19/9/89.___
<sub>Signature</sub> <sub>Date</sub>

## FOR BANK USE ONLY

Notes: Cheques should be made payable to the State Bank Minder Fund.

    Applications for Deposit to the Fund will only be accepted on this form accompanied by the relevant Statement of Termination Payment provided to you by your former employer, and a Roll-over Payment Notification from a superannuation fund or Approved Deposit Fund.

    This application must be signed by you or by your authorised attorney and if signed under a power of attorney, it must be stated that the attorney has received no notice of revocation thereof.

### Instructions for Lodgement

1. Sign application where indicated.
2. Mail or deliver your cheque, Application Form and Statement of Termination Payment and Roll-over Payment Notification direct to:

The Trustee, State Bank Minder Fund, State Bank Centre, 52 Martin Place, Sydney 2000 or any branch of the State Bank.

**Receipt** (Official acknowledgement will be sent to you shortly.)

Received the sum of $100,000 _____ being Deposit to STATE BANK MINDER APPROVED DEPOSIT FUND.

_____
<sub>Signature</sub>

STATE BANK OF NSW
402-204
-19 SEP 1989
INVESTMENT
ADVISORY SERVICE

Sample NSW State Bank Minder Fund deposit application   (see page 107)

AUSTRALIAN TAXATION OFFICE

# ROLL-OVER PAY

This form is to be completed w

*Please use block letters*

SURNAME: Citizen.

CHRISTIAN or GIVEN NAMES: John David

DATE OF BIRTH: 31 / 10 / 28 . ELIGIBLE SERVICE PERIOI

POSTAL ADDRESS: 100 Smith Street , S

I hereby apply to make a total "roll-over" payment amounting to $ 1

received from A.B.C. Engineering Supero

NAME OF ROLL-OVER INSTITUTION: State Bank

POSTAL ADDRESS OF ROLL-OVER INSTITUTION: 52 M

**ELIGIBLE TERMI**

| CONCESSIONAL COMPONENT | PRE 1/7/83 COMPONENT | POST 30/6 |
|---|---|---|
| $ | $ 85.000 — | $ 15, |

**AMOUNTS**

| CONCESSIONAL COMPONENT | PRE 1/7/83 COMPONENT | POST 30/6 |
|---|---|---|
| $ | $ 85,000 —. | $ 15, |

*To be completed by "roll-over" institution*

Name of "roll-over" institution: **STATE BANK MIND**

I *(full name)* Andrew John W

person of the above institution, declare that the amount of, $ 100

Signature of Aut

**N.B. A separate receipt should be issued in respect of that part (if any) o**

NAT 951-9.85    **ORIGINAL—TO BE RECEIPTED BY ROLL-OVER INST**

Sample Australian Taxation Office roll-over payment notification    (see page 107)

# NOTIFICATION

ORIGINAL

over" payment is being made

| FILE NUMBER AS SHOWN ON LAST INCOME TAX NOTICE OF ASSESSMENT | 731 . 999 . 810 . |

2010 .......... DAYS: POST 30/6/83 ... 13,400 ........ DAYS

NSW . 2000 .

O ─────────── including the tax instalment deducted, if any,

on Fund . and consisting of the components specified below, to:

Approved Deposit Fund .

ace , Sydney . 2000 :

MENT RECEIVED

| IT | UNDEDUCTED CONTRIBUTIONS | TOTAL ETP |
|----|--------------------------|-----------|
| | $ | $ 100,000 ── |

ED- OVER"

| IT | UNDEDUCTED CONTRIBUTIONS | TOTAL TO BE ROLLED-OVER |
|----|--------------------------|-------------------------|
| | $ | $ 100,000 ── |

J.D. Citizen ............ Date 19 . 9 . 89

# OVED DEPOSIT FUND

................................................................ an authorised

........................... has been received by the institution.

............................. Date 19 . 9 . 89 .

83 Component that relates to tax instalment deductions to be refunded.

TURNED TO THE APPLICANT AND LODGED WITH RETURN.

# The Macquarie Investment Bond Fund

This is an excellent investment opportunity for you. It has the tax advantages of a single premium life insurance policy plus the security of a fixed interest portfolio.

Tax is paid by The Over 50's Friendly Society at the low rate of 30 cents in the dollar **before** bonuses are declared.

**If you leave your funds fully invested for 10 years or more, you will have no tax liability on your bonuses, regardless of your own marginal tax rate.**

If you decide to cash in your Bond wholly or partially within 10 years, you will be entitled to a **rebate of 29 cents in the dollar** (30 cents from 1/7/1989) on your assessable accrued bonuses – effectively no tax payable for investors at lower marginal tax rates.

In addition, if you cash your Bond in Year 9 only ⅔ of your accrued bonuses will be assessable, and in Year 10 only ⅓, while all your assessable bonuses still enjoy the full 29 cents in the dollar tax rebate!

## Your Effective Tax Rate

| Macquarie Investment Bond surrendered in: | Normally 30.25% reduced to: | Normally 41.25% reduced to: | Normally 50.25% reduced to: |
|---|---|---|---|
| Years 1-8 | 1.25% | 12.25% | 21.25% |
| Year 9 | 0.83% | 8.17% | 14.17% |
| Year 10 | 0.42% | 4.08% | 7.08% |
| After Year 10 | 0.00% | 0.00% | 0.00% |

Tax rates apply as at July 1, 1988, and include Medicare levy of 1.25%.

Just look at the excellent performance to date achieved on members' funds:

## 12.85%
## Based on Average Returns over 3 years

| ACTUAL RETURNS AT 20% TAX | ESTIMATED RETURNS AT NEW 30% TAX |
|---|---|
| 1987/1988  10.40% | 1987/1988  9.10% |
| 1986/1987  13.10% | 1986/1987  11.46% |
| 1985/1986  15.05% | 1985/1986  13.17% |

\* 12.85% average return over 3 years

\* 11.24% average return over 3 years

Sample over 50s investment bond fund brochure   (see page 80)